Marios Kyriazis is a medical doctor who has also studied gerontology, the science of aging, at the University of London. He has a Diploma in Geriatric Medicine from the Royal College of Physicians of London and is also a Chartered Biologist, a Member of the Institute of Biology, thanks to his work on the biology of aging.

He is a certified member of the American Academy of Anti-Aging Medicine, the founder of the British Longevity Society, and has extensive experience in nutrition, supplements and anti-aging drugs. He is an accomplished medical and health writer, and an advisor to several national age-related organizations. He is considered by the UK media to be one of Britain's leading longevity specialists.

The Anti-Aging Plan

Stay Younger Longer

Dr Marios Kyriazis

ELEMENT
Shaftesbury, Dorset • Boston, Massachusetts
Melbourne, Victoria

© Element Books Limited 2000
Text © Dr Marios Kyriazis 2000

First published in the UK in 2000 by
Element Books Limited
Shaftesbury, Dorset SP7 8BP

Published in the USA in 2000 by
Element Books, Inc.
160 North Washington Street
Boston, MA 02114

Published in Australia in 2000 by
Element Books and distributed
by Penguin Australia Limited
487 Maroondah Highway, Ringwood,
Victoria 3134

Designed and typeset by Jerry Goldie Graphic Design
Printed and bound in Great Britain by
Creative Print and Design Group, Ebbw Vale, Wales

British Library Cataloguing in Publication
data available

Library of Congress Cataloging in Publication
data available

ISBN 1 86204 704 9

Contents

Acknowledgements

I couldn't take a single step forward without the help of the aging population of the UK, particularly the members of the British Longevity Society, the readers of *Yours* magazine and those enduring patients of mine whom I have monitored, studied and tried my ideas on over the years.

My thanks go also to my wife for putting up with my 'marshmallow brain' (psychologists call this 'total immersion') during the entire period it took me to write this book. And for helping me disentangle the horribly convoluted threads of scientific jargon from plain 'patient speak'.

To Dr Michael Perring of the Optimal Health Clinic in Harley Street, Dr Alan Hipkiss of King's College London, and the academic staff at the Age Concern Institute of Gerontology, University of London, for invaluable inspiration.

To Grace Cheetham of Element Books for her help and support.

And finally, to my parents, for helping me be there.

To Stella

Introduction

If you want to live a long and healthy life, and if you are 25 and over, this book has been written especially for you.

If you don't know much about the aging process, but would like to find out, now is the time to start. This book will take you through the necessary steps.

If you are very old or very young, you still need to take care of yourself. If you are worried about your future health, if you want to find out details about a particular age-related health problem and if you want to deal with it yourself, I hope that my book will support you in your quest. If you believe that there is nothing we can do to slow down aging, to prevent age-related diseases or to live healthily to a ripe old age, think again.

If you are an expert in this field, you will still be surprised, either positively or negatively, by some parts of this book.

Aging can be slowed down in certain parts of the body; sometimes it can be stopped for a while and sometimes it can be reversed – perhaps not dramatically at present, perhaps not even appreciably, but it can be done. This depends mostly on you, your choice of lifestyle, your knowledge of the subject, your motivation, persistence and patience.

The route to a youthful body, mind and spirit is long and always uphill. This book will guide you along it. The treatments and ideas may not be 100 per cent effective or complete, but they are based on how we currently understand aging. There are many relevant, practical ways open to you.

The desire to avoid aging is fundamental to the human race. We are a part of a long chain of events and endeavours which stretches back to the dawn of time and expands into the new millennium, forever.

How and why do we age? How can our attitudes affect aging? Can we prevent aging, and how? Aging can affect us in ways we don't even think of. Sometimes it stabs us in the back, at other times it stares straight into our eyes, smiling sarcastically. But we have always managed to fight back, using our brains, dreams and knowledge, both conventional and alternative.

As you will see from the following discussion, I believe that it is biologically possible to live to a healthy 120 years. If you are not planning to live that long, you are depriving yourself of what is naturally yours. Modern science can do a great deal to banish the most common age-related illnesses. The visions and fantasies of our ancestors may then become reality in the new millennium.

Part I

CHAPTER 1

The Process of Aging

Aging in Antiquity

Since humans first realized that their lives had an end as well as a beginning, their rampant desire to live forever became indomitable. Attempts to find the fountain of youth and the secrets of eternal life go back to the dawn of civilization. Many of these were strange and naïve, but they did have a dose of scientific basis.

The primeval interest in prolonging life revolved around three main themes:

The Antediluvian Theme

According to this line of thought, ancient people believed that in the very distant past the life span of the population was extremely long. The Bible mentions that Adam lived for 930 years, Noah 950 and Methuselah 969.

The antediluvian theme is found in almost all cultures, from the ancient Greeks and Romans to the Indian races. It is even alive today to some extent. The explanation of this extreme longevity, according to the beliefs of the period, was that people lived for so long because their gods granted them this privilege.

The Hyperborean Theme

This is based on the idea that certain individuals or races in distant lands lived much longer than the current life span. Hyperborean is Greek for 'beyond the north'. The ancient Greek belief was that there was a race living in a distant land 'beyond the north' which enjoyed an extremely long life span. Many other civilizations adopted this theme, which is basically a belief in a 'paradise on Earth', a land without disease, suffering and aging.

As recently as the early 1980s the Hyperborean legend was still firmly believed. It was thought that the inhabitants of Georgia, of a certain area of Pakistan and of the Vilcabamba area in Ecuador lived to exceptionally old ages. After researchers checked the records carefully, however, this myth was somewhat deflated.

As science and modern civilization reach the most distant parts of the Earth, the Hyperborean belief is declining steadily, though perhaps it will never die completely. Even today, sporadically, we see reports of people in distant lands living to be 140 or 150. Only a few months ago, I was approached by a national UK newspaper to comment on their discovery of 'a 148-year-old man somewhere in Asia'. As I will discuss later, the maximum possible human life span is only around 120 years.

The Fountain Theme

This is probably the best-known belief. It is that somewhere there exists a magic fountain that confers the gift of eternal youth and immortality. Taken more widely, this theme includes the search for a drug, a medicine or any other method of prolonging youth and life span. This theme is extensively followed today, with most of us taking something to help us maintain our health and vigour.

Countries like Hungary, Romania and Bulgaria have a long tradition in life-prolongation treatments using the fountain theme. Not so long ago, the Romanian drug Gerovital caused a stir in the murky waters of anti-aging treatment, attracting world-wide interest as an agent for restoring youth (*see* chapter 10).

In some Hungarian spas they offer refreshing treatments with water containing sulphur, carbon and other minerals. The actual spa treatment consists of hydrotherapy with natural or artificial mineral water, mud baths and dry carbon baths. The spa owners claim that their naturally radon-rich waters can revitalize worn-out cells and slow down degenerative processes like atherosclerosis. Maybe this is the real fountain of youth.

So, the human race has basic and fundamental beliefs about extending life span, and we are still bound by these beliefs to a degree today. If we want to be successful in our quest for longevity, we should exploit what our ancestors taught us. There is a great deal we can learn from them.

The Egyptian Quest

The ancient Egyptians were experts in the art of maintaining a youthful and beautiful skin. They had many recipes for preparing creams and potions to improve aging skin and make wrinkles vanish, some containing snake parts.

One of these recipes was found in the Edwin Smith Surgical Papyrus (approximately 1700 BC) and is entitled 'Recipe for transforming an old man into a youth'. I spent a lot of time studying the text of the papyrus, trying to see beyond the words into the ancient writer's mind. The recipe gives detailed information on how to prepare an ointment to make wrinkles disappear, a 'beautifier of the skin, a remover of blemishes and disfigurements and of all signs of old age'. It is amazing to note that so many thousands of years ago humans were concerned with the disfigurements of old age probably just as much as we are today. Four thousand years later, the magic potion remains elusive.

The most important ingredient of this Egyptian ointment is a type of fruit that is green and small, has a hard husk or shell and contains seeds. The scientists who tried to translate the ancient papyrus were unable to identify it. My guess is that this fruit is symbolic of anything natural, green, organic and coming from the earth. It is no coincidence that seeds are increasingly promoted nowadays as containing powerful anti-aging chemicals.

Shedding the Skin

The image of the snake keeps coming up in civilizations which tried to deal with aging. Many believed that the snake sheds its skin as a way of renewing itself and staying young forever.

The idea of shedding the skin as a way of regeneration does not seem to be confined to the ancient times. For example, even today the

Amazonian Indians believe that a certain type of tree sheds its bark as a means of staying young. This is the Capirona tree found in the upper Amazon, where local Indians told me that whoever sleeps under it will regain their health. The women use its bark to maintain a youthful skin.

It is interesting to notice that when scientists analysed the bark of the Capirona tree they found it to contain large quantities of vitamin E, which protects the skin and other organs from age-related damage. Many more life-prolonging plants must be there in the rainforest just waiting to be discovered.

The modern techniques of dermabrasion, or face peeling, use modern tools to get rid of the outer skin as a way of looking young again. So, ancient wisdom and modern technology are not complete strangers to each other.

The Tao of Longevity

The ancient Chinese believed that immortality doesn't actually mean living forever, but rather living for around 300 years – enough for some, you might think. In their attempts to discover the secrets of longevity they amassed a large amount of information on natural medicine and plants.

The Chinese believed that by reducing the size of an object, they could harness its life energy and use it to heal their own bodies. This idea of miniaturization to prolong life sounds familiar to me. Later on, you will see that nanotechnology (the technology of miniaturization) is a very promising tool (perhaps *the* tool) in the fight against old age.

The goal of Taoism, which developed in ancient China, is to harmonize human actions with nature – the Tao. The Tao has no beginning and no end. By living according to the Tao one participates in it and becomes eternal.

Taoists believe that immortality is not only possible but has been achieved in the past by disciples who have been through special training. To give an insight into the Taoists' ideas I will describe one of their most important and interesting methods for prolonging life – the respiration method.

Taoists believe that the entire world is a huge living organism, breathing like other living beings. So, by breathing the right type of air it is possible to absorb the Earth's energy and therefore maintain the body's own energy.

Before starting the breathing techniques in a comfortable and quiet room, trainees would fast for long periods, pray and meditate. Then they would learn how to breathe in and hold the breath for increasingly long periods. Immortality could be achieved when the breath could be held for the length of 1,000 normal respirations. Some practitioners could manage the length of over 100 respirations, but this was only possible because their metabolism was slow following the long periods of fasting and they did not require large amounts of oxygen.

There is a small grain of truth in these Taoist beliefs. Lowering the level of respiration, thus lowering the metabolism and the amount of oxygen in the body, reduces the exposure of the body to free radicals, the molecules which damage the organism and cause aging. Also, the mental discipline necessary to perform these breathing exercises super-charges the immune system and improves the ability to fight disease.

The Breath of Life

Moving on from the Taoists, there is the story of King David, who would sleep with young virgins in the hope of absorbing their revital-izing breath (Kings 1:1–4). It is mentioned, however, that he did not have intercourse with them.

This idea was taken up by the medieval Oxford scholar Roger Bacon. He considered that health and youth were contagious in the same way that some diseases are and thus could be transmitted through the breath.

There is a basic truth in these ideas. As long ago as 1959, it was shown that old male rats live longer if they are put in the proximity of young female rats. The scientific reason behind this effect could be that young, sexually active animals or humans stimulate other members of the opposite sex via sexual hormonal molecules called pheromones. Pheromones are carried through the air and are different from one animal to another. After the specific pheromone is picked up by the body, it boosts the secretion of sexual hormones and other chemicals from the brain which can have effects similar to conventional hormonal supplements (HRT for example). Although this is still not widely accepted by scientists, researchers are actively exploring this possibility.

As you can see from these ancient beliefs, throughout history a long natural life span has been an ideal. I believe that it can be achieved, but it takes some searching and patience. There are several different approaches to attaining long life and some are more success-ful than others.

Current treatments for aging promise a lot and many of these treat-ments are based on ideas developed by our forefathers. We are grateful to them for the heritage that plays such an important part in modern health.

But were do we go from here? Whether we like it or not, we are the millennium generation. Now is a symbolic time to pause for a while, study our past, relish our present and look forward to our future.

The Length of Life

It is a fact that life has definite limits. Nobody has ever reached the age of 900 or more, as claimed in the Bible. Not even the age of 180, as many claim in certain regions of the world. The highest limit of human life span lies around the age of 120. This is called the 'maximum life span'.

One well-documented case of a person living to the age of 121 is that of a Japanese man called Shigechiyo Izumi. He was born on 29 June 1865 in Asan on Tokumoshima Island, 820 miles from Tokyo, and died in 1986. His advice for a long life was to leave things to God, the sun and Buddha and to avoid stress. His diet was mainly vegetarian. Another case is that of Jeanne Louise Calment, a Frenchwoman who was born on 21 February 1875 and died on 4 August 1997 at the age of 122.

It is very difficult to confirm the age of anyone who claims to be over 100 years old. But in some countries (for example Sweden), where a very thorough investigation follows the death of older people, no one has ever been found to have reached an age higher than 110 years.

Why do some people claim to be very old and how do these claims arise? One reason is that some people who live in remote areas circu-late rumours that the 'oldest man on Earth' lives in their town or village in order to attract tourists.

Until 1978 the Vilcabamba valley in Ecuador was a tourist attrac-tion due to the claims that many people there were supposed to be over 130 years old. Many curious tourists visited the area in an attempt to meet these super-centenarians and to ask them their secrets of a long life. Scientific investigation, however, showed that these people were using the birth certificates of their fathers or grandfathers, not their own. This reduced the age of the oldest man from 140 years to just over 96. That is still quite a reasonable age, but tourists soon lost interest and took their money elsewhere.

Another reason for people claiming to be very old is the high social value and esteem that some countries bestow upon very old age. In the Abkhazian republic of Georgia in the former USSR, very old citizens are treated as local saints with all the privileges that this status entails.

In the case of this particular republic, it has also been suggested that in the past some men assumed the identities of older men in order to avoid military service in the Czar's army. It is no surprise, then, that one in 40 citizens at that time claimed to be over 100 years old.

Hunza in the Karakoram range in Pakistan is also a region with a high percentage of centenarians. It is an isolated community with a high degree of illiteracy and no written records, so it is quite impossible to substantiate any claims.

All the inhabitants of these regions have a few things in common. First, although no inhabitant has ever been proved to have reached an age higher than the maximum life span of 120, it is still true that the percentage of older people in these regions is higher than in the rest of the country, so they must be doing something right.

Secondly, their diet consists almost entirely of vegetables with very low amounts of meat. In the case of Hunza it has also been found that the water there is rich in selenium, an essential mineral that helps fight aging. A life-long diet low in calories (a procedure called 'dietary restriction') is probably a prime factor in helping these people live longer.

Thirdly, they keep exercising until very late in life in an attempt to earn their living in the prevailing harsh conditions. Social and physical activity is thought to play a role in keeping people healthy and in fine shape.

And fourthly, these people are all of European origin. The Georgians are white Caucasians, the Vilcabambans are principally of Spanish origin and the inhabitants of Hunza are, according to legend, descendants of the Greek soldiers of Alexander the Great. There may be genetic factors that (together with the lifestyles described above) improve the chances of survival of these people.

While it is true that the maximum limit on life span has remained unchanged (around 110–120 years) since the first humans walked the Earth, it is also true that the average life span has changed many times.

Most industrialized people nowadays have a reasonable chance of living to 75–80 years, if not more.

This average life span has constantly changed during the past thousands of years. Cro-Magnon men living thousands of years ago had a variable life span. For example, those who lived in the Djerdap gorges of the Danube had a life span of more than 40 years, whereas people in later periods who lived in the same area had a life span of only 20 years.

An explanation may be that members of the earlier group were living the life of hunter-gatherers, ie, small groups of people moving all the time from one place to another. Therefore, the chances of contracting diseases from each other were very small. When the practice of agriculture became more widespread, new settlements were formed with large numbers of inhabitants. The spread of epidemics was easier in these conditions. Those later people had a very small chance of living to old age because the risk of dying early from a disease was phenomenal.

We find similar fluctuations in the average life span through the years from the times of the Romans right up to the early 20th century. The main reason for these fluctuations is health care and the control of diseases. As we approach modern times, health care improves and the average life span expands. In the future there may be a day when the average life span will tease the limits of the maximum one. One of the problems, however, will be that the age of the population may well increase, but the health of people who are very old may not improve. Diseases related to aging may become more and more frequent, and the numbers of elderly people requiring health care may increase dramatically.

Some researchers don't agree with this scenario, however. They claim that medical and scientific advances will improve the health of the people and so there will be an increase not only of the life span but also of the health span (the health span is simply the amount of time an individual is healthy). Ideally, people would live to a healthy 120 years and then die quietly, not from disease, but simply because their flame had died.

What Is Aging?

In order to slow down your rate of aging you first need to know as much as possible about it, so let's explore some of the current ideas.

When I talk about aging, I refer to the aging of humans, unless I specifically state otherwise. Some aging mechanisms in animals or plants may be different. Don't be fooled into thinking that what affects aging in animals must necessarily affect aging in humans.

The branch of science studying the mechanisms of aging is called 'biological gerontology'. There are only a few biological gerontologists in Britain, Canada and Australia, but in the USA biological gerontology is much more developed and this is where most of the research is conducted.

Statisticians believe that aging is an increased chance of dying. Mathematical calculations show that after the age of 30, the probability of dying doubles every seven years. For example, if my neighbour has a 10 per cent chance of dying at the age of 30, this chance will become 20 per cent at the age of 37, 40 per cent at the age of 44, 80 per cent at the age of 53 and a certainty at 60. So, for this particular person, life would be too short. If, however, you start off with a lower chance of dying at 30 years of age, then you will be in a better position than my neighbour and you will certainly live longer.

How can you lower your chances of dying? This depends on you. By following certain sensible guidelines and making alterations to your lifestyle, it may be possible to avoid early aging and premature death. The secrets will be revealed later on.

Another way of seeing aging is as an ideal means of getting rid of people who can't have children anymore. This is a way devised by Mother Nature to make room for new generations when the old ones have fulfilled their purpose.

Research looking into the physiology of aging shows that after the age of around 35, the signs of aging start sprouting like rampant weeds. We begin losing muscle tissue, the amount of fat in our bodies piles up, our skin gets thinner and drier, and our strength slips away from us constantly year in and year out.

This view of aging is also supported by the fact that after the menopause, the signs of aging become much more obvious. In other words, when a woman is not able to have any more children, Mother

Nature withdraws all her protective support. (Of course, this refers to the animal kingdom in general and has nothing to do with those couples who for one reason or another can't have any children.)

But then, why do we live as long as we do? Why don't we just die after having children, but instead continue living for another 40, 50 years or more? Scientists think that this is due to a process called 'free-wheeling'. Nature wants to make 100 per cent sure that we live to an age to have children and then live for a bit longer to help them grow up, so a lot of effort is put into ensuring we reach the age of 30–35. Then, after this initial push, we just continue a life of freewheeling for another 40–50 years, slowing down gradually until we come to the point at which we stop, death.

This makes sense. If you want to build a house to last for, say, 10 years, you make an effort to build it properly and make sure that it can last for well over 10 years just to be on the safe side. When you stop repairing it after 10 years, the house will not just disappear overnight, but will slowly decay over the following 10 or 20 years. This process of decaying is comparable to aging.

Another theory sees aging as a product of civilization. Many thousands of years ago, the chances of somebody dying prematurely from accidents, disease, predators or wars were colossal. People who lived into old age were a curious exception in those societies. As civilization progressed, we managed to avoid several of these dangers and therefore most people lived long enough to experience aging. According to this theory, aging is not contrary to natural laws, because nature is not specifically opposed to the process. To put it in another way, it is not unnatural to die later in life. Civilization and technology caused the lengthening of the life span and unmasked the hidden natural signs of aging.

This process can be seen in the natural world, where very few animals live to reach old age, most being killed by predators, accidents or diseases. If, however, we take a number of these animals and protect them in artificial conditions, for example, in zoos or in houses as pets, then these animals will not die prematurely and with the passage of time they will start to show signs of aging.

How Do We Age?

So there are a few well-accepted explanations and answers to the question of why we age. But how do we age? What makes us age? There are many theories about this, but none is conclusive.

In gerontology meetings, scientists often joke that there are as many theories about aging as there are gerontologists. A few years ago, one of them actually sat down one day and tried to match the existing theories to the number of eminent gerontologists. The numbers matched reasonably well! So every gerontologist worth their salt will have their own theory.

However, it seems that no matter how many theories of aging exist, there are two general agreements:

a We age due to factors that damage our body
(eg, chemicals, toxic by-products of the metabolism, random damage, genes which affect aging).

b We age because this damage is not repaired properly
(eg, due to lack of energy, deficiencies of hormones, faulty genes or failure of the immune system).

When we understand more clearly the basic ways in which the body ages, then we will be in a prime position to fight aging. Let's examine more closely some of the most inspiring and up-to-date ideas on how aging happens.

Molecular Sharks

One such theory supports the view that aging is caused by undesirable by-products of our metabolism called 'free radicals' (FR). FR are the price we pay for breathing oxygen. During everyday metabolism, the oxygen in our body can give off FR which, if left uncontrolled, can be disastrously damaging to our tissues. Without oxygen we die, with it we age. It is a matter of balancing the two and finding a middle ground in which active health can flourish.

Organisms that have a low metabolic rate are said to age more slowly than the rest. Turtles, for example, age more slowly than mice. Certainly, the rate of living is important: animals that hibernate and therefore slow down their metabolism are thought to be extending their life. This may be due to the fact that these animals use less oxygen, which means a lower production of free radicals and therefore less damage. The breathing exercises of the Taoists come to mind here.

To be fair, free radicals in small amounts are normal and essential to our metabolism, but they have a tendency to react violently with many molecules in our body, such as proteins, enzymes and DNA, so their excessive production is able to cause widespread damage. Some people have named them 'molecular sharks' because they devour everything in their way. FR have also been called 'agents and products of doom' and 'molecular terrorists'. The process by which they cause their damage has been compared to the rusting of metal.

FR are not only responsible for causing aging but are also implicated in all those nasty age-related diseases like arteriosclerosis, cataract, Alzheimer's dementia, Parkinson's disease and arthritis. Their production is stimulated by reckless smoking, inconsiderate environmental pollution, unnoticeable radiation and an unsound diet. A few years ago, it was estimated that the genetic material inside each and every human cell receives around 10,000 damaging hits by FR every single day.

To prevent this kind of damage, our body has developed a mop-up system of chemicals which attack and destroy FR. Enzymes and other chemicals called 'free radical scavengers' or 'antioxidants' roam our bloodstream like hungry animals seeking their prey, identify free radicals and gobble them up.

In addition to this, the body has developed a series of mechanisms to repair the damage already suffered. Our repair rate can be up to 99.9 per cent effective, but this does worsen with the passage of time. So the damage caused by FR can build up progressively until it overwhelms the body, causing aging, disease and death. Perhaps we will never be able to stop this decline completely, but we can certainly slow it down.

Some scientists, however, are pessimistic about the use of antioxidants in slowing this decline. They point out that although many people supplement their diets with antioxidants, they still don't live any longer than those who don't squander their money on supplements. There may well be some health-stimulating effects from antioxidants, like the prevention of heart disease and of other age-related diseases, but they claim that more trials are needed to prove this beyond doubt.

Scientists who take this view believe the reason there is no evidence of any significant benefits in longevity is because the antioxidant supplement needs to be delivered to the exact point in the cell where the FR damage is and in great enough quantities to be able to counteract the damage. Also, antioxidants in our body are in balance with each other and taking too much of one may reduce the natural production of another.

I mention the views of these scientists to give you a sense of balance and to discourage you from thinking that blindly taking an antioxidant is necessarily a good thing to do.

On the other hand, all scientists are in agreement that taking care to dodge free radical damage by avoiding smoking and environmental pollution should be encouraged.

Nanotechnology

Damage by free radicals can, in theory, be repaired manually, or rather electronically. American researchers hope that by the year 2020 very small robots will be injected into our bloodstream, directed to the point of the free radical damage and ordered to repair it. These tiny robots, as small as an ordinary human cell, will also clear the skin of any dead material, fight viruses and cancer cells, and repair other age-related damage.

Human material can be attached to microprocessors to create the robot. The robot itself will be like a science-fiction hybrid with proteins and living material sticking out of specially prepared computer chips. I have seen samples of this stuff and I can tell you it looks really spooky.

Serious research into the science of nanotechnology is particularly active in Japan and new developments are being announced all the time. We will have to wait for years to see whether this vision becomes reality, but many computer specialists think that it is a real possibility.

Immortal Genes?

The current talk of the town in the gerontological community is the 'disposable soma' theory. This theory of aging is based on the interplay between energy, repair of damage and the survival of the species. Unfortunately, it does not have any immediate practical relevance to our everyday life, so I will mention it only very briefly.

This theory basically is that we age because there is not enough natural energy to maintain our body, only enough to maintain our genes. So we age and die but our genes are immortal, living forever in our offspring. Cancer cells are an exception to this rule, being able to live forever because they have the ability to steal energy from healthy cells in order to maintain themselves. Cancer causes death, while the genes create life. What a cruel and wonderful trick of nature, to use the same process for death and life at the same time!

Some people are better able to repair the damage to their bodies and this makes them able to live for a few more years than the rest. But they live on borrowed time, because whatever they do there will come a day when their allocated energy will run out and their genes will have to 'dispose' of their protective body (ie, die) and acquire a new body (their offspring). It is just like the chicken and egg situation. If a chicken is the egg's way of making another egg, then we are the genes' way of making more genes.

Hormones

Another theory of aging involves the endocrine (hormonal) system. This theory says that aging is due to an imbalance of the different hormones in the body, just like an orchestra performing on its own without a conductor. You can imagine the noise and confusion.

The idea that hormones are the key to aging has been a favourite one for decades. During the late 19th and the early 20th century, doctors performed testicular transplants from several species of apes to humans. Other experiments used similar procedures, for example injections of dogs' sexual hormones, in an attempt to rejuvenate old men.

A certain Doctor Voronof was the most famous advocate of these techniques. Another doctor, the eminent physician Charles Brown-Sequard, injected himself with testicular products from different animals. He reported an increase in mental power, increased muscular strength and a regularity of bowel function. Although all of these procedures caused a stir in the scientific circles of the period, none of those who tried them lived long enough to tell us the story in person.

What does science tell us about these treatments? The main active ingredient of testicular tissue is the hormone testosterone. This can miraculously, though temporarily, banish the effects of old age in some men, so there may be some basic truth behind these procedures.

Testicular tissue is still used today in the form of cell therapy in certain Swiss clinics. It is easy to find dried bovine testes or ovaries prepared in tablet form, for example, to treat problems related to sexual function. Swiss doctors are also especially fond of using injections of cells from embryos or from placentas in order to achieve strong immunity. They say that this is a natural technique, similar in principle to the one using genetic material such as RNA extracts (*see* chapter 10).

Apart from the sexual hormones (*see* chapter 9 for more detail) other hormones begin to dwindle with age. The most important of these are the pituitary hormones, the thyroid hormone and the thymic hormone. I'll examine each of these in more detail.

The Pituitary

The pituitary is a gland (a group of cells) in the brain. It is responsible for secreting a number of hormones and some regulating factors. Some of these hormones regulate other hormones in the body such as the growth hormone. Growth hormone itself is essential for growth and development, and a lack of it causes signs of aging.

Sex hormones are also regulated by the pituitary. These are:

a the oestrogens and progestogens, mostly active in women

b testosterone, mostly active in men

At a certain point in life, the lack of these hormones shows up in a variety of ways:

- hot flushes in women
- sexual problems in men
- hair loss

With the passage of time, the pituitary hormones become less effective and can't perform their duties as well as they should. This imbalance in the pituitary hormones is blamed on the presence of chemical clocks (*see* 'Melatonin' below) which may exist in the brain and which go progressively out of control, causing havoc in the normal interplay between the different hormones.

The Thyroid

The thyroid gland (thyroid is Greek for 'shield-like') has been compared by incurable romantics to a shield carried by the Knights of the Round

Table. This gland, found in the throat, is essential in regulating the body's metabolism.

An overactive thyroid makes the body go into 'fast forward' mode, causing shakiness, anxiety, irritability, a galloping metabolism (eating more but losing weight), a brisk heartbeat and so on. On the other hand, an underactive thyroid gland will cause the opposite effects: a slowing down of activities, weight gain, drowsiness, slow bowel movements (constipation) and a sleepy heartbeat.

A fast metabolism means that an increased amount of oxygen is used, aggravating the danger of free radical damage. With age, the changes in the concentrations of thyroid hormone affect other hormones and the final result is irreparable damage to the organism. In both cases, instead of protecting us, our shield betrays us.

The Thymus

This organ, normally situated not far from the thyroid gland, reaches its maximum activity early in life. It secretes a hormone called thymosin, which is necessary for the maturation and development of the immune system. With the passage of time, however, the levels of thymosin fall progressively. This is, according to some researchers, the key which unlocks the ravages of aging. A failure of the immune system, whether due to reduced amounts of thymosin or to other reasons, is at the heart of the aging process.

Melatonin

Every one of us carries time-measuring mechanisms inside our brain – even those people who are always late for appointments. Our internal biological clocks measure time, day and night cycles and even the cycles of the seasons. Aging is caused when these clocks go progressively out of control. It is alleged that melatonin can regulate them, so slowing the rate of aging.

Melatonin is produced by the pineal gland, a small gland in the brain that some cultures considered to be the centre of the soul. Others believed that it used to be our third eye, looking for danger or prey behind our head many millions of years ago.

Whatever the case, with age the concentration of melatonin falls, making the interpretation of time more difficult. Scientists who studied the passage of time in mature people concluded that time passes more slowly in old age. Older people can't calculate correctly its passing, thinking for example that 60 minutes have gone by when in fact only 45 minutes have passed.

Because melatonin interprets how the body perceives the passage of time, it is used to cure jet lag by normalizing the body clock. Its other main use is to help induce and maintain sleep. There is not sufficient evidence that it can affect aging in humans, as alleged.

Growth Hormone

Treatment with growth hormone (GH) opens up a more promising anti-aging avenue. It has been proven that the older we get, the more growth hormone we lose. Growth hormone is responsible for growth in children and for maintaining development in adults. One of its actions is to keep muscle, skin and bone tissues in a robust state.

The interest in GH as a life extension factor started some years ago. Researchers studied groups of men aged between 60 and 80. They found that a large proportion of these had a low level of GH in their bodies. The researchers also measured several other factors like the thickness of the skin, the weight of the muscles and fat tissues, the bone density and the blood pressure. They found that as people get older there is:

- a decrease in muscle weight
- an increase in fat tissue stores
- a continual thinning of the skin and of the bones

Following these initial measurements, they gave artificial GH to half the patients for several weeks. The other half received a dummy treatment. At the end of the study period the researchers repeated the measurements again.

The results took the researchers by surprise. They showed that in those men in whom the GH deficiency had improved, there was a real reversal of the signs of aging. Their skin became thicker and stronger, their muscles became as efficient as the muscles of 40 year olds, they lost body fat and their kidneys worked harder.

Other possible effects of GH include improvements in sexual performance and in the immune system. These effects are not maintained for long periods after stopping the treatment, so it is necessary to continue treatment for years to sustain the reversal of aging. The need for long-term treatment is in fact common to all hormone deficiencies. Compare, for example, the need for continuous treatment with HRT in menopausal women and the need for daily insulin injections in diabetics.

Following the trials, some American, Swiss and Mexican doctors were quick to start offering GH treatment for older men. A few in Britain are offering it too. More conservative scientists, however, have held back, being concerned about the possibly serious side effects of the treatment, both short term and long term. These include:

- fluid retention

- high blood pressure

- diabetes

- cancer

We are awaiting the results of more extensive studies.

One serious drawback of GH treatment is the enormous cost. In Switzerland, for example, it costs around $30,000 for a year's injections (or $9,000 for four months). The injections can be started at the medical centre and continued by the patient at home. Three times a week, the patient injects himself (rarely herself) with biologically engineered human growth hormone.

Not all patients are suitable for the treatment. Patients with diabetes, high blood pressure or cancer are barred.

GH is legally given to children who suffer from GH deficiency so it is not an outlawed treatment. The problem is that GH is not licensed for use in older adults and fear of the side effects makes most doctors unwilling to use it. The basic cost for four months' treatment at UK prices would be around £2,500 ($4,000). As more efficient ways of manufacturing GH become available, the cost of the treatment will fall considerably.

The concentration of GH can, in theory, be increased by taking certain supplements and these are discussed later on. The best way to increase GH levels in the body is, however, regular exercise.

In summary, the endocrine theory of aging blames aging on the changes in the different hormones in the body.

22

Failing Defences

The immunological theory suggests that we age because with the passage of time we lose the ability to fight disease due to defects in our immune system. This decline begins around the time of sexual maturity.

The immune system is a collection of molecules, cells and chemicals which work together to protect us from invading viruses, bacteria and toxic compounds. It also controls cells which have become abnormal and lost the ability to perform as they should.

The immune system can be divided into two main parts:

a the immune cells (cell-mediated immunity)

b the immune molecules (humoral immunity), also called 'antibodies'

The cells (mostly white blood cells) are responsible for identifying foreign material in the body and destroying it. Some of these cells are under the influence of the thymus gland which, with the passage of time, does not produce enough thymosin, making immune problems more likely.

In order to boost the thymus, scientists have used extracts of animal thymus gland to treat deficiencies in humans. Several treatments have been tried, some with a degree of success.

A newer treatment using more refined extracts makes use of a protein called thymic protein A. This is supposed to stimulate the thymus gland and to help boost the effectiveness of certain immune cells. This protein is available in powder form. Some doctors, however, think that as soon as this protein enters the stomach it is inactivated and so has no benefits whatsoever.

Apart from low thymosin, genetic factors, pollution, malnutrition, excessive stress and certain drugs all affect our immune system, making it less efficient.

One of the consequences of an aging immune system is the increased incidence of the 'auto-immune' diseases such as lupus, rheumatoid arthritis, certain skin diseases and others. This is due to the failure of the body to recognize what is 'self' and what is not. Therefore, with the passage of time, the defence mechanisms of the immune system become confused and attack almost at random, causing damage to both friend and foe.

An Aging Gene?

The genetic theory of aging says that hidden somewhere in the depths of our DNA there exist genes which are responsible for stimulating the production of 'bad chemicals' which finally cause the organism to age. In other words, aging is not the result of external damage, but of a built-in programme, a pre-set self-destruction mechanism.

According to this theory, some genes are inactive until later life, when they are suddenly switched on and make us age. Other genes actively keep us healthy in earlier years and then, out of the blue, turn against us. These are called 'pleiotropic genes'.

Scientists are not even sure whether such genes exist in normal humans, but they have found evidence that special aging genes do exist in worms and fruit flies. Control these genes and you make the fly or worm live much longer than average.

Several gerontologists believe that humans don't have special aging genes because nature didn't have enough time to develop them. As I have explained above, the signs of aging became apparent only during the past few thousand years, a very short period indeed on a scale which measures time in millions of years. So it wasn't necessary for nature to develop special genes in order to kill us, because we were certain to be killed by disease and predators anyway.

Whatever part genes play in the aging process, it is clear that longevity does run in families. People who have long-lived parents or grandparents are blessed with increased chances of living for many years themselves.

Telomeres

As you may already know, the molecule DNA is made of long strands of certain chemicals. These chemicals can be compared to the steps of a spiral staircase, in ever-changing complexity. Towards the end of the DNA molecule there are the telomeres. These are a repetition of the same steps of the DNA staircase over and over again, perhaps 9,000 times. Their function is to prevent mistakes during cell division when the original DNA divides into two 'daughter molecules'.

As an analogy, think of a long overseas telephone number, say, the number 00 441 604 630 779. It starts with a repetition of numbers, 00, and then continues with the meaningful part of the telephone number. The initial 00 acts as a sign: 'Here follows an overseas telephone number.' It is the same with telomeres, only the 00 equivalent is at the end, signalling: 'Here ends the DNA.'

The sequence of these telomeres is normally long, but starts shortening with age. In that case, when the DNA divides, the telomeres are not long enough to prevent errors, which progressively accumulate and eventually cause the DNA to malfunction.

Telomeres are looked after and kept long by an enzyme called telomerase. Too little telomerase causes short telomeres, which in turn cause damaged DNA to accumulate.

Brisk activity of telomerase is found in cells which are immortal – the cancer cells and the cells which contain our genetic DNA. Lowering telomerase may contribute to controlling cancer by causing devastation to the cancerous DNA. But low telomerase may also bring about reduction of normal DNA and age-related damage. At present, we just can't make telomerase reduce cancer without affecting healthy cells, but we can still find a use for it: high telomerase can be a sign of cancer and it can be used as a marker to find out if a patient is developing cancer or not, or whether a patient is responding to anti-cancer treatment.

25

Scientists are studying several substances which may be able to stimulate telomerase and lengthen the telomeres in an attempt to slow down aging. These are still at the experimental stage and not yet available to the general public.

In some experiments, scientists took telomerase, injected it into old cells and then found that these cells started becoming young again, in the biological sense. They believe that in the near future it may be possible to take human cells, repair them with telomerase and inject them back into the body to regenerate aging organs. Sceptics have, however, suggested that aging is not affected by telomerase so this treatment will not make any difference to our health.

A Summary of the Theories of Aging

The main theories of aging blame free radicals, a lack of energy, the falling levels of hormones, the state of the immune system and genetic factors. On many occasions these theories overlap, whereas at other times they contradict each other. It is likely that there are many different factors which cause aging, not just a single one.

Research interest is growing almost daily in this area and many scientists are hopeful that we will indeed find more effective therapies against aging soon.

In the meantime there are many different therapies, both natural and artificial, which aim at prolonging our life span. However, it isn't just the number of years that counts. What we should be aiming to increase is our youthful, happy, productive, healthy, high quality life span. In the following chapters I will focus on several ways to do this, based on the different theories of aging discussed above. For example:

- by being choosy with your food, you can reduce the damage free radicals inflict on you

- by upgrading your lifestyle, you can affect the way external factors downgrade your health

- by performing mental exercises you can increase the performance of your immune system

- by replacing your dwindling hormones, you can replenish your fleeing vigour and health

How the Body Changes with Aging

Quite a few people believe that if they have a health problem this is only due to 'their age'. Rubbish! You can be old without being ill, just as you can be ill without being old.

You will, perhaps, be surprised to learn that many so-called 'age' problems are not due to old age at all but to ordinary treatable diseases which can befall anyone, including children. To give you an idea of what is an age change and what is not, I will review some common changes to the body which occur with the passage of time. Don't despair if these sound gloomy. There are many things we can do to deal with each and every one of these changes.

The Mouth, Digestion and Bones

With age the mouth feels dryer. One reason for this is because the amount of saliva generally falls. The salivary glands (the organs which produce the saliva) still function normally, producing the same constituents necessary to aid proper chewing.

Another cause of a dry mouth is the side effects of certain drugs. Examples of these are water tablets (diuretics) and some blood pressure tablets.

With age the tooth enamel gets thinner and there is also a certain degree of gum infection in most people. The material which surrounds the teeth gets progressively laxer and so teeth lose their support. That is when they start falling out.

The absorption of nutrients and drugs from the gut becomes less efficient during aging. This means that you may be taking medicines or nutrients which are not absorbed properly by the body and are therefore useless. Kidney and liver function packs up, too, and these organs become sluggish at eliminating toxins from the blood.

The body fat increases and some drugs which are stored in the fatty tissue may take longer to be eliminated. This can cause disastrous side effects. The average 65-year-old woman's body is 43 per cent fat compared with 25 per cent at the age of 25. It is not all bad, though. Oestrogen hormones are stored in fatty tissues and this may be one of nature's ways of helping post-menopausal women to retain oestrogen after the menopause. So, putting on a little weight in later life may actually help in boosting the oestrogen hormones.

The requirement for food falls with age. People aged between 55 and 70 years need 5 per cent fewer calories than before. After this age, they need 7 per cent fewer for every 10 years. In general, the metabolism slows down. So, to avoid old age flabbiness you need to gently cut down on your calories over the years.

There is a progressive loss of calcium from the bones, which become more and more fragile with age (*see* 'Osteoporosis' below).

The Heart

During normal old age there is no change in the resting pulse rate (the heartbeat while we are sitting or lying down), but changes become evident when we start exercising. Unfit people will have a faster pulse rate on exercise because the heart (being unfit) will not pump enough blood with every stroke so it will need to pump faster to compensate for the increased demand for blood.

In addition, the lungs begin to lose their elasticity and the capacity for holding air is reduced.

27

Muscle

Our muscle strength constantly declines with age, but this loss can be slowed down by exercising. The loss of strength is about 1 per cent for every year above the age of 45. Muscle tissue also decreases with age and the use of oxygen while exercising becomes less efficient.

If you want to delay or reverse this muscle weakness, you need to exercise regularly. Trained elderly people are stronger than people of the same age who have not had any regular exercise in the past. There is no need to exercise hard in later life. Small amounts of regular exercise will be sufficient. If you are young, you need to exercise now to avoid weakness later on in life.

The Joints

With age, our joints become stiffer and movement becomes more difficult and more restricted. There is a reduction of the elastic tissue and a loss of the lubricating fluid between the joints. If the damage continues at a fast rate arthritis could result. Although this kind of damage is very difficult if not impossible to repair, it is possible to stretch the remaining healthy tissues around the joint to their limits, preventing further worsening. This can be achieved with regular exercise, which increases the flexibility of the joints. The answer is to stretch, stretch, stretch.

The Brain

Intelligence changes little in old age. People who had a high IQ when young will still retain many of their capabilities when they grow old.

The general personality does not change with age either but it gently evolves through time. Older people do not necessarily stay fixed in their ways. It depends on the individual and on social status. Research suggests that poor or working-class people are more likely to be inflexible and that older women tend to be more outgoing, tender and tense than men.

The ability to make judgements and to solve problems does not necessarily decline, even after 75 years of age, although the time needed to make a decision is prolonged. This is because the nerve cells of older people take more time to transmit information to the brain, like slow-burning fuses. As a result, any mental disadvantage in old age is more obvious when there is a time pressure or when a task becomes more complicated.

Increased familiarity with a task should make things easier.

Regarding memory, it is usually the retrieval of past information, specifically information held in the short-term memory, which could be affected by age. The learning process and the imprinting of new memories in the brain is not affected appreciably. It is possible to use different strategies to aid your memory (*see* chapter 6).

The Senses

Our vision and hearing abilities are not spared by age. There is an increased chance of developing cataracts and other eye conditions (for more details on vision, hearing and other sense changes, *see* chapter 6). Wax can build up in the ears, which may cause blockage of the ear canal and difficulty in hearing. This is not 'just old age' and it can easily be sorted out. Hearing loss in general should not be left untreated.

Sexual Changes

There is no significant decrease in either male potency (the ability to maintain an erection) or libido (the desire to have sex) with normal aging. Notice that I am not talking about frequency here, only about desire. In some cases, potency may be impaired due to drugs or disease, but this is not always an age-related process and it can affect anybody of any age.

As many as 70 per cent of people over the age of 60 can be sexually active. Regular sexual intercourse has been recorded between a man aged 103 and his wife of 90. However, there are some changes with age. In men the amount of ejaculate decreases with age and the amount of testosterone (the main sexual hormone in men) possibly falls, there is a reduction of the blood supply to the penis and it takes longer to reach a full erection. In women the vagina becomes dryer due to lack of oestrogen and orgasms become less intense. (For more details on how to deal with these, *see* chapter 9.)

These changes seem to matter little overall. A number of research projects have shown that in men, many of the negative points of age, such as low testosterone, testicular disease and low blood supply, are merely due to disease and not to aging itself. If men who are chronically ill or who are on medication are excluded from the statistical calculations, even in advanced age the sexual changes are nothing to write home about.

Researchers in one study found that the average age when people started to reduce their sexual activity was 68 in men and 60 in women, but other studies suggest even older ages. In general, sexual activities and habits continue into old age. People who are sexually active will continue to be so well into old age, while people who are not very interested in sex when young will not be very interested when old either.

The Benefits

Getting old is not only doom and gloom. There are several benefits which make old age much more enjoyable. In comparison with younger people, older people:

- sweat less
- sneeze less
- suffer less from allergies
- suffer less from travel sickness
- enjoy travelling more
- are less sensitive to pain
- have fewer nightmares
- have a better sense of humour
- are less likely to lose their temper
- have less stress and worry less
- can be slightly overweight and still be considered healthy
- are less likely to suffer from skin scars after injury

All of these are normal consequences of aging.

Conclusion

As you have realized by now, aging is not a disease as such, but a natural process which affects everybody. It may well be associated with some diseases, but many of these can be prevented or treated with great success. Aging is also associated with some changes to the body and to the mind which happen to all of us. These can also be prevented up to a point and some can also be reversed. The choice is up to you.

But before you can get on with your anti-aging routine, there is something else you need to bear in mind: the perils of social aging …

CHAPTER 2

The Effects of Aging

Many people believe that 'aging' inevitably equals 'disease'. This view is thought to be wrong by several eminent gerontologists. Aging is just another part of development, another life stage, like infancy and adolescence. You can grow to a glorious old age without suffering any significant medical problems whatsoever.

It is wrong, in fact, to see the so called Third Age as a time of decrepitude. If the First Age (childhood) is a time for preparation for life and the Second Age (adulthood) a period of productive labour, the Third Age (maturity) is a period of personal fulfilment and satisfaction. Only the Fourth Age (senility) is for infirmity and eventual death, but this period is not necessarily long (days or weeks) and even this should be shortened as much as possible.

Having said that, there are indeed some diseases which are more common in later life but these are not necessarily inevitable. For example, the three most common killers (heart disease, stroke and cancer) are diseases connected with the Western way of life rather than with age alone. African tribes which still follow a more primitive way of life don't have a high incidence of these diseases. The Masai bushmen, for example, have a very low incidence of ischaemic heart disease and heart attacks. What influences the development of these diseases is diet, lack of exercise and smoking.

Some other diseases, for example Alzheimer's senile dementia, are thought to be connected with the process of aging itself. The changes in the brain of patients suffering from Alzheimer's disease are similar to those seen in healthy elderly people, but are much more severe. It seems that if we all lived long enough we would fall into the claws of Alzheimer's dementia. But not all scientists agree with this scenario either, thinking that dementia is something completely separate from the process of growing old.

Dementia apart, no matter what happens to your body, if you have the right attitude, if you think 'young' and if you are always positive, then aging won't ruin your life.

How to Age Successfully

Social aging plays an important part in our health and so it is necessary to highlight certain relevant points. There are three main social theories of aging. These theories see aging in the social sense – how an individual interacts with society – and have nothing to do with the theories of the biology of aging discussed in the previous chapter.

The Disengagement Theory

This sees aging as the process of gradual withdrawal of an individual from the activities of life in order to leave space for new members of society. Society itself also plays a part in this process by pushing the individual to 'disengage' from active life by enforcing retirement and by discriminating against the older person in a variety of subtle and not so subtle ways. The withdrawal from active life is associated with the subconscious desire to start preparing for death. Many older people will say that their turn has passed and it is now the time to make room for a new generation. Those who disagree with this idea are better able to come to terms with their age, and they 'age successfully' in the social and medical sense.

It is certainly true that later life can sometimes bring social isolation and boredom. One way to deal with this is to have many friends or keep in contact with many relatives now, in order to reduce the chances of problems in the future. Don't neglect going out and visiting other people regularly to strengthen your social bonds.

During the past two years how often have you attended activities organized by a club, church, political or other organization? Being a member of an organization greatly reduces the chances of isolation in later life. It is not enough to just belong to a club, though – you should participate in activities that are held there as frequently as possible, no matter how old you are.

Be prepared for the later years, physically, emotionally, mentally, socially and financially. Don't disengage too soon, or better still, don't disengage at all!

The Activity Theory

A slightly different way of seeing aging is what social scientists call the 'activity theory'. Young people are usually active in all areas of life, but as they grow older they progressively abandon their activities. This can be due to the loss of a job, loss of members of the family, loss of friends or loss of hobbies due to physical limitation. But by becoming less active people lose their role and identity, ie they are socially 'aged'.

It is possible to recover some of these losses by keeping active with hobbies, a part-time job, a new course of study and so on. You should also try to maintain your identity through the years by adapting your style to avoid becoming 'just another little old person'. Keeping socially active and enforcing your presence in life will make other people see you as a precious member of society who has something useful to offer and who needs to be respected and valued.

Some people find that the passage of time makes them less confident about their abilities. This is bad news. You should be confident and believe in yourself no matter how old you are. Whatever happened in earlier years may have been very nice and interesting, but now there are many more happy years to look forward to.

The Continuity Theory

Finally, a third theory of social aging is the 'continuity theory'. Here, aging is seen as a continuous process from youth to old age. This theory claims that there are no clear-cut variations and no sharp changes in personality due to aging.

When people grow old, their characteristics do continue to evolve and improve according to circumstances, but the basic personality remains the same. A naughty little boy will become an awkward young husband and then a cantankerous old man. On the other hand, a cute little girl will grow up to be a fashionable woman and finally a coquettish older lady. As one pensioner put it: 'I accept that I am a retired man in receipt of a pension, but I am the same person I was when I was working as an engineering designer.'

One way to deal with any traits in your personality which may evolve to cause serious social problems is to be flexible and adapt easily to change. If you are too rigid and can't cope with change, you will probably have social difficulties later on in life. Try not to be stuck with the past, but accept modern changes. You may have traditional values, but adapt these to suit the world around you.

Happiness

Being happy is the cornerstone to general health and in particular to social health. Do you feel contented and happy with your life now? Are you happy with your partner or with not having a partner? If you had the chance to live your life again, would you change anything?

Feeling unhappy with your partner or with the lack of a partner may not only make you feel miserable now, but it can affect your future health as well. Ask yourself what it is that makes you unhappy, and what you can do about it. Don't leave things until it is too late. Do it now. Stop reading for a moment and think about it.

Many people would like to be able to put right earlier mistakes and consider that their earlier life has not been a success. But whatever your situation, it is never too late to get back onto the right track, and if you feel you have missed an opportunity earlier in life, be dynamic and try to catch up with it now.

One sign of happiness is the ability to look forward to the future.

Ask yourself these crucial questions:

1 Do you keep setting new goals?

2 Are you looking forward to the next five years?

3 Would you prefer to live in the 'good old days' or are you happy to live in modern society?

4 If you have an event or activity booked, do you look forward to it with enjoyment?

5 Are you hopeful that new developments in science will help you delay the signs of aging?

My comments on the questions:

1 People who keep setting new goals show that they believe in their future and that they have not yet given up hope. Even short-term (weekly or monthly) goal-setting keeps hope alive. This will make it easier for you to fit in with society and be better adjusted socially.

    Seek out new opportunities and new experiences in life. Try a new course, a sport you have never done before, a new part-time job. Write a story or a novel for a magazine, try out new concepts, go for new activities in politics/religion/science or art. Be a dreamer, seek new challenges.

2 If you think that the future is only doom and gloom, your thoughts will soon become reality. Growing old should be seen as just another stage of life, with many different opportunities for enjoyment. It is so exciting to experience this part of life and you should be looking forward to it.

    Don't take everything too seriously. Play, relax, don't get upset with little things, let go of your worries. Think of how insignificant you are in the universe. Nothing is important in your short life, apart from living it well, according to your values. Every day should be a great new adventure. Every day is a new opportunity to enjoy life.

3 We all experience constant changes in life. The ability to accept these changes and the new situations makes it easier to stay socially healthy. Many people prefer to live in the past and this is healthy up to a point. However, you shouldn't make the past your master. Even if you prefer the values of the past, act as if you are always happy and cheerful. If you smile, laugh and have the confidence to show you are happy, then you will feel happy.

4 To look forward to events is a sign of a natural positive thinker. Even if the event is expected to happen some time in the future and is not generally considered enjoyable, you can try and find the positive side of it and look forward to that. Always hope for the best scenario, be

optimistic and try to find enjoyment in what you do.
Never say, 'I'm too old for that.' If you can do it, go ahead.

5 Many developments in science can be used to improve
health in later life. There are hundreds of discoveries every
year which can help you maintain health and vitality. You
should be ready for these developments. Be curious. Don't
take everything at face value but read between the lines.

Our society worships youth only because old age was considered to be
worthless. But there are new ideas on the horizon. Youth is a difficult
age, with problems of inexperience and insecurity, whereas maturity is
for security, knowledge, professionalism, stability, wisdom and health.

Marriage and Death

The complex social and medical issues of disease become obvious when
we consider the following results of a research study. Married men, in
general, live longer than unmarried men. Specifically, unmarried men
between the ages of 45 and 64 have a higher risk of dying than those of
the same age who are married. (The term 'married' is taken in the traditional sense and doesn't take into account those men who are single and
live with a woman who is not their wife. This research project doesn't
make it clear whether married women also live longer than unmarried
women.)

So it seems that if a man wants to live longer he has to live with a
woman who is his wife. The reasons are not very clear, but could be
due to the support a wife gives to her husband. Married men have a
wife constantly encouraging (some say 'nagging') them to eat better,
exercise, smoke less, etc, whereas in general, the diet of single men is
not good. They may not have the time to cook, so they constantly eat
ready-made meals. This increases the chances of stress and disease.
Also, they probably smoke and drink more alcohol than married men.

In general, married people have more social contacts and this is
thought to improve longevity. Lonely people die prematurely.

Lastly, the (presumably) happy and regular sexual activities of
married men may be another reason for prolonged life.

There may be other reasons why married men live longer (for
example, genetic reasons in order to look after their children and ensure

survival of the species), but one thing is clear: health is a very complicated issue which is affected by many apparently unrelated factors.

Mental Attitudes

Our attitudes towards old age play an important part in our own longevity. Many people, even older people, consider advanced age to be a disadvantage instead of a positive asset. They expect old age to be a period of decrepitude and suffering instead of a period of new challenges and new experiences. Consequently, when a relatively minor disease strikes, these people think that the problem is due to old age and they don't try to fight back. This becomes a self-fulfilling prophecy because if the disease remains untreated, it will get worse and may cause serious problems in the future.

This is particularly true in the case of disorders which are difficult to see as being a distinct disease, such as:

- memory loss
- aches and pains
- incontinence
- social isolation
- cantankerousness
- general slowing down
- boredom

It is in these cases that we need to fight back. It is normal to be happy, pain free and disease free, even in late life, and that is what we should be aiming to achieve.

Fear of Years

Certain American psychologists believe that, due to our upbringing, we have an increased sensitivity towards aging. Women have been taught that success is being pretty, feminine, having smooth skin and looking after a family. So, if old age brings the opposite, then it is bad and should be avoided. Similarly, men are supposed to be strong, masculine, virile, have high-powered jobs and play competitive sports. Again, if age brings the opposite, then it must be bad and needs to be avoided.

Psychologists say that we need to counteract these thoughts if we want to come to terms with our own aging.

Accordingly, if you are a woman, meditate on 'male' images such as taking important decisions, being dynamic, playing male sports or driving macho cars. A man should think of 'female' images, such as being easily able to deal with emotions, being creative and making oneself physically attractive, especially through the use of beauty care treatments such as skin moisturizers, manicures and facials. The aim of this mental exercise is to reassert yourself as an individual and understand that being a woman does not necessarily mean having a beautiful face and being a man does not necessarily mean having an important job.

Are You Ageist?

Ageism is a prejudice and negative discrimination against old age. It is equivalent to feminism or racism. Ageism is deeply rooted in our society and it can be very difficult to spot. Older people can themselves be ageists without realizing it.

Sometimes, when I meet young people, I ask them the following questions:

- Do you think that as we grow old our health will get significantly worse?

- Does the sense of adventure decline considerably with age?

- Do you believe that most people over the age of 60 have no interest in sex?

- Do you estimate that about one in 10 pensioners lives in residential accommodation (old people's homes)?

Most answer 'yes' to all of these questions. This shows how ageist our youth is. If you answered 'yes' even once, then you are ageist too. The fact is that health, the sense of adventure and sexuality do not necessarily get worse with the passage of years. There are millions of older people who are completely healthy, are productive and enjoy life in general. Research shows that the majority of people over the age of 75 who have a partner have regular sexual intercourse. Only one in 25 pensioners lives in residential accommodation.

If you are still not convinced, consider this: two thirds of British adults believe that older people are not respected by younger people. Also, a questionnaire addressed to 16–25-year-olds revealed that they consider 'old' people to be those who are 50 and over. This tells you how ageist our youth is.

Many of you must have seen the British traffic sign depicting an old couple carrying walking sticks with the warning: 'Disabled People'. Who on Earth designed this sign? Why should age be a sign of disability? And, for that matter, why should we be careful of older people in particular? It is a different matter if there are disabled elderly people in the area, but a healthy able-bodied older person should not be treated any differently from anybody else.

Likewise, when I see the notice 'Please give your seat up to an elderly person' in trains and buses, I want to scream. Who is elderly? The Oxford Dictionary describes 'elderly' as 'a person past middle age'. Perhaps the sign should say 'frail person', drawing our attention to somebody who is physically weak and not merely to somebody who is over a certain age. I think it is insulting when people over the age of 25 offer their seat to other healthy people just because they appear to be 'elderly'. It is as if they are saying: 'Look at me, I am strong and fit, whereas you are so weak and pathetic that you can't even stand for a few minutes.' Children or very young people should show respect to senior citizens and offer their seat as a mark of gallant value, but not because they think that they are stronger or fitter than the older person.

Spotting ageism can be very difficult. Ask yourself the following questions and then think about the comments:

1 When you approach an important birthday (eg, 40, 50, 60) do you get anxious or upset?

2 Do you think that people of your age or older can be attractive?

3 Do you get on well with teenagers?

4 Do you think that the signs of aging on your body make you look bad?

5 Do you agree with women having fertility treatment after the age of 50?

Comments:

1 Landmark birthdays are a time for reflection. It is natural to think back and to compare the past, present and future. If you look forward to the future as well as looking back to your past, you are less likely to be affected by the passage of years.

   Research shows that people live longer if, on average, they are happy, non-smokers, intelligent, have a positive attitude to life and have a good social life. People who live longer are usually older than their spouse, are older siblings, have few children and continue working through to their retirement. They have long-lived parents, a young mother and up to the age of 40 they looked younger than their actual age.

2 People of any age can look attractive if they make some effort. If you think that people older than you still look attractive, it means that you believe that you can look attractive too when you are their age.

3 If you get on well with teenagers it means that you don't have any problems with looking youth in the face and accepting your own age. If teenagers get on well with you it is probably because you have a young mind and refreshing thoughts.

4 The physical signs of aging have different values for different people. Those who think that they are an asset have high self-esteem and are likely to look good in years to come. People who say that they feel 'old' are more likely to suffer from the effects of social aging. Instead of saying, 'I feel old,' say what you actually mean. You probably mean 'I feel tired or exhausted.' The two are not the same at all.

5 Some people will argue that if you agree with older women having fertility treatment it means that you are ready to accept the developments of science. This acceptance will make it easier for you to get new scientific treatments when necessary. It may also indicate that you accept modern society more easily. Not everybody agrees with this argument.

Computers and Learning

Another area where ageism comes into question is learning in old age. For example, many people think that it is impossible for older people to learn how to use computers. This attitude reflects earlier stereotypes about old age which portray aging as a period of decline, loss and dysfunction. Looking at current research we can see that not only is it possible to teach old dogs new tricks, but also possible to teach them things that they had never even heard of a few years ago.

Researchers from the University of Ulster in Ireland have proved that it is possible to teach 75-year-olds how to use computers to write their own life histories. Other researchers have successfully taught people over 80 years old how to use the Internet. Learning these skills improves the confidence, well-being and social contacts of older people. This research is marvellous news to those who believe that it is necessary to exercise the brain to maintain it in peak condition. It also shows that earlier stereotypes about old age should now be reconsidered in the light of modern research.

41

Your Personal Aging

If you agree with the comments in this chapter, it means that your personal aging is smooth and elegant. You have a very good chance of maintaining your social health and feeling good in the years to come. You can see many positive aspects of getting older.

If you disagree with the majority of my comments, social scientists would argue that you are aging poorly and unsuccessfully. You think that getting old is only doom and gloom. Try changing your attitudes, work on your relationships, your beliefs and on your appearance.

Conclusion

Making an effort to reduce the effects of social aging will prevent the very thing people are afraid of: disability and disease in older life.

There are two paths to total fulfilment. The first path is: 'Act as if you are going to live forever.' Start new projects, plant a tree to see it grow, no matter what your age is now. When my aunt was 90 years old, she emigrated to a different country, built a new home and started a new life. She is still happy and well.

The second path is: 'Act as if you are going to die at any moment.'

Don't miss any opportunities, enjoy each particular moment because you will never experience it again. If you don't stop to look at a rose now, somebody will cut it tomorrow and you will have missed the chance to give that little pleasure to yourself.

Philosophers say that incorporating the positive parts of these two pathways is the basis of all true personal happiness. Think about it.

Death and Hope

An old man who had travelled a long way carrying a huge burden of sticks found himself so weary that he cast it down and called upon Death to deliver him from his miserable life. Death heard him and came to his call and asked him what was the problem. The old man looked at him and, changing his mind, said: 'Please, sir, do help me lift up my burden and continue my travels!'

Aesop's Fable

One reason why people dread old age is the fear of approaching death. The realization that we only have a short time on this Earth and that death is not only inevitable but, most importantly, permanent, must be the most bitter discovery each one of us has to make.

The preoccupation with longevity and death is, according to religion, due to a decline in faith in divine salvation from death. We don't believe as widely as before that immortality is possible by divine action. So to avoid death we either ignore the problem altogether (ie, we put a taboo on it) or we try to find other ways of dealing with it.

For Christian believers, there is life after death so it doesn't matter if we die now, for we will live again in heaven forever. Similarly, for Muslims there is life in heaven awaiting the righteous. It is very comforting to know that if you live your life with a certain virtue, you will be rewarded by eternal life in Paradise. Some true believers in fact see their life here on Earth as an obstacle to eternal life and believe the sooner they finish it here the better. This, perhaps, is one reason why so many young believers are not afraid to die in combat.

For Hindus, there is the belief in reincarnation, that a person will come again on this Earth in another life. Reincarnation is a quite widespread belief and it may serve the purpose of cushioning the fear of death. Whether it actually happens or not, believers still experience a sense of internal tranquillity and a reduced fear of death. Why should you fear death if there is the guarantee that you will come back again in a different form? Why should you try and prolong this life when you have the opportunity to live again as somebody else?

Other religions like Jehovah's Witnesses believe that there will be a final battle between God and Satan and, following this, a period where aging will stop, ie, we will achieve immortality of the body as well as the soul.

But what about the non-believers, the agnostics and the atheists? It is a very soul-destroying conclusion to realize that life is finite and there is no hope of revival.

Cryonics, the freezing of human bodies in the hope that they can be revived in the future, suggests a way out of this by offering hope of a future life after a period of suspended animation. This theme of suspended animation goes back through the ages, with the fairytale of Sleeping Beauty probably the earliest example. In this, the princess lies asleep for many, many years and when woken up by the prince, she is as young as she was before she fell asleep.

These and other exotic ideas all attempt to satisfy our inability to face death and to reduce our fears regarding the finiteness of human life. As we grow older, it is only natural to begin to consider such matters. It is remarkable that many young scientists believe that there is no life after death and yet, as they grow older and realize the prospect of their own certain death, they begin to change their minds about their original theories and trust that there may be some hope after all.

Whatever our beliefs, coming to terms with death is a vital part of learning to live well. Another part is making the most of life, and that includes aging well. What can we do to stop or at least slow down aging? We can do many, many things. First, prevent it, then treat it and finally reverse it. Let's start with prevention.

Part II

Part II

CHAPTER 3

The Secrets of Anti-Aging

Every morning, Nustreddin Hodja (Hodja is the title for a wise Muslim priest) asked his young son to take their one and only clay pot and go to get water from the village well. Each time, before the boy set off for his journey, the Hodja used to hit him two or three times with a cane. The boy, curious, once asked his father, 'Why do you punish me?' The Hodja explained, 'It's all about you breaking the pot.' 'But,' the boy cried, 'I haven't broken the pot!' 'I know,' said the Hodja. 'But I hit you now to make you extra careful. If you do break the pot it would be too late and there wouldn't be any point in me punishing you. No amount of punishment would bring my pot back!'

The meaning of this story is, you've guessed it, 'prevention is better than cure'. So, what can we do to prevent age-related illnesses?

In theory, it is possible to prevent most types of heart problems, strokes and cancers, as well as some other diseases like killer genetic disorders and environmentally-induced diseases. According to some researchers, the prevention of all of these diseases would increase the average human life span by 10–30 years, making it possible to live comfortably to the age of 100–120 (ie, stretch the average life span to the limits of the maximum life span). According to this scenario, people would live their lives without worrying about dying prematurely. Life would be much easier because most of the elderly people (even those who lived to 100) would be comparatively healthy and therefore better able to enjoy their lives.

These predictions are now becoming a reality. By the year 2050 there will be 6 million people in Britain aged 75 and over. The numbers of people aged 90 and over will increase by an amazing 600 per cent. In the USA the number of people over the age of 65 will top 65 million by the year 2030. By investing in aging research and health strategies now we can make enormous savings in healthcare costs in the future.

After reaching the magic limit of 100–120 years, new diseases are likely to intervene to cause death. It is almost as if nature doesn't want us to live longer than this time limit and as soon as we eliminate one disease of aging, others appear. This causes considerable debate between scientists. For example some doctors believe that there is a limit on our average life span. It is only biologically possible, they say, to live to a mere 85 years and those who live to be over that age are just an exception to the rule, nothing more than freaks of nature.

Whatever our natural limit, it would be unfair just to expect a few hundred scientists to come up with new ways for improving our health. It is the responsibility of all of us to take care of ourselves and keep our body and mind as healthy as possible.

Most people in their younger years take good care of themselves physically with a lot of exercise, socially with a great many activities and mentally by studying at school or at college. After reaching middle age, however, it becomes harder to look after ourselves. It is during this period that we need to make that extra effort and take up a really healthy lifestyle. By avoiding disability in middle age, we increase our chances of living a healthy life well into our nineties and beyond.

Given the prospect of living another 20 years and being completely healthy, most people will happily grab the opportunity. People who don't make any effort to live longer should ask themselves: why die earlier than normal? Why die young? Not trying to live a healthier life is like driving a car with your eyes closed: you increase the chances of dying early, at a time when you are not supposed to.

Statistically:

- a 35-year-old man has another 40 years to live
- a woman of the same age can expect to live another 44 years
- a 50-year-old man is likely to live for another 26 years
- a woman of the same age another 30
- those in their early seventies can expect to live another 10 or 15 years on average

Researchers also say that people who live in the country or suburbs have a better chance of avoiding disease and therefore live longer than inner-city dwellers, who have more stress and suffer from more health problems.

Aging Well

Prevention

Prevention is always better than cure and today lifestyle evaluation organizations can even offer you practical prevention checks. The idea is that to be able to live longer we need to have near-perfect health and so should try to prevent illnesses before they appear. The checkup consists of a variety of tests, from the well-known standard blood, heart and urine tests to the more unusual like the measurement of some obscure hormones in the blood, the estimation of the level of the by-products of aging, mineral analysis, naturopathic screening and several other computerized tests.

Although the idea of prevention is very attractive, several more traditional doctors, particularly in the UK, say that there is no evidence to suggest that such a complete body health analysis helps people live longer. It may help in the early detection of some diseases like osteoporosis, but this can also be achieved by performing one or two simple and cheaper tests on people who are at high risk. As my medical trainer used to say, 'We should treat the patient and not the piece of paper with the laboratory result on it.' Conservative doctors say that if you feel generally well and if your basic medical checkup is normal, there is no need to embark on anything more complicated, unless there is a specific reason to do so.

In preventing age-related problems a lot depends on us. But what is your age now?

Your Biological Age

There are many scientific tests which assess the biological age of a person. These tests use special devices and measuring machines as well as extensive blood tests in the laboratory. It is also possible to evaluate your own age by using specially devised questionnaires, which are much simpler but not as accurate as the laboratory tests.

Do-It-Yourself Age Test

The following tests and questions are for general guidance only and are not meant to identify all possible age-related problems. The idea is to give you an overview of your own rate of aging and to stimulate you to improve certain areas of your health. The result is not supposed to pinpoint your biological age exactly, only to make you generally aware that there may be a problem which needs sorting out.

AGE TEST: 1

(This is not suitable for very young or very old people.)

1 Ask your doctor or nurse to check your blood pressure (or check it yourself if you have the equipment). Ask what the high value is (the systolic blood pressure) in millimetres of mercury.

If you are a man:

125 is average for a 30-year-old.

130 is average for a 40-year-old.

135 is average for a 50-year-old.

140 is average for a 60-year-old.

155 is average for a 70-year-old.

160 is average for an 80-year-old.

If you are a woman:

120 is average for a 35-year-old.

130 is average for a 45-year-old.

140 is average for a 55-year-old.

150 is average for a 60-year-old.

155 is average for a 65-year-old.

160 is average for a 70-year-old.

165 is average for an 80-year-old.

2 Use glasses if you are short-sighted, but not if you are long-sighted. Hold a newspaper at arm's length and concentrate on the normal letters, not the headlines. Bring the newspaper nearer and nearer to your eyes and stop where the letters start appearing blurred. Measure this distance exactly with a tape measure or a ruler.

100cm is normal for a 60-year-old and over.

40cm is normal for a 50-year-old.

20cm is normal for a 40-year-old.

10cm is normal for a 30-year-old.

3 Stand unsupported on one leg, with your hands on your hips and eyes open. Time how long you can stand without falling.

70 seconds is normal for a 30-year-old.

60 seconds is normal for a 40-year-old.

50 seconds is normal for a 50-year-old.

40 seconds is normal for a 60-year-old.

30 seconds is normal for a 70-year-old.

20 seconds is normal for an 80-year-old.

Do the same with your eyes closed.

1–2 seconds is average for an 80-year-old.

3 seconds is average for a 70-year-old.

4 seconds is average for a 60 year old.

9 seconds is average for a 50-year-old.

15 seconds is average for a 40-year-old.

20 seconds is average for a 30-year-old.

4 Gently pinch the skin on the back of your hand and hold it for about 40–50 seconds. Then let go and measure the time needed for the skin to retract to a level position.

> Less than 1 second is normal for a 30-year-old.
>
> 1 second is normal for a 40-year-old.
>
> 4 seconds is normal for a 50-year-old.
>
> 8 seconds is normal for a 55-year-old.
>
> 11 seconds is normal for a 60-year-old.
>
> 15 seconds is normal for a 65-year-old.
>
> 30 seconds is normal for a 70-year-old or over.

5 Warm up first, then see how many push-ups you can do in 30 seconds.

If you are a man:

> 25 is average for a 30-year-old.
>
> 20 is average for a 40-year-old.
>
> 15 is average for a 50-year-old.
>
> 10 is average for a 60-year-old.
>
> 4 is average for a 70-year-old.
>
> 2 is average for an 80-year-old.

If you are a woman:

> 12 is average for a 30-year-old.
>
> 8 is average for a 40-year-old.
>
> 6 is average for a 50-year-old.
>
> 4 is average for a 60-year-old.
>
> 3 is average for a 70-year-old.
>
> 2 is average for an 80-year-old.

6 Ask a friend to make a list of 10 male and female names at random. Study these for one minute, then cover the list up and write down as many names as you can remember.

> 8 names is normal for a 40-year-old (or under).
>
> 7 names is normal for a 50-year-old.

6 names is normal for a 60-year-old.

5 names is normal for a 70-year-old.

4 names is normal for a 80-year-old.

Score

Now calculate your biological age. For each of your answers, round your values to the nearest value shown in each test. Add up all the years based on your results. Divide this by seven. This is your approximate biological age.

If your biological age is lower than your actual chronological age, then your body is younger than average. If your biological age is higher than your chronological age, your body is older than average.

Another way to find out where you stand on the biological aging path is shown in the following age test.

AGE TEST: 2

1 Measure your waist and hips.

Waist (over belly button) is …

Hips (over the fattest part of the hip joints) measure …

Divide your waist measure by your hip measure. The result is …

If you are a man:

A score of up to 0.95 is normal.

A score of 0.96 and above is not normal.

If you are a woman:

A score of up to 0.79 is normal.

A score of 0.8 and above is not normal.

2 To calculate your body mass index (BMI):

Measure your weight in kilograms … (this is value A).

Measure your height in metres … and multiply this by itself (the result is value B).

Now divide value A by value B.

A score of 19–25 is normal.

Anything else is not normal.

Continue with the questions, answering 'Yes' or 'No':

3 Have you had a major illness in the last 10 years?

4 Have you ever had any serious allergies?

5 When you cut yourself, does the wound take a long time to heal?

6 Have you ever had frequent antibiotic courses for infection?

7 Do you catch a cold easily?

8 When you do have a cold does it usually take over three days to get better?

9 Do you get any of the following more frequently than once every six months?
Thrush, cold sores, mouth ulcers, skin infections.

10 Do you feel 'old'?

11 Do you have any heredity-related diseases in your immediate family (eg, heart disease, blood pressure, diabetes)?

12 Have any two of the following died before the age of 70: a grandfather, grandmother, father or mother?

13 Does your job or lifestyle involve any amount of danger?

14 Do you drive (or are driven) more than 10,000 miles a year?

15 Do you frequent a place where it is very noisy, dirty or dusty?

Score

Steps 1 and 2: No points for each 'Normal', one point for each 'Not normal'.

Questions 3–15: One point for every 'Yes' answer and no points for every 'No' answer.

Your total is ...

0–1 *Amazing.* Your body is younger than your age. Try to maintain it that way. Only constant effort will make sure that your body stays healthy.

2–3 *OK.* You are in good physical condition, but you can still improve it. A small degree of effort will defend your body against the ravages of age.

4–7 *Neither here nor there.* There are several ways in which you can improve your score. Look at the comments below and refer to the relevant sections of the book. Having an average score doesn't mean that you should feel satisfied with yourself.

8–15 *Awful.* Your body is older than your actual age. Pay particular attention to your answers and the comments and advice below. There are some risk factors which you cannot change but it is important to concentrate on those areas where an improvement is likely. See your doctor or other registered healthcare practitioner for further advice.

Comments

Steps 1 and 2 These check for obesity. Being overweight carries significant health risks but it doesn't make such an impact on health after the age of 75.

3–9 A strong immunity is a sign that the aging process has not caused much damage yet. The chances of cancer and infectious diseases are reduced. Immunity may be less than perfect in people with allergies and in those who catch infections easily. A wound that heals slowly marks an inability of the repair systems to deal with damage effectively. Try to keep your immune system in a healthy condition. Read the sections on immunity in other parts of this book.

10 Research shows that those who give up on life are more likely to suffer from the effects of age. Some connections do exist between mentality and disease.

11, 12 Longevity runs in families. If your parents or

55

grandparents lived a long healthy life, you have an increased probability of enjoying the same. The longer your parents lived, the better chance you have for a long life.

13, 14 To live a longer, healthier life you must also avoid early death by accidents. If you follow a high-risk lifestyle you have an increased risk of early death and disability. Spend some time looking at ways of reducing physical danger in your life. This is worth doing even if you lead a low-risk lifestyle.

15 Occupational diseases can shorten life. Noise, dirt and dust can cause several preventable diseases. It is not only up to the employer to improve working conditions, it is everybody's responsibility.

Compare your results in the first and second age tests. If they correspond, it means that your aging is balanced (either for better or for worse, but balanced nevertheless). If not, it means that some parts of your body age slower or faster than others. This could be a bad thing, so it's better to do something about it now.

Conclusion

Here is my advice on anti-aging lifestyles according to your age and sex. This general advice may be relevant to average, healthy people but it may not be particularly suited to you. It summarizes the advice given throughout the book in a few sentences. If in doubt, see your healthcare practitioner or refer to the relevant section of the book to expand on the details.

Men

AGED 25–40

Go to the gym for exercise or take a regular energetic swim or cycle ride or do another active sport at least three times a week. Check your testicles for any lumps. Avoid smoking and aim for fewer than 20 units of alcohol a week. Health supplements should include broad-spectrum antioxidants such as suitable doses of vitamins A, C, E and selenium. Practise safe, frequent sex.

AGED 41–55

Consider saw palmetto or other prostate supplements if necessary. Spend extra time taking care of your skin. Supplements may include more specific 'anti-agers' such as carnosine and pycnogenol (*see* chapter 10).

Exercise should include less energetic gym training and more outdoor activities such as tennis, golf and walking. Start brain exercises and chi kung two or three times a week. Now is the time to do something about your bulging stomach with regular abdominal exercises, diet, massage and holding in the muscles constantly.

AGED 56–70

Continue taking, or considering the use of, prostate supplements (saw palmetto, nettle root, *Pygeum*). Think about your new life in retirement and avoid the pitfalls of social aging. Increase your social activities and consider a course of study, a part-time job or a new hobby. Aim for regular walking, swimming or home exercises.

Have suitable checkups with your doctor, optician and dentist. Your choice of supplements may include isoflavones, antioxidants such as vitamin E, Q10, plus carnosine. Use ginkgo biloba for brain health, if required. Think about osteoporosis and take over 1,000mg of calcium a day. Consider growth hormone releasers. Continue chi kung training. Do daily stretching exercises to keep the joints in top condition.

AGED 71–80

Your lifestyle should include all of the above plus the following. Contemplate extra anti-aging drugs such as DHEA or pregnenolone. Review your illnesses and any prescription medication regularly with your doctor. Avoid routine if possible. Continue with calcium supplements and isoflavones. Perform regular low-intensity brain exercises.

AGED 80 PLUS

A healthy lifestyle is still essential. Biologically speaking, smoking doesn't matter much by now, but regular exercise does. Continue the supplements as above and aim for low-level but regular brain exercises. Look after your appearance and personal hygiene. Pay extra attention to your diet, which should contain enough fish or chicken protein, pulses and vegetables. Consider travelling, perhaps adventure travelling. Enjoy yourself and don't leave any health problems untreated.

Women

AGED 25–40

Exercise should include energetic gym exercises or training at home. Use moisturizers regularly and consider anti-aging creams. Avoid the sun or sun-beds. Look after your hair. Try to find a suitable partner and establish a stable relationship.

Use antioxidant supplements such as vitamins C, E and selenium. Pay attention to your weight. Consume high calcium foods. Get regular check-ups for general health including cancer of the cervix. Start chi kung or yoga.

AGED 41–55

Protect yourself against the sun and use antioxidant creams, moisturizers and antioxidant supplements. Carnosine and vitamin C supplements are better, but also consider Q10 and isoflavones. Get extra help from hormones such as DHEA and growth hormone releasers. Start dong quai or isoflavone supplements if necessary.

Perform facial muscle exercises. Drink extra quantities of water or green tea and aim for larger portions of dark-coloured fruit and vegetables. Continue eating high calcium foods and start calcium supplements. Exercise should include swimming, brisk walking, aerobics and sports.

This is the best stage in life. Find new interests/hobbies or start a new career. Look after your weight and slightly reduce your calories (as we age we don't need as many calories as before). Consider memory boosters if needed. Rethink your sex life to allow for problems related to the menopause. Look after your emotional self and do regular brain exercises, meditation and visualization.

AGED 56–65

Choose exercises such as daily swimming and walking rather than dangerous sports such as skiing or horse riding to reduce the risk of bone fractures. Other suitable forms of exercise include yoga, t'ai chi or chi kung. Try aquarobics. Stretching exercises will keep your joints supple and mobile.

Health supplements should include DHEA, carnosine and calcium, 1,000mg a day at least, with at least 400iu vitamin D. Don't avoid the sun completely to help your body manufacture the desperately needed vitamin D. Strict dieting may not be that important but avoid excesses. Red wine is fine. Have fun with your life.

Sex problems should be seen as medical problems and not as 'just aging'. Your skin still needs moisturizers. Treat medical problems properly as they arise and learn to adapt your life to live with them if no cure is available at present. Plan ahead for possible medical problems.

AGED 66–76

Aim to increase and strengthen your social activities to avoid isolation. Do mental exercises at least four times a week even for a few minutes at a time. Brain supplements are ginkgo, DHEA and phosphatidyl serine. Continue calcium and antioxidants with carnosine or similar.

Do what you enjoy instead of worrying too much about your lifestyle. Look after your appearance. Many women discover new interests and new directions during this period. Try more sedate hobbies, preferably new ones. Painting, country walking, travelling, reading and discussing the book afterwards, doing volunteer and charity work are all beneficial.

Be on the lookout for osteoporosis, heart disease, breast cancer and arthritis. Explore alternative anti-aging treatments if you wish. Be careful to avoid problems which may appear later in life such as immobility, chronic diseases, malnutrition. Be prepared for possible bereavement.

AGED 77 PLUS

You could have another 20 years or more to enjoy, so you need to continue with a healthy lifestyle. Widowhood may be a problem, but try to keep in touch with friends or relatives to avoid isolation and loneliness.

Treat all your medical problems as effectively as possible and have regular check-ups with your doctor, nurse and optician. Continue walking regularly at least four times a week. Perform mild mental exercises every day. Take supplements such as vitamins C, E and selenium. There is no need to avoid the sun, which is needed for vitamin D, the bone booster.

CHAPTER 4

Time-Busting Nutrition

Luigi Cornaro was an Italian nobleman born in 1467. He led a life of sensual pleasures, overindulgence and extremes, as many of us do today. By middle age he was crippled with gout, stomach pains, fever and arthritis. It was then that he suddenly decided to change completely and live a life of restraint.

After some time, his health levels returned to normal and he lived to the ripe age of 98. He wrote four books on health and longevity, the latest being completed when he was 95. His classic treatise 'How to live one hundred years' advises:

> The two rules for maintaining health and prolonging life are quality and quantity ... A regular life preserves man to the age of a hundred and upwards ... A proper diet is the most important factor in achieving long life ... Eat what you like when you like, and die young.

Remember, this was written over 500 years ago! The importance of a proper lifestyle and dietary habits was recognized by this nobleman at a time when the majority of the population hardly reached the age of 40. Even today the validity of his suggestions can't be denied. One of his main suggestions, to eat less and in moderation, is now considered by some to be the key to long life.

A bit later on, an Englishman called Thomas Parr was reputed to have lived to the age of 152 by adopting a meagre vegetarian diet and drinking sour whey. He was said to have married when he was 120 and his wife boasted that they had regular intercourse. King Charles I invited him to his palace to ask him the secrets of his longevity and treated him with great hospitality. Unfortunately the king's diet of meats and other rich food did not suit Mr Parr, who died shortly afterwards.

So you see, eating can not only sustain life, but also kill you. The correct nutrition will help you achieve the best possible health.

However, there is a difference between healthy eating and anti-aging eating. Eating for general health is a vague concept which doesn't address any particular health problems but rather promotes overall health. Anti-aging nutrition, however, is specific to youth and longevity on the one hand and to age-related diseases on the other.

Certain foods are particularly effective in helping to boost our body's defences in the fight against aging. Other foods are useful in defying age-related diseases such as arthritis and osteoporosis. These foods can easily be included in our everyday diet, but we need to make the effort to choose them wisely and to consume them regularly in order to enjoy the maximum benefits.

A substantial part of anti-aging nutrition is devoted to fighting free radical damage.

Free Radicals

The theory that aging is caused by free radicals is currently the best known in the scientific and anti-aging communities. Several dietary antioxidants can boost the performance of the body's own free radical scavengers, the 'mop-up molecules' which neutralize FR and therefore minimize the damage they cause. Examples of the most common and best known antioxidants are:

- vitamin E
- vitamin C
- beta carotene
- selenium

Other free radical scavengers are less well known but equally effective.

61

These include chemicals such as:

- pycnogenol
- carnosine
- grapeseed extract
- isoflavones

These will be discussed more fully in chapter 10.

Another extremely efficient free radical scavenger is the chemical superoxide dismutase, or SOD for short. Cutting-edge research has found that SOD supplements can help prevent heart attacks and arthritis, and can slow down aging. A study of centenarians has shown that people who live to be over 100 years old have high levels of natural SOD in their blood.

However, other researchers warn that taking very high levels of artificial SOD supplements on their own may produce more problems than benefits. It is best to take these supplements in balance with other antioxidants such as vitamin E or vitamin C. In this way, the potency of each individual antioxidant is increased and the effects are much more powerful.

To reduce production of free radicals you should aim to avoid taking iron supplements. Iron is important in preventing certain forms of anaemia but it should only be taken on medical advice. It is not an all-purpose 'pick-me-up'. Several research projects have made scientists aware that too much iron in the blood can boost the effectiveness of free radicals, helping them to cause even more damage.

Anti-Aging Foods

Several foods can help us live longer, look younger and generally fight the aging process. Certain foods can also help in reducing the risk of age-related diseases, such as stroke, Alzheimer's dementia, osteoporosis, cancer and heart disease.

Phytochemicals

One group of anti-aging foods is the large group of phytochemicals. Phytochemicals are natural substances found in fruit, vegetables and other plants or plant products. They have antioxidant properties but can also fight the aging process in many other ways.

Phytochemicals are divided into four large groups:

1 flavonoids (also called polyphenols), which are further divided into two principal sub-groups: isoflavones and anthocyanidins, though there are other smaller groups such as the lignans

2 carotenoids

3 chlorophyll

4 betacyanin

Carotenoids are, as the name suggests, found in carrots, but also in many other plants and include the vitamin beta carotene. I am not going to discuss chlorophyl and betacyanin here because they are not that important in aging, or at least not yet. I will concentrate on the flavonoids, as these are currently a hot topic in the field of anti-aging medicine.

As mentioned above, flavonoids are broadly divided into isoflavones and anthocyanidins. Isoflavones play an important role in the menopause and will be discussed in more detail later on. Anthocyanidins include chemicals from bilberries and cranberries, as well as from grapeseed and pine bark (pycnogenol). These chemicals are sometimes also called OPCs (oligomeric proantocyanidins). They are used to help prevent macular degeneration, to prevent infections and to improve circulation. They are potent antioxidants, 50 times stronger than vitamin E. Anthocyanidins prevent free radical damage to proteins, cell membranes, collagen and DNA.

Scientific research on the effects of anthocyanidins shows that they are also effective at reducing joint inflammation, that they improve the fragility of the small veins of the skin, thus preventing easy bruising, and that they help maintain healthy skin. They also help prevent heart disease by improving the supporting materials collagen and elastin within the wall of the arteries. Certain anthocyanidins are used in cream form to help protect the skin from sun and age-related damage.

Pycnogenol, a particular type of anthocyanidin, is becoming increasingly popular in the field of anti-aging medicine. It has strong antioxidant properties and it is used to combat free radical damage to the skin, heart and brain. However, tablets containing pycnogenol can sometimes cause mouth ulcers.

Strong concentrations of a variety of phytochemicals are present in:

- garlic
- grapes and berries
- herbs and seeds
- tomatoes
- pomegranates

Garlic lowers blood pressure and cholesterol, and prevents stroke and heart disease. It has been used for thousands of years to promote health.

Grapes and berries should be eaten regularly, at least once a week. Strawberries, blueberries and red grapes contain 20 different types of natural antioxidants.

As for herbs, thyme, rosemary, frankincense and oregano are all good antioxidants and anti-aging factors. Researchers from Scotland have been using herbs in order to fight age-related damage in mice and other laboratory animals. Thyme oil and some other herbs are also available in capsule or liquid form. Instead of sprinkling salt on your food, use dried mixed herbs for taste.

Seeds from pumpkins, sesame and sunflowers contain natural anti-aging substances and should be used regularly as part of an age-defying diet. Chew the seeds thoroughly to break the husk.

If you look into this subject, you will be surprised to discover how many different edible types of seeds are on the market. A single seed has inside it the power to create a whole new plant, complete with flowers or fruit, so you can imagine how it can energize your health.

Raw tomatoes contain lycopene, which is a powerful natural anti-cancer chemical. Sun-dried and tinned tomatoes are also very useful, but

How to eat odourless garlic

Put some unpeeled cloves of garlic in a cup and sprinkle with olive oil. Microwave for 30 seconds. Unpeel and eat with meals.

cooked tomatoes or tomato sauce are the best. Lycopene is better absorbed in the presence of oil, so, for example, eat tomatoes sprinkled with olive oil. Tomatoes also contain other types of phytochemicals which have antioxidant properties.

Pomegranates contain the agent virucide which can kill more than 1,000 million viruses in a few minutes. They may be helpful in shortening the duration of colds, flu, cold sores and other viral infections.

People who eat one chocolate bar (40g) a week are likely to live, on average, one year longer than those who don't eat chocolate at all. Researchers reported in the *British Medical Journal* that chocolate contains the antioxidants phenols which help lower the risk of heart disease. Eating chocolate three or more times a week, though, causes an increase in the death rate.

There are many different types and groups of phytochemicals. All of these are strong antioxidants and they can be used in reducing the risk of cancer.

65

Flavonoids

Flavonoids also have other effects. Research has shown that regular use of flavonoids reduces the risk of heart disease and can soften the symptoms of the menopause. Flavonoids are abundant in:

- citrus fruit
- apples
- strawberries
- pears
- mangoes
- broccoli
- onions
- dark beer
- red wine
- tea
- grape juice

Natural Hormones

Another group of phytochemicals is the phyto-oestrogens. These are natural hormones found most commonly in soya products, such as:

- soya beans
- tofu
- tempeh
- soya milk
- soya butter

Research into the effects of phyto-oestrogens shows that these can help reduce the risk of breast cancer and improve menopausal symptoms. Researchers who studied the effects of soya protein in the diet found that it reduces hot flushes, night sweats, irritability and vaginal dryness.

Soya beans contain the phytochemical genistein (a flavonoid) which, according to some scientists, can help fight cancer of the prostate and reduce the risk of thickening of the arteries (atherosclerosis).

Many phytochemicals, including phyto-oestrogens, are also available in tablet or powder form. Examples of products easily available in health shops are:

- bilberry extract
- grapeseed extract

How to increase your intake of soya

- When making hamburgers or other dishes requiring mince, use soya protein mixed with mince instead of mince alone.

- Eat soya beans both dried and green, in salads.

- Use tofu, tempeh (soya bean cake) or roasted soya nuts.

- Use soya milk and soya flour in cooking.

    (It is best to avoid soya bean oil as it is too fatty and may cause indigestion.)

- pycnogenol
- soya powder

These supplements are prepared using natural sources. They are useful because they make up for the low amount of natural anti-aging ingredients in the Western diet. You should remember, however, that what is 'natural' may not necessarily be good for you, and some natural products can have side effects similar to those caused by synthetic drugs.

The Benefits of Alcohol

Alcohol, in particular red wine, if drunk in moderation has several health benefits. Apart from alcohol, red wine contains many different types of antioxidants and other anti-aging substances, such as catechins. Reservatrol is the name of another miracle wine chemical you are going to hear more and more about in the future. Drinking two glasses of red wine a day was shown to protect against heart disease.

Beer and other types of alcoholic drinks may also have anti-aging effects if drunk in moderation. Certain scientists believe that it is better to have one or two alcoholic drinks a day than having no alcohol at all. Consuming more than this amount is, of course, not recommended. These observations are based on research which shows that teetotallers are more likely to have heart disease than people who consume a small amount of alcohol regularly.

Fatty Acids

Fat is essential to life. Without it our skin would shrink and sag, our cells would disintegrate and our brain would stop working. What we need to avoid is too much of the wrong kind of fat. Consuming the right type of fat, on the other hand, can optimize our fight against aging.

Take for example, omega-3 fatty acids. These are the essential agents which help lower blood pressure, prevent abnormal clotting of the blood and prevent thickening of the arteries. In this way heart attacks and stroke can be prevented. Other age-busting effects of omega-3 fatty acids include an improvement in rheumatoid arthritis and in osteoarthritis. Consuming omega-3-fatty acids regularly can reduce the risk of cancer of the bowel or cancer of the ovaries.

Tuna, salmon, pilchards, herring, trout, anchovies, whitebait, sardines and mackerel are rich in fatty acids. It is best to eat these kind of fish frequently – twice a week can reduce the risk of heart disease substantially – but there is also the alternative of taking fish oil supplements in the form of capsules.

Another source of essential fatty acids is flax oil and flax seeds. These are available from health food stores. Flax seed extract can also be taken in capsule or liquid form.

Omega-3 fatty acids can also be found in perilla oil. This oil prevents certain types of heart disease, fights chronic inflammation and maintains the cells in good condition. Perilla oil comes from the beefsteak plant known as *Perilla frutescens*. It is frequently used by East Asians and it is available from some health shops in capsule form. Perilla oil doesn't cause indigestion, which is a problem commonly encountered with other forms of oils.

Natural Supplements and Drugs

First, a word of advice: if you are considering taking any supplements, check with your doctor or a suitably qualified nutritionist beforehand. Many people take supplements without being sure exactly why they take them. It is best to take a combination of supplements suitable for your own particular health needs, not just some that you saw advertised somewhere. As I said before, a 'natural' product may still have significant side effects in sensitive people.

There are several dietary supplements used by millions of people to help counteract some of the effects of age. These supplements usually work together. The most important ones used to fight aging are (in alphabetical order):

Amino Acids

The use of amino acids (building blocks of proteins) as dietary supplements is back in fashion again. The amino acids cysteine, glutamic acid and glycine combine to form glutathione which prevents age-related damage to the body.

Glutathione is one of the most important antioxidants produced by the body during everyday activities. It is found in fresh fruit and vegetables but cooking can destroy large amounts of it. Researchers found that people who lived to be over 100 years old are endowed with high concentrations of glutathione in their blood and are therefore well protected against aging. Most people over the age of 60, however, have low glutathione and this makes free radical damage more likely. One study showed that almost 80 per cent of patients admitted to hospital with chronic disease have low glutathione in their blood.

Too much fat in the diet increases the need for glutathione, which struggles to neutralize the fat-related damage. Scientists use glutathione measurements in the blood to help to estimate the biological age of the individual.

Glutathione comes in tablet form, but good natural sources include:

- avocado
- watermelon
- asparagus
- broccoli
- potatoes
- carrots
- tomatoes
- fresh lean red meat

Very recently, carnosine, a chemical similar to amino acids, was found to be effective in reducing age-related damage in the brain and in other parts of the body. Carnosine is found in red meat and chicken, but is also available in tablet form. Carnosine deserves a whole book praising its age-busting actions. For the moment, *see* chapter 10.

Beta Carotene

Research shows that beta carotene is an antioxidant and anti-cancer agent. It takes part in the fight against some types of cancer such as lung and stomach cancer. It is found in carrots, spinach, broccoli and other green vegetables, sweet potatoes, apricots, cantaloupes, pumpkins, mangoes and tangerines. The darker the colour of the fruit or vegetable, the higher the beta carotene content. Beta carotene is also found in calf's liver, cod liver oil, corn, cheese and eggs.

Beta carotene is part of a large group of nutrients called carotenoids. Research shows that it may work better in association with other antioxidants such as flavonoids.

Chromium Picolinate

This is a chemical which controls insulin and balances glucose in the blood, helps lower cholesterol and supports immunity. It can also reduce sugar cravings. Chromium levels decrease with age and this, scientists believe, can cause problems with the glucose in our blood. Many people who are on a diet also use chromium picolinate in an effort to boost their weight loss. Some swear by it, others swear at it.

Chromium is found in brewer's yeast, broccoli, barley, liver, kidneys, grains and mushrooms. Different strengths of chromium supplements exist in tablet form. If you are diabetic, ask your doctor before taking chromium supplements.

Co-Enzyme Q10

You will find this little devil almost anywhere in the body. No wonder its scientific nickname is ubiquinone, for it is present ubiquitously. It is usually made inside our bodies but its effectiveness wanes after the age of 40. Q10 is involved in energy production and it is an antioxidant. Some people prefer to think of it as a biological spark plug, super-charging the cells.

Q10 is increasingly used to protect immunity, to prevent brain damage and to improve heart or muscle weakness. Recently it has also been used in order to improve age-related damage to the gums.

Good sources are sardines, mackerel and other oily fish, soya beans, nuts (particularly almonds and walnuts) and spinach. It may also be taken in tablet form.

Used together with vitamin E, Q10 has been proven very popular as a general anti-aging supplement. Women who tried this combination have told me that, for some unknown reason, it makes them feel sexually excited, particularly over the clitoris area. Don't ask me why this happens!

Selenium

The antioxidant selenium is the most important mineral in fighting the effects of free radicals. According to some scientists, selenium can help fight cancer and heart disease, improves immunity and fights viruses.

Selenium can be taken as a food supplement together with other antioxidants or it can be taken in the form of selenium-rich food, mostly Brazil nuts but also grains, radishes, mushrooms, tuna, garlic, beef, oysters and halibut.

Vitamin B12

This comes in different forms. A particular form, methyl-cobolamin is promoted as being effective in reducing brain cell damage, as well as protecting the nerves from free radical injury. Vitamin B12 is thought to protect against the effects of the amino acid homocysteine, which plays an active part in causing heart disease. I will return to the dangers of homocysteine later on.

Sources of vitamin B12 are clams, beef or lamb's liver, mackerel, pilchards, sardines and other oily fish. It is also available in tablets, capsules or lozenges.

Vitamin C

This is the best-known antioxidant. Vitamin C destroys free radicals before they enter the cell and is therefore a good preventor agent. An intake of large amounts of vitamin C has been advised by some scientists in order to combat aging.

Vitamin C can be found in fresh fruit and vegetables, eaten raw. The best sources are citrus fruit such as oranges, grapefruit and tangerines, but vitamin C is also present in guava fruit, kiwi, blackcurrants, paw-paw and mango. Other sources are tomatoes, Brussels sprouts, potatoes and red peppers. Many people also take large amounts of daily supplements in tablet form, but this has not been endorsed by mainstream scientists.

Vitamin E

This is another well-studied antioxidant. It protects the cell membrane against free radical attacks.

Vitamin E is found in soya beans, avocados, wheatgerm, spinach, liver, blackcurrants, nuts, mainly almonds, and green tea, which also contains vitamin C, the phytochemical catechin and other polyphenols. Many people use green tea as an antioxidant to improve their immune system and to help fight cancer. While on the subject of green tea, it is possible to get green tea extract in the form of a capsule which, the manufacturers claim, is as strong as 10 cups of tea.

It was recently shown in trials that low vitamin E concentrations in the blood increase the risk of heart attacks. Likewise, large trials involving more than 130,000 people have shown that supplementing the diet with 100 units of vitamin E a day can substantially reduce the risk of heart disease.

Vitamin K

This vitamin affects clotting of the blood, but it also influences the bone strength and the health of the arteries. A specific form of vitamin K is found in green vegetables, cheese, liver, yogurt, cauliflower, Brussels sprouts, tomatoes, spinach, broccoli, beans, lean meat and soya.

Low vitamin K in the blood may be associated with an increased risk of osteoporosis and extra supplements of this vitamin may be necessary to boost bone health.

In a few experiments, vitamin K was found to play a role in Alzheimer's disease, but it is too early for definite conclusions yet.

Vitamin K is available in tablet or injection form, but it is not widely used as a health supplement at present. My guess is that its potential benefits will be recognized in the near future. In the meantime, it may be worth choosing vitamin K-rich food from the list above.

Zinc

This mineral nourishes the immune system and stimulates the thymus gland which, in turn, also sustains immunity. As a bonus, it also plays a part in the fight against free radicals and accelerates wound healing.

Zinc is found in seafood (mainly oysters), cereals, nuts and seeds. It is also available in pill form on its own or in a multi-vitamin combination. Suitably prepared zinc supplements, usually lozenges, are sometimes used to fight cold and flu symptoms. Some people find it effective, others don't.

Tips to preserve vitamins in vegetables

- Tear rather than chop lettuce, cabbage, etc.
- Don't soak the vegetables too long in water.
- Avoid peeling and slicing (but wash thoroughly).
- Avoid boiling – use steaming or stir-frying instead.
- After boiling vegetables, use the water for soups, gravy or sauce, as it is full of vitamins.

Recipes

To give you a general idea of a good anti-aging diet, here are a few recipes containing some of the ingredients discussed above.

Tuna and Pasta Bake

275g (9½oz) pasta

1 small onion

15ml (3tsp) virgin olive oil

200g (7oz) tuna

150g (5½oz) sweetcorn

75g (2½oz) low fat cheese, grated.

For the sauce:

15g (½oz) cornflour

570ml (20fl oz) semi-skimmed milk or soya milk

Pre-heat oven to 400°F (205°C), mark 6. Boil the pasta. Sauté the onion, add tuna and sweetcorn. Then add the cooked pasta. Add cornflour mixed with milk, top with grated cheese and heat for 15 minutes.

Serves 4, 454 calories per serving.

Chicken with Apricots

2 chicken breasts, grilled or boiled

150g (5½oz) apricots, sliced

10g (¼oz) cashew nuts

6 cloves of garlic, crushed

honey

Stir fry the apricots, nuts and garlic in olive oil, add some vinegar and 1 tsp honey, mix and serve as sauce for chicken. Add a dash of lemon juice and ground ginger.

Serves 2, 400 calories per serving.

Vegetables with Brown Rice

1 small onion, chopped

5ml (1tsp) perilla oil

50g (2oz) brown rice

1 chopped tomato

175ml (6fl oz) water

mixed herbs

1 vegetable stock cube

50g (2oz) mushrooms

50g (2oz) red peppers

50g (2oz) runner beans

Cook the onion in oil, add rice and cook for a minute. Add tomato, water, herbs and cube. Simmer for 30 minutes. Add mushrooms, peppers and beans. Simmer for another 10 minutes.

Serves 2, 290 calories per serving.

Boiled Vegetable Mix

1 stick of celery

50g (2oz) carrots

50g (2oz) courgettes

40g (1½oz) broccoli

40g (1½oz) broad beans

40g (1½oz) artichokes

2 large tomatoes

Boil all the vegetables together, drain, serve. Use mint and parsley to garnish.

Serves 2, 50 calories per serving.

Fish Soup

300g (10½oz) whitebait

1 carrot, sliced

1 small onion, sliced

1tbsp tomato paste

1tsp olive oil

1 small sliced potato

50g (2oz) brown rice

parsley

lemon juice

Boil the fish in a pan. Sieve and put the broth back in the pan. Sauté the vegetables with the fish and then add to the broth. Add the rice. When the rice is cooked, add tomato paste, olive oil, salt and simmer for five minutes. Add lemon juice and garnish with parsley.

Serves 2, 280 calories per serving.

Lentil with Rice Pilaff

100g (4oz) lentils

50g (2oz) brown rice

1 large onion sliced in thin rings

olive oil

1 litre (35fl oz) water

Soak lentils overnight. Cook for 15 minutes in a pan with water. Add the rice and cook for another 15 minutes or until most of the water is absorbed. Fry onions in olive oil and mix with pilaff.

Serves 2, 250 calories per serving.

Broad Bean Salad

150g (5½oz) broad beans

1 clove garlic

1 stalk fresh fennel

flax oil

white wine vinegar

black olives

Either boil fresh green broad beans for 40 minutes or use tinned ones. Strain and put in a bowl. Add crushed garlic. Beat the oil and vinegar and pour over the beans. Sprinkle with fennel and garnish with black olives.

Serves 2, 70 calories per serving.

Chicken and Spinach Salad

2 small chicken breasts, boiled or grilled and chopped into small pieces

100g (3½oz) spinach leaves

walnuts

parsley

1 grapefruit, segmented

radishes

Mix all of the above in a bowl. Dress with olive oil, mixed with thyme and black pepper.

Serves 2, 250 calories per serving.

Easter Salad

½ small lettuce

6 spring onions

2 hard-boiled eggs

olive oil

1 cup white wine vinegar

dry herbs

Tear lettuce and cut spring onions (including their green leaves) into big pieces. Add sliced eggs. Beat olive oil and vinegar and add dry herbs to taste.

Serves 2, 250 calories.

My Father's Recipe for Home-Made Bread

570ml (20fl oz) tepid water (approximately)

250g (8½oz) bran

200g (7oz) wheatgerm

1 kg (2¼lb) wholemeal bread flour

3tsp natural yeast

sugar and salt, 1 tsp each

3–10tbsp of any, or all, of the following: aniseed seeds, alfalfa seeds, pumpkin seeds, black cumin seeds, poppy seeds, sunflower seeds

First, mix all of the dry ingredients in a large bowl. Add the tepid water at intervals and mix very well until the dough does not stick to your fingers. Form into any shape (round, square or long, but without any cracks, otherwise the bread will fall to pieces during cooking). Put on a baking tray and cover with a towel for half an hour in a warm place. Cook in a pre-heated oven at 350°F (180°C) for up to an hour.

Bean Soup

200g (7oz) black-eyed beans

200g (7oz) carrots

1 chopped onion

garlic cloves, crushed

thyme

parsley

vegetable stock cube

Sauté the carrots, onion and garlic in a pan. Add 285ml (10fl oz) boiling water, thyme and beans and cook for 2–3 hours on low heat. Sprinkle with parsley.

Serves 2, 200 calories per serving.

Pasta with Shrimps

140g (5oz) spaghetti

100g (3½oz) shrimps

1 chopped onion

1 glass white wine

1 glass fresh orange juice

zest of 1 orange

black pitted olives

oregano

sunflower oil

Sauté the onion in sunflower oil, add shrimps, wine and the orange juice, bring to the boil. Cook the spaghetti. Add sauce to the spaghetti, sprinkle with olives and oregano.

Serves 2, 360 calories per portion.

Other Ideas
Breakfasts

To include:

- tea, (preferably green tea), mineral water or fruit juice, avoid coffee,
- orange, tangerines, grapefruit, all mixed with orange juice and garnished with mint
- mushrooms and tomatoes, grilled, on toast
- cereals with skimmed milk, sprinkled with raisins and orange slices
- wholemeal toast with yeast extract, banana
- bran flakes with chopped banana and dried apricots
- baked beans on wholemeal toast, half a grapefruit
- a boiled egg, home-made bread and soya margarine
- apricots, figs, apples and pears mixed with low fat yogurt
- slices of orange with oatmeal pancakes
- wholewheat toast with cottage cheese, half a grapefruit
- oatmeal with raisins and peach slices

Snacks

- dried apricots, figs, prunes, dates
- carrots or celery stalks
- low fat yogurt with nuts and raisins
- fresh fruit salad with apples, oranges, nectarines, pears
- exotic fruit salad with melon, kiwis, pineapple, mangoes, lychees and rose water
- berry salad with strawberries, raspberries, loganberries, gooseberries
- fennel seeds, pumpkin seeds or sunflower seeds
- blended apple with cashew nuts, spread on wholewheat crackers

79

Lunch

- jacket potato with tuna and sweetcorn or beans
- sardines in pitta bread
- thick cubes of sliced tomatoes with mozzarella cheese, garnished with olive oil and herbs
- thick sliced tomatoes with olive oil, mint and lemon juice
- green salad, cream cheese, thick slice of wholemeal bread
- carrot and orange soup (made with carrots, onion and olive oil, and topped with low fat yogurt), low calorie bread with peanut butter
- salmon sandwich with watercress, apple or banana
- lentil soup and spinach omelette
- tuna mixed with tomatoes and cucumbers in pitta bread, tangerines
- tomato soup, turkey and salad, rice cakes (crispbread)
- ciabatta bread with grilled bacon, sun-dried tomatoes and light cheese spread
- cucumber, tomato, radishes and watercress salad, dressed with olive oil, lemon juice and vinegar, and garnished with thyme and fresh parsley
- Greek salad: thickly cut tomatoes, cucumber, onion (or spring onions) and fetta cheese, dressed with olive oil, vinegar, lemon, parsley and black olives

Dinner

- mezze with whitebait, houmous, tzatziki, tomato, cucumber and olive salad, pitta bread, herrings and grilled halloumi cheese
- chick peas with brown rice pilaff
- lentil, oatmeal, walnut, sage, onion and thyme bake
- baked stuffed tomatoes, boiled cracked wheat, with or without tomato sauce

- avocado and prawns, boiled salmon, rice and celery
- boiled chicken with lemon juice and black pepper with rice and sweetcorn
- tuna fish with spring onions and white bean salad
- bean soup, grilled salmon, broccoli and boiled potatoes, tomato slices
- grilled herring, beetroot, potatoes, with papaya or mangoes
- mixed green salad, poached salmon, cracked wheat, natural yogurt
- pasta with shrimps in orange sauce, fruit
- grilled chicken with jacked potato, red cabbage, apricots
- stir-fried broccoli, mushrooms, carrots, spring onions, peppers, small pieces of chicken breast, brown rice

81

Desserts

- strawberry or raspberry jelly
- banana and low fat yogurt
- Greek yogurt with honey
- apples and bananas garnished with raisins and nutmeg topped with honey
- baked apples with cinnamon
- peaches finely chopped, mixed with chilled orange juice, topped with honey and almonds

Drinks

- pure unsweetened grape juice
- tomatoes, blended with Worcestershire sauce, mineral water, mint and some sugar
- apricots blended with apples, bananas and mangoes and mixed with orange juice

- Airan drink: thoroughly mix two or three tablespoonfuls of Greek yogurt with cold water in a large tumbler; add a small amount of salt and dry mint

- soya drink: mix $^1/_2$ part frozen pina colada, $^1/_2$ part water, 250g ($8^1/_2$oz) soya protein powder and stir well

- brain drink: chop and blend watercress, 3 celery stalks, half an apple, 3 carrots, fennel and parsley; add mineral water, mix well

- mint tea made from fresh mint boiled in water

- herbal drink made from boiling water with thyme, rosemary and mint

Dietary Restriction

Over the past several years research has confirmed that there is a way not only to live to an 'ordinary' old age but to live longer than anybody has lived before. This has been confirmed time and time again in hundreds of experiments. The way to do it is quite simple: just eat 30 per cent fewer calories than the amount usually consumed. But there is a catch. The experiments were mainly performed on laboratory animals like rats, mice, flies and monkeys, not humans.

The original experiments involved two groups of laboratory animals. The first group was allowed to eat as much as they wanted. The second group (consisting of animals from the same family, identical to the animals in the first group) was allowed to eat only a certain amount of calories. This amount was from 30 to 70 per cent less than the calories consumed by the first group.

The results were always consistent: the calorie-restricted group lived longer than the ordinary group (up to 100 per cent longer) and, in addition, the diseases connected with aging seemed to be less frequent and less severe than in the ordinary group.

We don't know if the results can be applied to humans with the same certainty. But some indirect research has given a glimmer of hope. Small groups of volunteers who were on a diet for religious or weight reduction purposes agreed to take part in experiments to see if their diet made their bodies age more slowly than people who were eating normally. The results showed that some changes in the bodies of these volunteers were indeed similar to the changes seen in the laboratory animals. It is still too early to draw any long-term conclusions from this.

Other experiments performed by American scientists who took part in the Biosphere 2 project confirm these results. The Biosphere 2 project was an experiment designed to study, among other things, how humans can cope living in a completely self-sufficient environment. Those who took part in this experiment also tried a low calorie diet for some months. They noticed that on this diet their cholesterol and insulin were reduced, they lost excess weight and other signs of aging were reversed.

Although research on humans has not been as extensive as research on other animals, there are some scientists who suggest that dietary restriction (DR) may work in all humans as well. They suggest that if we apply these research results to humans we may see that with a controlled diet of about 1,700 calories daily for women and 1,900 calories for men, it may be possible to extend the maximum life span to about 150 years or more! These calorie requirements should be reduced by 2 per cent for every 10 years past the age of 35. There is no need to stay on a diet forever. All that is needed is to generally restrict the amount of food consumed and to follow certain guidelines. At least this should help those who want to lose excess weight!

Many centenarians living in several parts of the world do claim that their long life is due to their diet: a very low amount of calories and a large amount of fruit, nuts and other basic foodstuffs such as beans and corn, but very little meat. This is, in effect, a lifelong dietary restriction regime, as recommended by some experts in the field.

Nobody knows exactly how calorie restriction works. Certain scientists think that if we eat less food, our metabolism will have less work to do and it will slow down. Long-lived animals have a slow metabolism, as opposed to animals who live for short periods and have a very fast metabolism.

Other scientists believe that by eating less food, we limit the amount of free radical production and so the damage caused by free radicals is reduced. There is no doubt, however, that DR works in all the animals studied so far and many people hope that it may work in humans as well.

The Human Diet

The aim of a DR regime is to have menus containing a reduced amount of calories as well as an assortment of antioxidant supplements, vitamins and other anti-aging factors. It is 'under-nutrition without malnutrition'.

The weight loss should be gradual and not abrupt. However, if you wish to start such a regime, it is important to consult a doctor first and to receive guidance from qualified nutritionists. This diet is not suitable for pregnant women or those who are breast-feeding. What can go wrong with calorie restriction diets includes:

- hunger pangs

- impaired fertility

- long-term danger of osteoporosis

- a reduced ability to react to stress, injury or infection

People who support dietary restriction say that at least 50 per cent of the calories should come from starchy food. This kind of food contains fibre with some vitamins but, more importantly, almost no fat. Starchy food is very filling and generally nutritious without providing too many calories. High starch foods are bread, cereals, baked potatoes, pitta bread, rice and pasta.

Fluids are also important. We need to drink at least two litres of fluid every day, mainly water. This helps to eliminate the toxic metabolic waste, helps improve kidney function and also helps reduce the appetite in people who feel very hungry.

Dietary restriction supporters use the following way to calculate their calorie requirements:

- First they find what is called their 'set point'. This is what their ideal weight was when they were 25 years old.

- Then, they try to adjust their weight to 10 per cent below their 'set point'. The degree of weight loss should be approximately 230g (8oz) every month.

- When they reach a body weight which is 10 per cent lower than their set point, they try to maintain it by adjusting the calories in their diet.

Calorie Counting

almonds, 25g (1oz)	130	mackerel, grilled, 100g (3½oz)	260
apple, 1	40–50	nuts, dried, 30g (1 oz)	170
apricots, dry, 5 pieces	50	oatmeal, 25g (1oz)	110
apricots, raw, 100g (3½oz)	50	orange, 1	40–50
banana, small	50	pear, 1	40
beans, baked, 100g (3½oz)	70	pitta, wholemeal, 1 slice	75
beans, kidney, red, 25g (1oz)	30	potatoes, boiled, 2 small	90
beans, runner, 100g (3½oz)	15	potatoes, boiled 200g (7oz)	150
bread, wholemeal, 1 slice	75	radishes, 60g (2oz)	8
broccoli, 25g (1oz)	10	raisins, 25g (1oz)	70
cabbage, 100g (3½oz)	5	rice, brown, 25g (1oz)	35
carrots, 25g (1oz)	10	salmon, steamed, 100g (3½oz)	220
chicken joint, 100g (3½oz)	210	satsuma, 1	20
celery, 100g (3½ oz)	5	sesame seeds, 15g (½oz)	80
cod, baked, 100g (3½oz)	110	spread, low fat, 1 tsp	15
cucumber, 100g (3½oz)	10	sunflower seeds, 15g	90
grapes, 100g (3½oz)	50	sweetcorn, 100g (3½oz)	5
grapefruit, 1	20	tomatoes, 1	5
haddock, 100g (3½oz)	110	tomato juice, 100g (3½oz)	20
halibut, 100g (3½oz)	150	tuna, in brine, 100g (3½oz)	135
lentils, 45g (1½oz)	100	walnuts, 25g (1oz)	150
lettuce, 100g (3½oz)	10	yogurt, low fat, 100g	80

On the other hand, people who enjoy eating usually can't see the point of living a life of constant restriction in order to gain a few extra years. It would certainly be ideal to discover how DR works and then use suitable tablets or other easy procedures to achieve the same result, instead of having to go through a lifetime of limitation.

Menus

Here are a few examples of low calorie menus containing antioxidants and other anti-aging factors.

For an average 45-year-old male, approximately 1,770 calories:

Breakfast

55g (2oz) bran cereal with skimmed milk and 30g (1oz) raisins

Total: 270 calories

Lunch

cottage cheese salad made with 170g (6oz) cottage cheese, 30g (1oz) walnuts, 110g (4oz) lettuce and olive oil

1 slice of wholemeal bread, 1 apple and 1 large orange

Total: 550 calories

Supper

medium bowl of tomato soup

150g (5½oz) grilled haddock, 100g (3½oz) broccoli, 150g (5½oz) sweetcorn, 50g (2oz) brown rice, 6 small new potatoes

1 pot low fat yogurt with apricots

Total: 750 calories

Snacks

25g (1oz) almonds, 100g (3½oz) carrots

Total: 200 calories

For an average 50-year-old woman, approximately 1,500 calories:

Breakfast

75g (2½oz) plain yogurt

2 tsp brewer's yeast

1 wholemeal toast with soya margarine

Total: 280 calories

Lunch

lentil soup with rye crispbread

mushrooms on toast

1 fruit

Total: 300 calories

Supper

75g (2½oz) salmon

80g (3oz) broccoli, 100g (3½oz) sweet potatoes, 50g (2oz) brown rice, 120g (4oz) spinach, 50g (2oz) soya beans

fruit salad

2 glasses of red wine

Total: 650 calories

Snacks

500ml (16fl oz) soya milk, fresh grapes, carrots

Total: 260 calories

Age-Related Diseases Where a Suitable Diet May Help

Many health problems can be prevented by the correct nutrition. Osteoporosis can be helped by adequate intake of calcium, heart disease by controlling dietary fat and by reducing cholesterol, diabetes by avoiding too much sugar and by losing any excess weight.

Special benefits of anti-aging nutrition may include an improvement of the immune system which fights infections, a healthier brain, a body which looks younger than its actual age, and generally a more enjoyable life.

Aim to have six servings a day of grain-based food, such as brown rice, pasta, bread or cereal. Complement this with three servings of milk, yogurt or cheese and two servings of meat, fish or poultry.

Good nutrition after the age of 30 does not only depend on what we eat but also how we eat it. After a certain age, changes in the way our body works can make us prone to follow a less than ideal diet and this can increase the risk of certain age-related diseases.

The senses of smell and taste start to decline after the age of 35. This is partly due to changes in the sensory nerves of the nose and tongue, which are sometimes damaged by smoking or by infections. A healthy lifestyle and special sense exercises should help maintain a good sense of smell and taste.

The sensation of thirst also decreases slowly over the years. This may lead to dehydration, particularly in hot weather or during an illness. On average we need to drink about 6–8 glasses of fluid a day.

With the passage of time we lose our ability to taste salt. This means that we may be adding too much salt to our food to make it palatable. You should be careful and judge your use of salt with your eyes, not rely too much on your taste.

Also, with aging, some people experience a dry mouth. A helpful trick in this situation is to look at the plate of food for one or two minutes before actually starting to eat. This should increase the production of saliva and make eating more pleasant.

Chewing and Digestion

Healthy nutrition can also be affected by tooth disease. It is important to follow a good oral hygiene programme, visit the dentist regularly and try to maintain good teeth. Otherwise, chewing can become a problem, with consequent malnutrition, imperfect digestion and bowel problems. Proper chewing (33 times every mouthful, my grandfather used to say) helps break down the complex constituents of the food and prepares them to be absorbed by the bowel.

Indigestion is made worse by poor mobility, age-related changes to the acid secretion in the stomach and by anti-inflammatory drugs given for pain control.

The extract of globe artichoke (*Cynara scolymus*) is promoted as being effective in reducing the effects of indigestion and improving stomach upset. It helps break down fat and stimulates the flow of digestive fluids from the liver (bile). It helps eliminate alcohol, protects the liver against the effects of alcohol, stimulates normal mobility of the bowel and also reduces cholesterol.

Artichoke contains the active ingredient cynarin, a naturally occurring substance. This is treated chemically and marketed in capsule form.

Artichoke extracts are also thought to be good antioxidants and research is currently under way to study the effects of cynarin on reducing atherosclerosis. This may be suitable for those at risk from liver damage due to too much alcohol, gallstones, problems with bile, or those who have had hepatitis. It is well tolerated and has no significant side effects. In practice, though, not everybody who tried it found it effective.

Aloe vera can also aid digestion, reduce excess acid in the stomach and reduce the risk of ulcers.

Dietary Advice for the Brain

A diet high in fruit, vegetables, starch and protein, especially fish, is thought to be important for the brain. Soya protein is particularly useful. A good breakfast energizes the brain after an overnight fast, but avoid fatty food or coffee. Supplements for the brain include antioxidants such as vitamin E, together with beta carotene, co-enzyme Q10, ginkgo biloba and selenium.

Other vitamins which may be helpful in maintaining a healthy brain are the B vitamins. These include riboflavin, thiamin and niacin. Sources of these vitamins are flour, kidneys, liver, potatoes, yogurt and oily fish.

Some scientists suggest that high vitamin C consumption can

reduce the risk of developing brain failure. This is due to the antioxidant effects of the vitamin on the arteries of the brain.

A good brain-boosting diet will be more effective if incorporated into a healthy lifestyle including good physical and mental exercises. For mental exercises, dementia and brain supplements, *see* chapters 6, 9 and 10.

A Diet to Increase Immunity

The immune system fights diseases and other aging damage to the body. A healthy immune system means a reduced likelihood of suffering an age-related disease. Apart from brain exercises to improve immunity, certain foodstuffs may make a difference.

Antioxidants, particularly vitamin E, are worthwhile. A low fat diet containing omega-3 fatty acids from fish oils is thought to improve certain components of the immune system. Vitamin A is also necessary to maintain the immune system in good condition. It is present in liver and fortified margarines.

The mineral zinc may help as well. The recommended dose for men is 15mg per day and for women 12mg per day. Taking more than this amount can actually have a negative effect. Zinc is found in seafood, wholegrains, seeds and nuts.

Nayad, an extract from yeast cells, is believed to help revitalize tired immune cells. Another herbal extract, echinacea, is also thought to energize the immune system. Echinacea is available in tablet, capsule or liquid form.

Too much alcohol can reduce the concentration of zinc in the body and thus worsen immunity. Also smoking, lack of exercise and depression can take their toll on the immune system in general.

A Cholesterol-Lowering Diet

A diet which contains a low amount of cholesterol is ideal, but we also need to eat more foodstuffs which actually help lower cholesterol in the blood. Some of these are carrots, oatbran, dried beans, garlic, avocados and virgin olive oil. Research has shown that these foodstuffs reduce the chance of developing heart disease and stroke.

Try to avoid white bread, chips and crisps, salami, butter, lard and suet. Ice cream, creamy soups, salad cream, jam, sweets, fatty meats, sausages, pork pies and pâté are also off the menu.

Choose these instead: wholemeal bread and pasta, rice, fish, fresh fruit and vegetables, chicken, turkey, sunflower cooking oil, low fat milk and yogurt, mineral water, tomato juice, home-made soups and nuts.

A study of several thousand women has found that those who ate 140g (5oz) of nuts a week had a lower risk of developing heart disease than those who did not eat nuts frequently. Although nuts contain a high amount of fat, this is the 'good' type of fat which is essential for robust health. Eating almonds and walnuts reduces cholesterol in the blood.

Having a slightly high cholesterol is not as important in older individuals as it is in younger people. In a study of nearly 1,000 people aged 70 and over, no connection was found between high cholesterol and death from heart disease.

Before you have your blood taken for a cholesterol test, consider this: people who sit down for 20 minutes before a cholesterol blood test have, on the whole, lower cholesterol than those who stand up for 10 minutes just before the test.

A Diet to Prevent Cancer and Heart Disease

The Alliance for Aging Research in the USA recommends that for the prevention of heart disease, cancer and age-related damage we should take each day:

- 1,000mg of vitamin C per day
- 400iu of vitamin E per day
- 17,000–50,000iu of beta carotene

This is considerably more than the recommended daily allowance in the UK.

Fish oils may protect against lung cancer in smokers. Those who eat fish at least twice a week are less likely to develop lung cancer or other lung diseases than those who don't consume any fish oils at all. The parts of fish rich in oils are the eyes, bowels and brain.

More nuts, olive oil, porridge and small quantities of red wine can reduce the risk of cancer and heart disease. These are the results of a study comparing mortality from cancer and ischaemic heart disease in vegetarians and non-vegetarians.

Women who have a diet high in fibre have a low risk of developing breast cancer. The reasons for this are not clear but it is suggested that fibre may bind to and inactivate the hormones which are associated with breast cancer.

Flavonoids, which are very effective antioxidants, can halve the risk of heart disease. Important sources of flavonoids include fruit, onions, green tea and red wine.

Extra virgin olive oil reduces the stickiness of the blood and helps with blood circulation. It also contains strong antioxidants.

Diet and the Prostate

Researchers believe that overweight men who consume large amounts of food are twice as likely to develop prostate cancer than men who are not overweight. In some countries, such as Japan, the cases of prostate disease are very low as compared to the US. This is thought to be due to the Japanese diet which is high in fish, vegetables and soya and low in fat and red meat.

Other researchers believe that a diet high in rye can protect against prostate cancer. Rye is easily available from rye bread. Vitamins C, E and beta carotene are also recommended. Evening primrose oil together with amino acids has also been used.

Soya can help reduce the risk of prostate cancer, probably because of its high content of phytochemicals, which block the hormones implicated in this cancer. Lack of a phytochemical, lycopene, was found to be the most common deficiency associated with prostate cancer risk. Lycopene is mainly found in tomatoes.

Avena sativa is a plant extract used by many men to protect themselves against prostate problems. It is mostly found in oats.

Zinc supplements in tablet form or from food containing zinc, such as grains and seeds, may also play a part in reducing the likelihood of prostate cancer. Pumpkin seeds in particular contain a high concentration of zinc.

Diet and Arthritis

There are many drug treatments for arthritis and nutritionists suggest that a proper diet will also help reduce some of its symptoms.

To treat arthritis, fat in the diet should be reduced. Forget fried food, butter puddings or pastries and avoid too much alcohol.

Arthritis sufferers should choose protein from fish and poultry rather than from red meat. Other sources of suitable protein include beans and pulses, nuts and skimmed milk.

Carbohydrates should be obtained from wholemeal bread, cereals, wholemeal pasta and brown rice, rather than from refined sugar.

Herring, mackerel, salmon, cod and haddock, eaten at least three times a week, or fish oil supplements in capsule form are highly recommended by some specialists. These fish oils contain omega-3 fatty acids which help reduce morning stiffness and tenderness of the joints. Evening primrose oil and flax oil, which also contain omega-3 fatty acids, work wonders for some people.

Finally, if you suffer from arthritis, it would be a good idea to lose that excess weight which puts unnecessary strain on your poor knee, back and hip joints.

A Diet to Prevent Osteoporosis

Thinning of the bones associated with aging can be prevented or at least slowed down by adopting a few lifestyle changes. One of these is to maintain a good intake of the mineral calcium. It is important to have a diet rich in calcium starting early in life. However, a good calcium intake is also essential later on.

Foods high in calcium include dairy products, green leafy vegetables, almonds, cereals, beans, tofu, sardines and whitebait (eaten with its bones). Alternatively, use calcium supplements in tablet/capsule form.

Vitamin D is essential in maintaining healthy bones. Sources include oily fish and fortified breakfast cereals or it can be in tablet form under medical supervision.

Diet and Cataracts and Macular Degeneration

These are two common causes of loss of vision in later life. Age-related blindness may be prevented by a diet rich in vitamins A, C, and E according to research performed at Harvard University. The risk of developing macular degeneration (age-related loss of vision) was 43 per cent lower in those people who had been taking these vitamins regularly. Lots of other antioxidants, zinc and selenium are also considered to be useful. In addition, spinach was found to prevent cataract in a large study published recently in the *British Medical Journal*. Green vegetables taken four or five times a day may prevent cataract in susceptible individuals.

An increased amount of fat in the diet may predispose towards developing macular degeneration by blocking the small arteries in the eye.

Look for the chemical lutein and the anthocyanidins in bilberry extracts if you want your eyes to look good.

Those who have relatives suffering from cataract or macular degeneration should consider asking their doctor for extra antioxidant supplements in order to lessen their chances of developing the disease themselves.

Diet and High Blood Pressure

To help maintain normal blood pressure a standard recommendation used to be to avoid excessive salt in the diet. The Western diet contains as much as 10 times more salt than the amount we actually need and it takes only a few weeks to modify our taste and enjoy low salt food. However, recent research into the effects of salt on blood pressure has given controversial results. No relationship has been found between salt consumption and blood pressure. Until the debate is over, however, it is best to avoid too much salt in the diet, or use salt substitutes. If you want to titillate your taste buds use dry herbs, red pepper or aromatic plants instead.

Garlic and calcium supplements are thought to help maintain normal blood pressure. Losing excess weight and taking regular exercise are both essential in lowering blood pressure. Food supplements in tablet form include high potency antioxidants, fish oils and magnesium.

Conclusion

It is possible to enjoy the benefits of a good anti-aging nutrition by making the right choices yourselves. But I would recommend working in association with a qualified nutritionist or with any other expert in anti-aging. Some nutrients may not suit certain people, and supplements may be taken even when there is really no need for them.

Anti-aging nutrition works better if it is part of a general plan including suitable physical and mental exercises. So it's on to these next ...

CHAPTER 5

Keep on the Move and Manage That Stress

As you already know, good nutrition alone is not sufficient to help us achieve good health. Regular exercise is also essential. Exercise helps us achieve a firm body, strong and supple muscles, agile joints and a sharp brain. It makes us look younger and healthier, feel better and balances the different hormones in the body.

If you are not completely convinced about the benefits of exercise, consider this: if you exercise moderately every day (brisk walking, dancing, swimming) and one day you suddenly put yourself under a lot of physical strain, your risk of suffering a heart attack is increased only twofold. If, on the other hand, you don't exercise at all and then you put yourself under sudden physical strain, your risk of a heart attack is increased by a staggering hundredfold.

Exercise does not have to be performed at the gym only. You can get some benefits if you try to be active during your day. For example, doing housework enthusiastically for periods of 20 minutes or more, without breaks, should make your heart speed up to beneficial levels, maximizing the use of oxygen by the muscle.

Gardening, suited to your own circumstances, as energetic and continuous as possible, running or walking on the spot, weightlifting with books or tins of food and climbing up and down the stairs a few times, should all provide enough stamina to slow down the effects of aging.

Whatever your age, you need to exercise. For example, post-menopausal women who exercise regularly live longer than those who don't exercise. An American study of over 40,000 women aged between 55 and 70 years showed that the risk of dying prematurely decreases according to the amount of exercise done.

Research also suggests that older people who live in nursing homes can experience a significant improvement in their mental and physical condition if they exercise regularly.

Many people who work hard and long hours claim they can't find enough time to exercise, but even 5 or 10 minutes of brisk walking a day will make a lot of difference to your health. You owe it to yourself to allow a few minutes a day for a bit of exercise. I see many busy people who ask me for lifestyle advice and my conclusion is more or less the same every time: their main problem is lack of exercise. I believe that even the busiest businessman on Earth can find a few minutes a day for simple exercise.

If you don't have much free time, the easiest way to start exercise is to go for brisk walks and then build up from there. Every day go a little further or a little faster. Then add more forms of exercise to your routine. The best are swimming and home or gym exercises.

Vigorous exercise stimulates the body to produce free radicals which, as you know, have no place in a healthy lifestyle. Accordingly, several trainers recommend taking antioxidants before and after exercising to help reduce this production of free radicals. An extra dose of vitamin E or a multi-antioxidant preparation should be enough.

Oriental Exercise Techniques

Apart from the usual exercises available, I believe that oriental exercise techniques are very useful and should be used by everybody who wants to achieve long life. Here I am going to mention three of these techniques: yoga, t'ai chi and chi kung. All three have particular benefits in the fight against the aging process. My personal favourite is chi kung, but all oriental techniques offer something to our health.

A Basic Breathing Exercise

- Sit on a chair with your back straight. Allow your hands to gently rest on your abdomen.

- Take a slow deep breath through your nose and feel the changes in your abdomen and chest during the breathing movement.

- Breathe out slowly, feeling the movements of your abdomen with your hands.

- Repeat three or four times.

Yoga

Ideal for its anti-aging benefits, yoga is a well-known Indian technique. Special yoga exercises are suitable for stretching the joints and ligaments, and some forms of weight-bearing yoga exercises help prevent osteoporosis.

Regular yoga practice helps relaxation and certain positions also boost the circulation of blood to the brain, kidneys, liver and to other vital organs. Yoga breathing exercises maximize lung capacity. The exercises are not used in order to build up muscle but to enhance general physical and mental suppleness. When you exercise you need to be aware of your breathing and try to concentrate on your inner spiritual health.

If you are new to yoga, start by reading a book describing the basic concepts (*see* 'Further Reading'). You need, however, to practise regularly, join a class or have private lessons if you wish to reap the full benefits of the exercises.

There are thousands of body positions and postures in yoga. At the last count over 80,000 different postures were identified. Here I am going to mention only a few:

Simple Yoga Positions

1 While standing, or sitting if you are tired, take a deep breath and at the same time raise your hands up just above your head. Then lower them together while breathing out.

98

2 Lie on your stomach. Breathe gently in and out a few times. Then raise your head and shoulders up as far as comfortable, breathe in, and then, while breathing out, come back to original position.

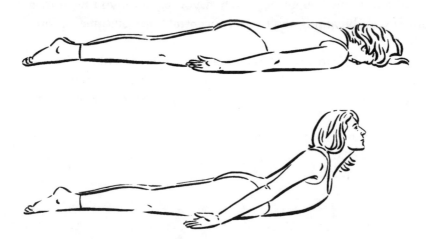

3 Sit on the floor with your knees slightly bent. Breathe in and raise your arms as in position **1** . While breathing out, bend forward and touch your knees with your head and rest your arms on the floor.

This movement should be finished by the end of the breathing out cycle. Breathe in and go back to original sitting position. Repeat.

Other Exercises
For Finger and Wrist Flexibility

- Sit on a chair with your back straight. Hold your arms stretched in front of you, with your palms facing the floor. Keep your arms stretched throughout.

- Extend your wrists so that your fingers point to the ceiling.

- Return to the original position and then flex your wrists so that your fingers are now pointing at the floor. Repeat.

- Now repeat the same movements with one hand facing to the floor and the other to the ceiling, alternately. Repeat a few times.

Squatting
This exercise improves the blood circulation and stiff joints.

- Stand up straight with your feet slightly apart. Hold on to a chair with your right hand.

- Keeping your back straight, squat, bending your knees all the way, and keeping your heels off the floor.

- Gently straighten up again. Repeat five times.

If you suffer from knee problems you need to be careful to control the weight on your knees and not just drop your weight suddenly onto them.

T'ai Chi

This is an ancient form of exercise for both the body and the mind. It is particularly suited to older people because there is little threat of muscular or bone injuries. Younger people can also get great benefits from regular t'ai chi sessions. These include better sleep patterns, a reduction of stress and toning of the muscles. Those who suffer from arthritis, back pain, muscle diseases and certain diseases of the nervous system may also experience an improvement during t'ai chi exercises. As for the mental benefits, a better memory, sharp mind, spiritual calmness and control of emotions are the prizes to take home after t'ai chi sessions.

T'ai chi is practised by the Taoists, who were mentioned earlier. The Taoists are great experts in all longevity matters and we can learn many tricks from them to help us live a long and healthy life.

I am going to describe a few basic t'ai chi postures just for starters. There are many more exercises and the easiest way to learn is by enrolling in a suitable class with a trained teacher. Otherwise you can learn from a book.

Start practising in front of a full-length mirror. Keep your body straight, but avoid tension. Think of your legs as the roots of a tree, your body as the trunk and your arms as the branches.

The Eagle Posture

Stand with your feet together, the heels touching each other. Let your hands hang by your side without any tension. Look straight ahead and relax. This is it.

The Dragon Posture

From the Eagle posture, take
one step forward with your
right leg. Bend your right
knee and keep your left leg
straight. Put most of your
weight onto the right knee.

101

The Monkey Posture

From the Dragon posture
move your weight to your
left leg and slightly bend
the left knee. Pull your right
foot all the way back,
keeping it flat on the floor.
When it can go no further,
raise the toes of your right
foot up while keeping the
heel touching the floor.

The Riding Horse Posture

From the Eagle posture, spread your legs sideways by a little more than the width of your shoulders. Bend both knees gently and put your weight on both legs equally.

These are merely four examples. From these postures you may progress to reach more postures using your hands. For example, from the Dragon posture do the following exercise:

Turn your hands to face downwards and gently circle them to face upwards. Keep your elbows close to your body and your left hand slightly behind the right. After this, allow your hands to swing to your right and follow the turning of your body to the right.

Or, from the Monkey posture:

Keep your hands facing each other with fingers straight. Bend your left arm and lift your left hand slightly up to the level of your left breast. Lower your right hand down to the level of your left knee.

These postures can then be incorporated into a full sequence of exercises. For example, the 'Play the Guitar' sequence starts with the Dragon posture, continues with the Monkey posture and ends with a modified Dragon posture.

Finish the exercises by adopting the Eagle posture.

By combining the different postures it is possible to perform dozens of sequences of movements. Remember to guide your mind during the exercises to use your inner strength. T'ai chi experts have such a disciplined mind that they can perform all the exercises in their brain, while remaining absolutely still.

Chi Kung (or Qi Gong)

This is one of the best anti-aging oriental techniques I have come across. It is an ancient system of movement, breathing exercises and meditation to heal body and mind. This method has been used for 4,000 years. It was, and still is, a favourite exercise for Taoists, those experts on longevity.

Chi means 'energy', while kung means 'art'. Chi kung practitioners claim that, if practised regularly, it:

- increases blood flow to the brain and to the skin

- lowers high blood pressure

- helps maintain a good sense of balance

- strengthens the bones

- supercharges the sex hormones

- restrains the biological effects of the aging process

Scientific studies have shown that while normal people breathe on average 12–16 times a minute, chi kung practitioners breathe less often than that, sometimes just five times a minute. This is a sign that their metabolism is balanced and slowed, reducing the effects of free radicals to a minimum.

Chi kung should be practised following certain rules. You need to practise regularly, when you are relaxed, and not before or after a heavy meal. Practise outside in the fresh air if possible, preferably away from pollution, in a large park, in the countryside or by the seaside. The best time for practising is at sunrise and at midnight, but morning or evening times are still acceptable.

Practise meditation, breathe correctly and relax during the exercise. The exercises are not just physical but are mental and spiritual at the same time, so you are able to kill three birds with one stone.

Here are some examples of basic chi kung exercises to get you started. If you develop an interest in this method (which you should!), then it is best to find a local class or get a relevant book to give you more information on other exercises.

Chi kung, like t'ai chi, should be performed not only with the body but also with the mind focused on the procedure.

Lifting the Sky

- Stand up straight, somewhere quiet, and relax for a few seconds with your arms hanging by your side (**1**).

- Smile, using the muscles of your face deliberately even if you don't feel the need to smile.

- Extend your fingers, bend your wrists upwards all the way and, while still keeping your arms straight downwards, bring your hands together so that the fingers of one hand touch the other (**2**).

104

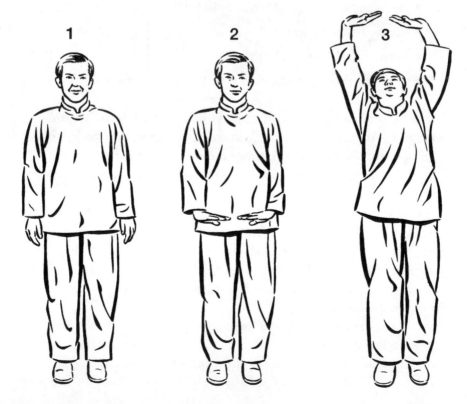

1   2   3

- While still holding this position, move your arms gently forwards and continue all the way upwards until you reach above your head (**3**). Remember, your wrists are still at right angles and fingers are touching. Breathe very calmly through your nose.

- While your arms are still above your head, push up as if you want to lift the sky up. Continue breathing gently and keep thinking happy, calm thoughts.

4

- Continue keeping your arms straight, and straighten your wrists, and then start lowering them, not in front of you, but by your side, as if you are drawing a big circle and you are in it (**4**).

- When your arms are by your sides again, relax and think happy thoughts.

Repeat the whole exercise about 20 times for the best results.

Pushing Mountains

- Stand up straight, with your arms hanging by your side. Extend your fingers, pointing upwards with your palms outwards (**1**). Bring your palms up to the sides of your chest with your elbows bent and pointing to your back.

1

2

- Breathe in gently and then push your hands out slowly, breathing out, both hands at the same time, fingers still together and pointing upwards, and imagine that you are pushing a wall or a mountain away from you (**2**).
- Bring your hands back to your chest and start again.
- It is important to feel the energy of your movements. Don't force yourself but feel that you have the strength to push a mountain away. Repeat this routine 30 times and then gently drop your arms to your sides.

Big Windmill

- Stand up straight with your arms hanging by your sides. Just concentrate on your right arm.

- Circle your right arm gently forward and all the way up, continuing backwards until you reach the original position. Breathe in gently during your forward arm movement. Breathe out during the backward movement. Take time and don't hurry yourself. During this movement think of energy flowing into your body, visualizing the energy fighting the aging process and making you young from the inside.

107

Repeat with the same arm about 10 times and then move on to the left arm.

Carrying the Moon

This exercise is especially for combating aging and increasing youthfulness and vitality.

- Stand with your body bent forward with your hands hanging just below the knees and your chin almost touching your chest.

- Stay in this position for three or four seconds, thinking of the energy flowing along your spine towards your head.

- Straighten up again gently, with your arms straight in front of you, bringing your arms forwards and all the way up above your head (**1**). Breathe in during this movement. Continue arching your back backwards as far as is comfortable for you.

- With your arms still at the highest point above your head, bring your thumbs and index fingers together to touch each other, making the shape of a circle (full moon).

108

- While still in this position, bend your head all the way back and look through the circle you have made with your thumbs and index fingers, as if you are looking at the full moon, while breathing gently for a few seconds (**2**).

- Straighten your body again, bringing your arms gently to your sides, drawing a full circle with your arms with you at the centre of it (**3**). While doing this, think of all the negative energy flowing down from your head to your body and legs, then escaping from your feet into the ground.

Ideally, you should concentrate on one technique, for example, chi kung, and practise this regularly, at least three times a week. In my opinion it is best not to mix the different techniques. For example I prefer not to perform chi kung exercises one day and yoga another.

Stress

Exercise can prevent many health problems and a good mental attitude can prevent equally as many. Quite a few people are afraid of stress, but a positive use of stress can actually add years to your life instead of taking them away.

Mind over Body (Psychoneuroimmunology)

The idea that the mind can extend life is not new in the Western world. The 18th-century philosopher William Goodwin stated: 'We become sick and die partly because we expect it and consent to it. If we believe in immortality, our beliefs will come true.'

We Westeners still deal with illness and old age mainly from a physical point of view, showing very little interest in the mental or spiritual aspects. Only recently have we begun, slowly but surely, to come round to more fundamental ways of thinking, realizing that mental powers are not only real but can help cure disease.

Scientific evidence comes from the relatively new branch of medicine called psychoneuroimmunology (PNI). This examines the effects of the mind (hence 'psycho') mediated through the brain and nerves (hence 'neuro') on the body and particularly on the immune system (hence 'immunology').

It is now well accepted by open-minded scientists that our thoughts can influence some parts of our immune system and make the treatment of disease much easier. For example, it was shown in experiments that in certain cancer patients who had a positive state of mind, the treatment with drugs worked much better than in patients who were resigned to their fate and expected the worst.

Along the same lines, it is possible to argue that a positive mental outlook and the right state of mind will have some effect on the aging cells and organs of the body. There isn't much scientific evidence to support this but, in theory, it is possible. By creating a positive mental state, we may be able to affect the immune system, delay the onset of some diseases and therefore delay the time of death.

A radical group of people go much further than this, hundreds of miles further. They claim that we age and die only because we think about aging and death. If we stop thinking about aging, and concentrate only on thinking about eternal life, then we will live forever, as simple as that. This is the Immortalists movement which is slowly flourishing in the US and is attracting a lot of ridicule from conventional (and not so conventional) scientists.

Leaving the Immortalists aside, I believe that it is worthwhile taking on regular positive mind training, as long as this is done within reason and as long as you are realistic about the results. It is certainly spiritually refreshing to use something else as well as drugs and pills for avoiding disease in later life.

Contrary to what many people think, stress could actually be good for aging. Some researchers think that it makes us live longer and here is the proof. Centenarian studies from around the world have shown that most people who lived to be over 100 years old had led a strenuous, hard-working and burdensome life, with a certain degree of stress and many crises to cope with. This doesn't mean 'excessive' stress but a sensible degree of stress which is perceived as demanding but comfortable by the individual. And I don't mean mental stress alone, but any type of stress, including physical and nutritional stress.

One way this may be explained is the following. During periods of stress or starvation, nature panics and spends more energy in trying to maintain the body in good condition. It is a disadvantage to die young, because young people can still have children and so improve the survival of the species. It makes sense that during periods of stress it is better to repair the damage and save the body rather than to waste the energy resources in reproduction.

That is why stress stimulates the body to repair itself more efficiently and therefore minimize age-related damage. This has been studied with animals in the case of calorie restriction treatments which reduce the amount of food to animals for many months, extending their life spans. In these cases, nutritional stress triggers the repair mechanisms, so aging damage is reduced.

For example, in calorie-restricted animals (animals which are under nutritional stress but not malnourished) the free radical damage is reduced, blood cholesterol returns to normal and the repair of collagen becomes more active.

Another study has shown that certain centenarian groups in Georgia consuming an average of 1,768 calories per day, boast low incidence of atherosclerosis as well as low incidence of other age-related diseases. Considering that we, in the West, consume over 2,000–2,500 calories a day, you can see why we die young.

However, I should make clear that the stress, be it mental or physical, should be controlled and kept under a certain limit in order to have any benefits. Very high levels of stress contribute to the well-known illnesses such as heart disease and mental problems. A steady, comfortable and low level of stress in our life may be sufficient.

Perhaps doctors should advice patients not only to pursue physical stress by performing comfortably demanding regular exercise, but also to:

1 Seek mental stress with daily brain exercises and by pursuing unfamiliar experiences

2 Seek nutritional stress by consuming a good quality yet low calorie food

3 Seek social stress by being active, setting new targets and trying to achieve them

4 Seek spiritual stress by remaining alert and suspicious, unsatisfied with easy solutions and by searching for new directions

Excessive stress on the other hand should be avoided. If you feel that you are under a level of stress which makes you feel uncomfortable, try the following ways to banish it:

• flotation sessions (*see* chapter 8)

• laughter therapy

• relaxation and meditation

• massage or self-massage

All of these help reduce the hormones related to excessive stress and boost natural chemicals which relax the mind.

You may also wish to try herbal supplements containing melissa or valerian. These two plants can be used together or on their own and have a calming effect on the nerves. They are also used to promote better sleep.

Aromatherapy oils, especially used during massage treatments, are very good for reducing stress.

If you become able to take the positive effects of stress and use these to your advantage, then your chances of living a long and healthy life will be greatly improved. If you let stress overcome you, then you will have no defences against the aging process and it will eat you alive.

Now is the ideal time to turn to the different ways leading to super brain health.

CHAPTER 6

Boosting Your Brain Power

The Aging Brain

Aging of the brain happens to all of us irrespective of how healthy we are. If we are unhealthy, however, the process is swifter.

The claws of time destroy our senses, too. Loss of even a minor amount of hearing or vision will put extra pressure on the other senses to work flat out in order to pump suitable information to the brain.

We need to adapt to this loss and make the necessary changes. For example, if you are a 50 year old, don't insist on having the same mental pressure as a 20 year old. Adapt your lifestyle to allow more time for decision-making tasks, driving routine or demands on your memory.

Mark Twain joked that 'Being old is no different from being young, as long as you are sitting down.' I would paraphrase this and say that being old is no different from being young as long as you allow yourself more time. Think about this and apply it to your everyday life.

Our brain tissues, chemicals and thinking processes change throughout life, some for better, some for worse. Specialists who have studied the biology of the brain have found that in older people's brains there is an increased amount of biological junk, called 'senile plaques' and 'neuro-fibrillary tangles'. The amount of this material increases as the years go by and it becomes particularly abundant in the brains of patients suffering from Alzheimer's dementia. Is this material the cause of dementia or is it a result of it? The jury is still out on this one.

Lipofuscin is a distinctive age-related junk material which accumulates inside the brain cells, affecting memory and other brain processes. This material is related to damage caused by free radicals, and scientists believe that it may cause cells to malfunction.

While you were reading these last few paragraphs, you probably lost several dozen brain cells. Thousands of our brain cells perish every day, but this is not as many as was once believed. The good news is that only some areas of the brain suffer this loss. In other areas there is almost no change at all.

Our brain cells die from a natural process called apoptosis, meaning that their death is orderly and controlled by the organism. Dead brain cells are removed tidily and the remaining cells are able to form new connections to try and compensate for the loss.

The ability to form new connections plays an essential role in maintaining our brain in fine shape. As an example, think of a company employing 100 workers. When two or three of these workers leave their job, the rest will have the ability to cover for them and the ultimate efficiency of the company will remain unaffected. If, later on, another two or three leave, the rest will still be able to cope effectively. And so on, up to a point. However, if they all left at once, the rest would be running around like headless chickens.

This important ability to compensate for lost brain cells disappears in very old people and in patients with Alzheimer's dementia. Fewer connections between brain cells means less brain function. In many experiments, scientists have showed that people who started mental exercises while young and who continued through to old age have a good chance of maintaining a healthy brain by stimulating the formation of new connections between the cells.

On the other hand, research evidence also suggests that a boring environment can accelerate the loss of connections between brain cells and reduce the formation of new ones. During experiments, rats which were kept in boring and monotonous environments had a very low ability to form new connections in their brain. When similar rats were moved into new cages with slides, ramps, different colours, etc – the rat equivalent of Disneyland – they developed new interests, lost excess weight and their brains cells sprouted new connections.

This means that we need to help our brain help itself by keeping it stimulated, avoiding constant and prolonged routine and by performing brain exercises.

Other Changes

Fortunately, our ability to make logical decisions and to assimilate general knowledge is preserved throughout life. In solving mental problems, the correct result can be reached by both young and old individuals, but older people take more time. This need not be a disadvantage – in many areas of life wisdom and experience win out over quickness of thinking.

A small mental decline may start from the age of 20 or 30. The rate of loss and the rate of change are not the same for everybody but vary, depending partly on genetics but mostly on external stimulation. Various components of the brain age more slowly than others. As a result, certain parts of memory may be affected early whereas others may continue functioning brilliantly. A very small loss of age-related memory is sometimes referred to as 'benign senescence forgetfulness', which is an almost normal event in aging.

Young people use their memory in a particular way which may not be suitable for older people. Older people need to exercise different parts of their brain which still function properly if they want to keep up. Many people are not aware of this and fail to use memory training frequently enough. Yet if they don't exercise their brain, their memory may worsen, and this will make them more worried and even less likely to exercise. This is a catch-22 situation. If you are in this situation, get out as quickly as possible. Learn about your brain and use this knowledge to support your memory. Help your brain learn about itself.

Poor diet, boredom, depression, anxiety and lack of physical exercise can make memory worse. Flagging memory can also be due to diseases, vitamin deficiencies, too much alcohol, thyroid problems and drugs. If you are worried about your memory it is best to see your doctor as soon as possible to prevent any problems in the future. It may not be 'just old age' causing your memory to fail.

Check your Memory

Answer 'True' or 'False':

a   I frequently keep forgetting what I am supposed to be doing.

b   I find it difficult to learn new things.

c   Concentrating for a few minutes on a particular task becomes more and more difficult.

d   I feel mentally exhausted at the end of the day.

e   I use 'er' and 'um' very frequently when speaking.

f   I frequently can't put my brain into action.

g   Sometimes I lose track of time.

h   I frequently forget people's names, even those well known to me.

i   I am frequently unable to recognize a person known to me if I meet them in an unfamiliar setting.

Award yourself no points for every 'False' answer and one point for every 'True' answer.

Score

0–1 Your memory is, in general, healthy.

2 and over. Your memory is running low. More problems are likely in the future unless you do something about it now. Think, contemplate, meditate. In earnest.

The Workings of Memory

Can memory be improved? Of course it can. Memory is like a muscle: if you don't exercise it, it weakens. Exercising your memory should start early in life with regular mental games, such as puzzles, crosswords and reading.

Most commonly, the information is already sitting in the brain but we lose access to it for some reason. This is when we talk about 'retrieval' problems. Less commonly, we may have problems with registering new memories in the brain. This is called an 'assimilation' problem.

To give you a better idea of these problems, I will discuss in simple terms how memory works. The remembering process can be divided into three different parts:

- encoding
- storage
- retrieval

Encoding means to imprint or to transfer information into the memory banks. The information, after being picked up by our senses, is sent to the brain through nerves which transform the information into coded electrical signals.

When a particular piece of information arrives at the storage area of the brain, it is somehow stockpiled into the memory banks. This is the stage of storage. It isn't clear how storage works, but scientists think that short-term memory and long-term memory may involve different processes.

For short-term memory, a kind of self-help action between the communication pathways of brain cells may take place. As an example, think of a field of grass. If people walk over it many times in a certain direction, they will create a pathway. Others will be able to see the pathway and use it to arrive at their destination quickly. When people stop passing through, the grass will slowly grow back and delete the pathway, making it difficult for other people to find their way. In the brain analogy, if the pathway is not used again and again, it will switch off after a few minutes, hours or days. The memory will then be lost. The process is called 'synaptic facilitation', but you may want to think of it as 'keeping the channels open'. Synaptic facilitation is responsible only for short-term memory.

Long-term memory, on the other hand, works differently. It may involve a permanent change in the shape of special memory proteins which get twisted, bent or otherwise changed to encode and hold the information long term. When we try to remember information which was encoded and stored a long time ago, our brain asks these proteins to provide the information they hold.

These are the most commonly accepted theories regarding memory, but are not 100 per cent proven. There may be other mechanisms of storing information in the brain which at present remain elusive.

The third stage is the task of retrieval. During this stage, our brain pinpoints the information we want to retrieve and makes it available for use.

There is something special here about rhymes, poems and songs. We are normally better able to remember a song than a series of words or numbers. This is because the memories of the sound or rhythm are encoded in addition to the memory of the words.

Very old people or patients with dementia who may not remember much of their past may still be able to recite poems or songs from their childhood. I have personal experience of this, from a relative who in her late nineties was demented and unable to remember everyday events. Yet she would sit in her bed mumbling on her own, reciting complicated folk poems and ballads using rhyming 15-syllable lines which she learned as a child, talking of heroes, princesses and dragons, passion, love and death.

Brain in a Bottle

If your memory is going, don't despair. There are dozens of different pills aimed at boosting brain function. In fact there is a befuddling variety of nutritional supplements and products offered to those who want to keep their wits about them.

The claims range widely, from 'Memory Fuel' (to improve memory and concentration) to 'Designer Brainfood' (which feeds the brain, improves speaking and writing). Some firms offer brain cocktails like 'Albert's Ale' (named after Albert Einstein and aiming to make the user as clever as he was). If you want to try it, mix 10 drops of ginger extract, 10 drops of red clover, 1 teaspoon of phosphatidyl choline (available from health shops), mixed with grape concentrate and organic apple juice. Tell me if it works.

Many chemicals are touted as effective 'mind-enhancers' (also called nootropics), including hydergine, piracetam, ginseng, phosphadytidyl serine, ginkgo biloba and vinpocetine. These and some others are discussed in detail later on (*see* chapter 10).

Ginkgo and vinpocetine are obtained from plants. Another plant used to improve memory is *Bacopa monnieri*, also known as the Indian brahmi plant. This contains the active ingredients bacoside A and bacoside B. It has been used for thousands of years in India as a tonic to treat mental problems, lack of concentration and crumbling memory.

This plant is mentioned in three Ayurvedic texts as being effective against brain problems. Modern research on it has been performed mainly in India over the past 50 years. Experiments in rats have shown that it is a brain stimulant, it improves the time necessary to take a decision and boosts memory. No side effects have been found.

The brahmi plant is thought to be the first modern Ayurvedic brain supplement to be introduced to the world, following an initiative by the World Health Organization to stimulate development of traditional plant remedies. This product was launched in 1996 in India and is slowly being promoted around the world.

Many conventional scientists believe that these supplements are useless. Many don't know enough about them and are unwilling to recommend them. Others examine what research there is and maintain a healthy scepticism. Yet other eminent scientists promote these treatments as miracle cures. Do they work? I personally know dozens of people who have used these supplements without improving one bit. But I also know dozens of others who think that they are wonderful. I think the solution to this dilemma is to try the treatment yourself. If you believe that it is working for you, continue it. If it doesn't work in two or three months, throw it away.

How to Remember

Now you know something about how memory works, you can make use of this knowledge to help you remember better.

Taking pills is the lazy way of memory boosting. There is a more difficult way for those who want to achieve their full potential: memory exercises.

Chunking

Most people have the ability to recall around 5–7 'chunks' or bits of information at any one time. But if we use this ability wisely and organize our approach, we will easily be able to remember long lists of items. The best technique to use here is actually called 'chunking'.

If, for example, you have to remember the contents of your shopping list, you should mentally divide the items into groups. If, say, you want to buy kiwi fruit, bread, bananas, biscuits, cornflakes and pineapple juice (six items), you can divide this into two groups: fruit and bakery. It is, you would agree, easier to remember two items than six. When you get to the supermarket you start with the first group and work your way through the items included in that group: kiwi fruit, bananas, pineapple juice. Then you tackle the second group: bread, cornflakes and biscuits. You can, of course, take a written list with you, but this is an exercise for your memory, not merely for your convenience.

Mental Imagery

Chunking can be used on its own or it can be supplemented by another trick called 'mental imagery'. The brain remembers images much better than written words. So, if you relate the items on your list to mental images, you will be able to remember them much more efficiently. You can either just remember the image of the item in your brain or you can try the following example.

Say you have pineapple, bananas and apples on your list. A way to remember these is to mentally go through your house and put each of the above items in a conspicuous place. You open your door from the outside and walk in. On the doormat somebody has left an apple. You enter the sitting room. Where you usually keep the fruit, there is an enormous pile of pineapples. You then go upstairs and almost slip on a banana left by somebody on the staircase.

If you wish, you can try remembering more items using this method. You can, for example, imagine the house of your friend or somebody very familiar to you and fill it in with other items from your shopping list. Try it a few times and, as you get more confident, add more items on your mental list to see how many you can remember. I have to say, however, that some people don't like this method because it involves substantial mental effort.

Context

The previous two tricks are good for remembering lists of things. If you want to remember past events, you need to use a different technique: context. All you have to do with this is to restore the surroundings related to the particular event.

For example, you want to remember what clothes you had on during an outing two weeks ago. Why you should want to remember this I don't know, but in any case, you do. You should try to mentally recreate the events of that particular day. Were you alone or with relatives? Which relatives? Where did you go? Was it cold? Was it raining? Do you remember a particular detail such as your shoes getting wet or dropping food on your shirt?

Spend some time thinking around the subject, comparing dates, images and events until you come to a conclusion. Remember, this trick is not only useful for answering practical questions, but it also exercises the brain.

Elaboration

In order to help improve the encoding of memories you could try the following: amplify the subject, ask questions and talk around the particular theme.

For example, if you are invited to go to the theatre next Saturday evening, it may be difficult to just remember the day, time and place. To make your brain better able to digest the details, discuss it either with yourself or with somebody else. Find out details such as:

- who else is going

- what the play is about

- how you are going to get there and back, and so on

This will help you register the whole subject in more detail in your memory banks and you will be in a better position to remember the details when the time comes.

Organization

This psychological trick is used for organizing memories into logical sequences. Here again mental images play a vital part. To help you remember certain details, try imagining yourself in the relevant situation and run the details through your mind.

For example, you are going to visit some friends and stay with them for the weekend. If you don't want to forget anything important, think of everything in sequence as if you were actually going away now:

- First, you need to know how to get there. Do you have their address, a map and a means of transport?

- Then you arrive. Have you remembered to bring a little present – flowers or wine?

- Then you sit and chat. Did you bring your holiday photographs or your daughter's new painting to show them?

- Afterwards you change for dinner. Do you have suitable clothes, shoes, make-up?

- If you are staying the night, did you pack your nightwear, slippers and toileteries?

Continue along the same lines until you mentally arrive back at your home. I have followed this method myself and I have never, not even once, gone up the road and then come back again because I had forgotten something. The only problem is that you need to really think very hard and consider all possibilities and all events, in sequence.

Knot in the Handkerchief

Not much psychology here! I know several people who actually tie knots in their handkerchief to help them remember things. The idea is that if you suddenly remember an important detail and you don't want to forget it, leave something in a noticeable place to remind you.

For example, if you are reading in bed and you suddenly remember an important appointment just before you fall asleep, put something that is to hand, say your shoe, inside your book and leave it on the floor. When you get up next morning you will see this strange combination and this will remind you of your appointment.

Observation

There are quite a few ways to super-tune your powers of observation. A well-known game is to look at several items for a few seconds and then, without looking, write down a complete list of these items. Other exercises are:

To improve the registration of memories in your brain, spend some time in the evening, preferably well before you go to sleep, trying to recall the day's events as vividly as possible.

Take a picture, look at it for a few seconds and then write down as many details as you can.

Alternatively, look at a stranger for a few seconds when you are out and then imagine that you are called by the police to describe that person.

Short-Term Memory Training

It is possible to improve your short-term memory by using several exercises. Try one of the following or, better, devise a few of your own that will make you use your imagination and remember a vast amount of details for a few seconds, minutes or hours.

Exercise 1

Underline all three consecutive digits that add up to 17:

26475859735241636476879806584673524254757687 98067

89675643543243637292010384756757698679605409 13836

72183941050985482121214365101027435572810183 64528

Exercise 2

Look at the following list for five seconds and then see how many words you can remember after covering it up:

pen

mobile phone

tree

washing

books

flapping

gun

aunt

fall

My guess is that you couldn't remember more than five or six words. If you want to remember more, make up a short story:

I had my pen and my mobile phone in my hand, and I was under a tree with my aunt's washing flapping in the wind. I read in my books that a man with a gun had a fall.

I agree that this takes much longer than five seconds, but the idea is that, with training, you will become able to make up stories in your mind without even thinking much about it. The story doesn't have to make logical sense but it will jog your memory in the short term.

When you finish this exercise, ask somebody to give you another list of unrelated words and try to make these into another story. Have fun with it.

Exercise 3

A similar way of remembering things is by learning lists of words. For example, try to remember these: cat, shirt, dog, biscuits, trousers, lemon, tie, giraffe, bread, peppers, snake, coat.

At first, this looks very difficult. But if you separate these words into three groups such as 'animals', 'food' and 'clothing', you will be able to organize your thoughts. This uses the technique of chunking in order to help learning.

Your list will look like this:

cat, dog, giraffe, snake

shirt, trousers, tie, coat

biscuits, lemon, bread, peppers

Spend some time trying to remember these. If you wish you can use mental pictures – for example a dog running after a cat and a giraffe with a snake on its neck.

These are just a few exercises which, I hope, will stimulate you to start regular long-term memory training. They will help refresh your memory and learning abilities, and after some training you will be able to use the tricks subconsciously. It takes some time to get used to them and to decide which trick to use and for what occasion, but they usually work well.

You have to keep exercising your memory well into very old age to prevent it from worsening. Look out for other exercises in memory books or come up with some of your own.

Revitalize your Mind

I can't remember where(!), but several years ago I came across the following little poem. I kept it because I think it describes my ideas in a nutshell. Here it is:

Age is a quality of mind.

If you have left your dreams behind,

if hope is cold,

if you no longer look ahead,

if your ambitions are dead,

then you are old.

Anonymous

126

It is important to keep the mind active at any age. If the human brain does not get enough outside stimulation, it becomes so desperate for new information that it starts creating it itself. In experiments using sensory deprivation when most outside stimulation of the brain was cut off, volunteers started having hallucinations and weird brain patterns, indicating that their brains made up information and fed it to themselves.

Explore Yourself

Contemplate the following questions and then spend a few minutes musing over my comments. These questions apply to you in particular if you are 30 years old or over.

1 How frequently do you watch the news on TV or listen to it on the radio?

2 Do you believe that old age should stop people being extravagant?

3 Do you get bored with ordinary routine?

4 Do you usually find it easy to initiate conversation with others?

5 Do you like hoarding things in case you may need them later on?

6   Do you have to think creatively and use your brain during your day?

7   How frequently do you read science, literature, philosophy or other similar books?

8   In general, do you believe that people's memory worsens beyond control as they grow old?

9   Do you keep yourself informed of the latest developments in science, fashion, politics or world affairs?

10   Do you feel out of your depth when having to handle a new video recorder, new computer, new mobile phone or similar?

Comments

Keeping informed on the national and international situation implies that you have a healthy interest in the world around you, which keeps the brain nicely stimulated. Do make a point of watching the news and then discussing it with a partner or a friend. On the other hand, also take regular 'media holidays'. For one day a week, avoid reading the papers or watching television to give your mind a rest from the constant news and advertisements.

Many older people, including those over 85 years old, feel that life is full of intellectually stimulating events and worth living to the full. This attitude maintains a sharp mind and avoids boredom.

Social characteristics such as a worsening of conversation skills, and unnecessary hoarding may be the early signs of brain aging.

Research suggests that a brain which is stimulated and challenged regularly will perform well even in very old age.

Stimulating activities can be very simple, for example:

• Think how to reposition the furniture in your sitting-room.

• Write a letter to your local paper on an issue important to you.

• Start a new part-time or evening course.

• Finish reading this book and write a long letter to me with your comments.

Reading books shows that you have an interest in learning new things, which in itself keeps the brain active. It is never too late to start reading stimulating books regularly. From certain books you will also be able to get information about new anti-aging treatments which you may find useful in maintaining your health.

Don't over-stimulate your brain, however. This can cause stress headaches and will dull the thinking process. If you are satisfied that you have had enough then it is time to stop for the day.

It is often difficult to handle technical equipment, and unfamiliarity always makes matters worse. However, you need to keep up with some technological advances which make life easier.

The questions continue:

11　Are you able to take decisions easily?

12　How much time do you put aside for your hobbies?

13　Do you usually sleep well?

14　Do you frequently feel like crying?

15　Have any of your older close relatives ever suffered a stroke or significant memory loss?

16　Were you educated to higher education or university standard or did you have a basic education?

17　Do you have a pet?

Taking a quick decision shows a sharp mind and a personality liking an element of risk. People who manage to carry these qualities with them into old age are fortunate. Those who don't should exercise them. If, however, you have been a slow decision-maker all your life, it will be very difficult to change as you get older.

Leaving aside time for your hobbies is one of the most important steps to avoid excessive stress. It also indicates that you've got your priorities right, that you care about yourself and therefore you keep yourself well.

Depression may manifest itself as memory loss, difficulty in sleeping and loss of appetite. Mild to moderate depression can easily be treated but if you think you are depressed, you need to make sure that you see somebody for advice.

Physical exercise and low cholesterol diets improve blood flow to the brain. A family history of atherosclerosis (thickening of the arteries) shows an increased risk of brain failure.

Research shows that low education is associated with an increased risk of Alzheimer's dementia. It is never too late to take up education in order to exercise the brain.

Having a pet is a good way to reduce mental stress.

Mental Exercises

Regular mental exercises make things happen inside us. Research evidence shows that:

- They maximize the power of the immune system.
- They boost morale and self-image.
- They may help the body fight aging damage, although the actual scientific evidence for this is not very clear yet.
- They make you confident to face old age in a positive way.
- They reduce excessive stress and balance some of the body's physiological functions.
- They speed up specific cognitive functions. For example, they regulate emotions, refresh and clear the thought processes, improve the outlook and keep the intelligence in admirable shape.

Recent research points out that regular mental exercises adjust certain special chemicals in the brain, called neuropeptides. Examples of these are VIP (vasoactive intestinal peptide), substance P, GABA (gamma-amino-butyric acid) and other exotically-named chemicals, all of which have the power to energize body and mind.

It is difficult to pinpoint exactly which exercise benefits which areas of the brain, so I am only going to concentrate on general mental exercises here.

Positive Thinking

One type of mental exercise is positive thinking. Examples are described below. Positive thinking is probably the most promising anti-aging activity you can do.

In order to start positive thinking exercises you need to follow certain procedures. First, find out what exactly concerns you about growing old. Tick those statements which apply to you.

I am concerned about growing older because of:

- fear of disease (cancer, deafness, etc)
- loss of income, loss of job
- isolation
- pain
- fear of death
- the possibility of going into an old people's home
- wrinkles, grey hair, loss of hair
- weakness
- becoming a burden to others
- being unwanted
- loss of memory/intelligence
- becoming incontinent
- loss of status
- loss of mobility
- loss of spouse/friends
- loss of independence
- being treated like a child

Are there any others which are important to you?

Keep your answers in mind while reading about the following exercises and see whether your concerns improve with time.

Relaxation

Don't go into mental exercises stone cold. Warm up first. You can do this through relaxation exercises. It doesn't matter what kind of relaxation you perform, whether it is a routine from a relaxation tape, from a book or your own individual form of relaxation. But you need to be relaxed to reap the full benefit of these exercises.

With the following exercises, make sure you read them through a few times and understand what you have to do. There is no point in interrupting the exercises every few minutes to read on and remind yourself what to do next.

One of the most convenient and easy relaxation exercises is the following, although I must say that some relaxation experts don't agree with this method any more.

- Lie down on the floor in a quiet room with dimmed lights. You must feel comfortable and warm, be wearing loose clothing and have taken off any shoes or spectacles. Close your eyes and calm down for a few minutes.

- Now start a series of clenching and relaxing your muscles.

  Start with your feet. Curl up your toes and feel the tension for a few seconds. Now let go and notice the difference. Repeat once more.

- Press your feet strongly to the ground and feel your calf muscles tighten up. After a few seconds relax and feel the difference between the relaxation and the tension. Repeat once more.

- Press the backs of your knees towards the floor so that your heels just rise from the floor. Feel the tension in your thighs and then let go. Repeat once more and notice the relaxation of the muscles.

- Tighten your buttocks hard and let go after a few seconds. Always notice the difference between the clenching and the relaxed muscles. Repeat.

- Pull in your abdomen as hard as you can. Let go and then repeat once more.

- Make a fist as tight as you can and notice the tightness in your forearm. Let go and then repeat once more.

- Tighten your elbows by bending them up towards the shoulder. Let go and then repeat once more.

131

- Moving on to the shoulders, pull these up towards your ears, hold tight for a few seconds and let go. Repeat and feel the difference between tension and relaxation.

- Lift your head up from the floor, hold it up for a few seconds, then relax. Repeat once more.

- Tighten your lips and let go into a smile. Do the same with your eyes by closing your eyelids tightly and then letting go. Repeat once more.

- Before you finish this relaxation session, let your mind go quickly over your body, starting from the feet, moving on to the calves, thighs, buttocks, abdomen, hands, elbows, shoulders and face. Check mentally to make sure that all these still feel relaxed and comfortable.

Now you can proceed to do the mental exercises described below. It is important to wait for a few minutes before you get up, though, because your blood pressure will be low and if you stand up suddenly you may feel dizzy.

The following brain exercises are suitable for anybody over the age of 25 who is reasonably healthy. If you suffer from any form of psychiatric or psychological disease it is best to check with your doctor before you start the exercises.

Positive Affirmations

By repeating one of the following affirmations several times a day it may be possible to smash through your subconscious barriers and hammer the message to your brain.

The affirmations should be positive and in the present tense (for example say: 'I am confident' and not 'I will be confident'). Keep the sentence short and simple.

A good idea would be to write down your affirmation several (say, 30–40) times a day instead of mentally repeating it.

If you run out of ideas as to what sentence you might use, go back to your 'I am concerned about growing older because ...' list. You can use your answers as the basis for positive affirmations.

Some examples of positive affirmations are:

- I love life and living.

- I am confident that I am destined to live for many years.
- I have important contributions to make to society.
- I am always younger than somebody.
- I live for today, because it is the youngest I'll ever be.
- I accept myself at any age.
- I am going to stay healthy for as long as possible.
- I can understand things better.
- I am … years old and it's nice.
- Thank God I don't have the problems of a younger person.
- New developments in science are there to help me if necessary.
- The past is over. I look forward to the future.
- I have everything to live for.
- I have no intention of dying now.

An example taken from the 'I am concerned about growing older' list would be:

- I am not afraid of cancer.

Positive Daydreaming

After an initial period of relaxation, while sitting comfortably some-where quiet, let your imagination run wild.

You can think of any scenario you like but the general idea could be that your body is fighting the negative effects of age. For example:

Imagine that you are sitting in a quiet hospital room. Now imagine that you are leaving your body and you are floating in the air above you. Leave all your worries and problems with your body. Imagine that the door opens and many scientists wearing white coats come in and start working on your body. They are using electronic gadgets with flashing lights and bleeping noises. They are blasting away all the aged cells in your body and all the bad effects of old age (wrinkles, white/grey hair, disease, etc). You don't feel any pain at all but you realize that you are beginning to feel better. All those scientists keep on hunting down every small abnormality in your body and repairing it. Your immune system is getting stronger and stronger and your healthy cells are fighting the weak damaged cells. Your body is bursting with energy.

Think about the damaged old cells being repaired and all those toxic chemicals being eliminated from your body. The scientists are giving you injections with powerful chemicals to help with this repair.

You may want to concentrate on a particular area of your body which has signs of aging (for example, arthritis), or you may try to revitalize your body as a whole.

Finally your body wins and feels healthier and stronger. Keep daydreaming until you are completely satisfied.

Wait for a few minutes and get up gently.

In this example, you should think of the damaged, aged cells as weak and pathetic, and the scientists as strong and efficient. The scientists and their treatment will inevitably win over the weak aging cells. Instead of scientists, some people prefer to use the image of God, or any other image connected with power and wisdom (Mother Nature, etc).

Keep daydreaming for at least five minutes a day.

Self-Persuasion

Think of yourself 10 or 20 years from now. What are you going to look like? Will your hearing be worse, will you be suffering from any illness? You may be, but on the other hand you will be more experienced, your current problems will not exist any more and you will be feeling healthy and energetic.

Imagine that you are completely satisfied, with enough free time for your favourite hobby and for work if this pleases you. You will still feel strong and refreshed, refusing to let yourself be 'old'. You will have time to travel and do anything you want without the pressures of your current life.

Try to make yourself feel excited about the life awaiting you when you are older. When you feel revitalized, finish the session.

Anti-Youth Meditation

While in a relaxed state, think back to when you were a child or a teenager. Concentrate on all those events and situations which you have conveniently locked away in your memory's attic – your inexperience, all those worries about the future, the problems at school, your shyness, mistakes, uncertainty, failures. Would you really like to go through those experiences again? Try to think of as many problems and terrible experiences as you can.

After a few minutes, think about the present and relish the difference. Now you are wiser, more confident about yourself and more experienced.

Exercises which do not necessarily need relaxation beforehand are:

135

Positive Self-Talk

Every morning stand in front of the mirror and look at yourself. Say to yourself positively and enthusiastically:

Good morning [name]

We are going to have a nice day today and live life to the full.

[or] We are going to do something really interesting today and have fun. A lot of interesting things are going to happen to us today.

Do this for 30 seconds a day. Use a loud voice if possible. This may make others in your house think that you are mad, but after a short time you will be surprised at the results.

Guided Attention Technique

Think of any random word, take its last letter and find a new word beginning with that letter. For example:

paper, robot, tin, name, eternity, yellow, water

If you really want to make your brain sweat, avoid using each word more than once and try to be as quick as you can. As you become more confident, aim to produce words relating to specific categories such as names, car makes, countries and capital cities. Time yourself and see how many words you can produce in two minutes.

This exercise helps sharpen up the thought processes while at the same time improving judgement and the retrieval of information from the brain.

The Object Uses Test

In this exercise you need to write down as many unusual uses of everyday items as possible. For example, write down five unusual uses of a shirt. It can be used as a head cover in the sun, as a bandage, to help start a fire, as a duster, to mop up water from the floor ...

Other items could include a pen, chair, a mug or a shoe. Do this exercise alone or in a group three times a week for 5–10 minutes at a time. The sillier, the better, but don't go overboard.

This helps enrich the thinking processes and encourages creativity.

Mindfulness Training

For this exercise, you need to decide on a controversial subject and then argue the case opposite to your own opinion.

For example, if you support homosexuality, write an essay or discuss with a partner all the disadvantages of it. Criticize it and find arguments to support the other side. You don't have to believe in what you say, as long as you are able to put forward an argument which is clear and makes sense.

The exercise makes you think of issues which you have hidden in some dark areas of your brain. It is spring cleaning for the brain, bringing out into the open parts of your personality which you may not be aware of.

A similar exercise involves occasionally reading a book or magazine which you don't usually read. If you are a man, for example, have a look at a woman's magazine every couple of months or so (some men do this every week!), if you are a pensioner, read a teenager's magazine, and so on. Make an effort to choose something different every now and then, something that may make you see things in a different light.

Thinking of Past Times

You need to put aside a considerable amount of time and effort for this exercise.

Using a notebook, write down as many positive events as you can remember from your past. Create a file or a dossier with photographs, letters, certificates and so on to remind you of your past.

This will also help you remember your achievements and it will prove to you that your life has not been a waste. You have achieved many things.

You don't necessarily have to show this to anyone else. It is for your own use. If, however, it makes you feel good, then do show it to others.

Include any positive events that you can think of such as holidays, important letters, awards, hobbies, financial achievements, sporting prizes, etc. Try to live your life now so that you will be able to add more achievements to your dossier in the future. You have a remarkable personal history – don't erase it.

Stimulation Exercises

When we are stuck in a routine, we become accustomed to everyday life and we miss out on new information. It then becomes difficult to appreciate new experiences. If you want to change the pattern of information flow to your brain, try something unusual every now and then.

For example, once or twice a month, as a mental exercise, have 'technology-free days', aiming not to use modern technology at all if possible. Walk instead of taking the car/bus, eat raw food instead of cooked food, read instead of watching television, write to somebody instead of using the telephone, talk to somebody instead of listening to the radio, etc.

This should stimulate your brain into new ways of seeing life, away from things which you take for granted. It makes you think about how to cope with new situations and also makes your brain work overtime to identify modern technological aids which you need to avoid during the exercise.

Creativity Exercise

For this exercise, read a story from a book, newspaper or magazine. Then think about it for a few minutes and write down or discuss with a partner these points:

- If you were a film director how would you make the story into a blockbuster film?

- How would you use the images from the story and what parts you would have to omit because they are not visual?

- Using well-known actors, who would be a good actor for each person in your imaginary film?

- What kind of music would you use and when?

Flash Meditation

Every now and then, stop thinking about your daily problems and take your mind away from everything except an ultra-trivial detail. Concentrate on this insignificant detail and think about it for a few seconds, without thinking about anything else at all.

For example, concentrate on the ridges on your house key. Think how these were made, who made them, what material they used. Maybe just concentrate on your breathing, thinking about the air going in and out of your nose. Whatever detail you choose, this exercise will train your brain to rest quickly in times of overload and will make you pay more attention to details.

Physical Exercise and the Brain

Remember, the brain is affected not only by mental exercise, but also by physical exercise. The benefits of physical exercise are never ending. Apart from its effects on the muscles, the lungs and the heart, physical exercise can also keep the brain in fine shape.

How does it do that? The answer is simple if you believe that the body influences the mind and that the mind influences the body. Physical exercise improves confidence and self-esteem. It drains away feelings of anxiety, depression and stress. In short, it makes you feel good.

Other possible mental benefits of regular physical exercise, based on the latest research:

- It enriches the dopamine levels in the brain. (Dopamine is the chemical which is depleted in Parkinson's disease.)

- It balances worn-out supplies of glucose in the brain. Therefore the brain has more ready-made fuel to burn during mental effort.

- Regular moderate physical exercise boosts the body's natural defence mechanism, the white blood cells which combat infection.

- There is evidence that regular physical exercise can help the brain cells develop better connections. This is essential in maintaining brain sharpness and can even play a part in restoring age-related memory loss.

139

It Makes Sense

Our brain is just like a computer. In the case of computers, information about the world is collected by using a keyboard, a touch-screen, a camera or other similar sensors. It is flashed to the central processing unit via wires and then stored safely in the memory. When necessary, information is processed and then transmitted to the outside via screens, printers, etc. The same basic mechanism is true for the human brain. Information is gathered by the eyes, ears and other senses, sent to the brain through nerves and stored in appropriate areas of the brain. When necessary, the brain dispatches this information through speech, expression, actions, etc.

You don't need to be Bill Gates to realize that if the keyboard, mouse or touch-screen is damaged, then it would be impossible to feed information into the central computer. The retrieval of information would then be impossible because the details wouldn't be there in the first place.

The same is true with the brain. If the eyes, ears and other sense organs are not in tip-top condition, then the information fed to the brain will be less than perfect. It follows that if you wish to have a good memory and competent brain, you need to make sure that your information-collecting systems, ie, your senses, are in good working order. Open your eyes, unblock your ears, deploy your taste buds, activate your nose, experience your sense of touch, and gather, gather, gather information from the world around you like a dry sponge soaking up water.

Here I will present some ways in which you can do this, but some of the exercises are not suitable for people who take medication for heart and balance conditions. Check with your doctor first.

Vision
How Vision Changes with Age

Age-related changes to our vision include an increased chance of developing cataract (clouding of the lens of the eye), macular degeneration and an increased sensitivity to glare. It doesn't end there. With the passage of time, the lenses of the eyes become less elastic, resulting in presbyopia (long sightedness). This is good news if you suffer from myopia, because the two conditions cancel each other out and the result will (hopefully) be an improvement of vision.

What you can do to improve visual age-related changes:

- Have your eyes regularly checked by an optician. If you do need glasses, wear them and have them checked every now and then.

- Older drivers are particularly affected by glare, especially at night. To protect your eyes you may need to use special anti-glare glasses while driving. (Some people, however, do not find these glasses helpful.)

- To improve concentration and eye discrimination while

you observe something, re-run the details of the scenery or the events in your mind after a few minutes to make sure that you remember the details.

- A varied, balanced diet will make a positive difference to your eyes. Go for food high in antioxidants such as vitamins C, E, beta carotene, bilberry extracts and pycnogenol.

- Give your eyes a rest every so often. If you use a computer screen or watch television for too long, either close your eyes for a few minutes, or, better, turn your eyes towards empty space and let your gaze wander without fixing on anything in particular.

- Avoid visual routine. Look at something which is coloured differently from your usual environment. If you have to live in a place which is painted white or dull grey, try looking at bright, dazzling colours every now and then. Do the opposite if you live in a very colourful environment.

- Illuminate yourself. The eyes of a healthy 60-year-old need three times as much light as those of a 20-year-old.

Scanning and Focusing

When we stare at something, the small muscles which move our eyes try to focus on the item we are looking at, jerking automatically from side to side until they fix on the image. This process is called 'fixation'.

As we grow older, the number of jerks before the eye can 'zoom in' properly increases and the time between each jerk lengthens. If a young person needs, for the sake of argument, 10 eye jerks in 2 seconds to focus on an object, in 40 years' time the same person will need 20 eye movements in 6 seconds to focus on a similar object.

This means that when an older person is scanning an area, it will take longer for all the information to be fed into the brain compared to the time needed by a younger person. Therefore, if you are looking for somebody in a crowd, in order to do a proper search you will need to allow yourself more time for your eyes to focus on the area you are scanning.

Peripheral Vision

When we are looking at something, we see not only the object in front of us but also other objects out of the corners of our eyes. What we see when we are looking at something straight in front of our eyes is known as 'central vision' and what we perceive around that object is 'peripheral vision'.

For example, looking at this book now, straight ahead of you without moving your eyes from it, what you perceive out of the corners of your eyes is your peripheral vision.

With the passage of years the range of peripheral vision narrows. Some scientists think that this reduction is comparable to wearing blinkers. This means that older people should not rely too much on the visual information coming from the corners of their eyes, because this information will be reduced and will not correspond to the full picture.

As an example, some drivers fail to see traffic signs because they are just looking straight ahead and the images from the corners of their eyes are being missed. The thing to do is to keep turning the head gently and scan the whole area in front in order to get the whole picture properly.

Hearing

Age-Related Changes

The ability to hear high-pitched sound declines with age. Also, there is a loss in our ability to hear consonants, though our ability to hear vowels is preserved.

The causes of hearing loss include ear infections, injuries, the age-related form of hearing loss called 'presbyacusis' and other, rarer, medical conditions. Presbyacusis affects one in three people over the age of 65 and it may be due to life-long exposure to noise, minor infections and other small, repetitive damage. So, if you are still young, now is the time to help prevent this by avoiding ear-splitting noise. You may like dancing to deafening music, but my guess is that when you are older only a hearing aid will bring music to your ears.

Slight loss of hearing, which is normal in later life, can affect memory in two ways:

a It causes people to mishear what is said and the information does not reach the brain in the first place.

b It makes the act of hearing more difficult and leaves less time to comprehend and store the information in the brain. This makes it harder to remember what was said. Therefore, slight loss of hearing can make conversation slow and less rewarding.

Hearing Aids

Almost half of older people who have a hearing problem find this can easily be treated with hearing aids, yet only one in 10 uses them. The reasons for this include the stigma of wearing a hearing aid and the fact that the person may be unaware that there is a problem and that there is an easy solution.

Newer devices are being developed all the time, including some which can be screwed into the skull.

Tips to overcome hearing impairment

- If you have a hearing problem, admit it.
- Look the speaker face to face with your back turned to the light.
- Reduce background noise.
- Have a hearing test and use a hearing aid if necessary.
- If you wear a hearing aid, have it checked regularly for flat batteries.
- Slow the pace of the conversation down gently to suit you.
- Shouting is not usually necessary.
- If you can't follow the plot, change the subject of the conversation to something more familiar to you.
- Don't be afraid to ask other people to repeat something if you don't understand.

Do-It-Yourself Hearing Test

1 Do you often mishear words during a conversation with somebody who is unfamiliar to you?

        Yes 1   No 0

2 Do you feel that your hearing is better in relation to television programmes than radio programmes?

        Yes 1   No 0

3 Do you frequently have buzzing or other noises in your ears?

        Yes 1   No 0

4 Have you had frequent ear infections?

        Yes 1   No 0

5 Have you been in a noisy environment for long continuous periods in the past?

        Yes 3   No 0

6 Do you feel more comfortable if you look the person you are conversing with straight in the face?

        Yes 3   No/Indifferent 0

7 Do other people frequently comment that they hear sounds which you don't?

        Yes 3   No 0

8 Do other people mention that your hearing is poor?

        Yes 3   No 0

Score

0–1: Your sense of hearing is likely to be normal.

2 and above: You may suffer from a degree of hearing loss. See a doctor to check for wax, infections and other causes. You may need to have a formal hearing test.

Hearing Exercises

There are several exercises to increase input of meaningful sounds to the brain. These will also help prevent memory loss and will keep the brain nicely stimulated and challenged.

Exercise 1: A Sound Exercise

Have frequent and regular periods of silence in your house.
On the other hand, if you usually have to live in a quiet
environment, have periods of extra noise to stir your senses up,
for example put the radio or the television on loud for a while –
not for too long, though.

Exercise 2: Noise Attention Exercise

This exercise will help you pay more attention to sound.
Sit quietly and relax for a few minutes. Then attempt to
discriminate the different noises and sounds from around you.
Most people are able to pick up anything between three and
eight various noises. Examples are the central heating creaking,
cars passing, your own breathing, the noise of the fridge, your
clothes rustling, the neighbour's child screaming, etc.

Do make an effort to perform this exercise at least once a week.
You will then become more aware of the different sounds
around you and you will be in a better position to remember
the particular situation easily.

Exercise 3: 'Heavyweight' Hearing Training

(also called 'Message Shadowing')

Spend a few minutes listening to the radio or the television
when somebody is talking, just to put your brain in gear. News
broadcasts are ideal for this exercise. Then listen for a fraction
of a second and repeat in a loud voice what the newscaster has
just said, like instant translators do. While repeating, listen for
the next sentence and repeat it immediately. Do this for as long
as you feel comfortable.

This is a tremendous exercise for stirring up many parts of the
brain: sensing sound, understanding words, speeding up
information processing and improving short-term memory and
decision-making abilities.

145

Smell and Taste

Age-Related Changes

Healthy people can identify over 10,000 different odours. The odour molecules touch the nerve endings (sensors) in the nose, which communicate directly with the memory centres. So it is true that a smell directly stimulates the memories.

However, the senses of smell and taste start to decline after the age of 45. This is probably due, in part, to a low concentration of zinc in the blood. It is also due to the changes in the sensory nerves of the nose and tongue, which are sometimes damaged by smoking. Other causes of decline are diseases such as Alzheimer's, underactive thyroid or folic acid deficiency. Generally, women do better than men in smell and taste tests.

Audit for your nose and tongue:

1 Have you had frequent nose infections, sinusitis or a nose operation?

        Yes 1   No 0

2 Do other people in the same room notice odours that you don't?

        Yes 1   No 0

3 Have you ever been told that you smell (either bad or good) without your realizing it?

        Yes 1   No 0

4 Do you smell petrol or exhaust fumes when you are out in a busy street?

        Yes 0   No 1

5 When you are walking in the park, do you notice the smell of freshly cut grass?

        Yes 0   No 1

6 Are you or have you recently been a smoker?

        Yes 2   No 0

7 Does your smoke alarm go off before you can smell anything burning? (Answer 'Yes' if you don't have a smoke alarm.)

        Yes 1   No 0

8 Have you ever had any head injuries?

> Yes 1   No 0

9 Do you enjoy eating your food?

> Yes 0   No 1

10 If you eat garlic, onions or curry, can you still smell the odour in your mouth after you finish eating?

> Yes 0   No 1

11 Do you frequently make an effort to smell flowers/your food/other scents?

> Yes 0   No 1

Score

0–1: Your senses of smell and taste are healthy.

2 and above: Your senses of smell and taste are starting to give way. Avoid smoking, since it can destroy the olfactory nerves in the nose. Folic acid supplements may help. See your doctor just in case there is something seriously wrong.

Here are some suggestions for making the most of what you have left of your senses of taste and smell:

Exercise 1: Taste Sessions

With eyes closed, taste one of the following:

- lemon juice
- wine
- mineral water
- sugar
- cotton wool
- plastic
- other unusual (clean and safe) objects/materials

The aim of the exercise is not to guess what the object is but merely to experience the taste sensation and to think about it for some seconds.

Exercise 2: Reminiscence

Think back to an event in your childhood and re-create the details in your mind. The purpose of the exercise is to re-create the particular smells associated with that event. For example, can you remember, when you were on your way to school, what the smell of your clothes or of your friends was like? If no smell comes to mind, try another scene and spend three to four minutes on each memory.

To help with this exercise, it is possible to use special aromas for reminiscence, containing smells from yesteryear. If you are over the age of 50 or 60, you may choose the smell of a hospital during the war, for example, a washday smell or the smell of an old teapot and others. If you are younger, try re-creating your own smells. For example, I use the smell of new leather to remind me of my schooldays, when I would carry a brand-new school bag every September (no synthetic plastics in those days).

Exercise 3: Odour Rotation

Once or twice a week use a different soap, perfume or after-shave and other perfumed items to keep your sense of smell active and interested. Use natural air fresheners instead of artificial ones to avoid stimulating your nose with the wrong chemicals. Use aromatherapy oils to energize your sense of smell or your memory, or to give your mood a boost.

Our sense of smell gets used to environmental odours and, after a while, we fail to notice a particular odour even when other people who have just come into the room can smell it straight away. This is called 'tolerance development'. If you keep rotating the different smells, your nose will be subjected to new challenges every time and the smell sensors will have to keep active.

Touch

Some Age-Related Changes

We don't usually pay much attention to our sense of touch, although this is a very important channel for sensing external information.

Like all senses, the sense of touch changes with age. The speed of transmitting information from the skin to the brain slows down and the touch sensors under the skin become slightly less sensitive. This means that we need to allow ourselves more time when feeling something. We also need to use as much skin surface area as possible (ie, use the whole palm of the hand, or even both hands) in order to increase the number of skin sensors feeling an object.

Touching Questions

1 With your eyes closed can you identify by touch the different keys on your key-ring?

        Yes 0   No 1

2 Have you ever been in a job using vibrating equipment?

        Yes 1   No 0

3 Do you frequently use your hands to feel for items?

        Yes 0   No 1

4 Have you done a lot of manual work in the past?

        Yes 1   No 0

5 Is the skin on your hands thin or thick?

        Thin 0   Thick 1

6 Take two similar pieces of paper and fold one of these in four. Can you feel the difference in thickness?

        Yes 0   No 1

7 Can you identify five different denomination coins by touch alone?

        Yes 0   No 1

Score

0-1: Your sense of touch is likely to be healthy. Try to maintain it that way.

2 or more: You may experience difficulties in using your sense of touch. Make a special effort to perform touch exercises (*see* below).

Touch Exercises

To improve the function of the different nerve pathways which are involved in the sense of touch try the following exercise:

> Sit somewhere quietly with a partner. Close your eyes and ask your partner to give you different objects to feel. Take the object in your hand and guess what it is.

> If you want to make this exercise more difficult, try to identify the object by only touching it lightly with your fingertips rather than holding it in your hand. If you can't guess what the object is, feel it with both hands and notice how many more details you can sense. Items to identify could be pens, coins, different keys, books, banknotes, shoes and so on.

> A variety of this exercise involves the same set-up but instead of trying to guess what the item is, you just feel the object and spend a few seconds thinking about its characteristics – hard, round, soft, etc.

> Massage helps revitalize the sense of touch. It also lowers blood pressure, helps angina and stress, and increases well-being. 'Pet therapy' – touching or stoking a pet – has similar effects. It also strengthens the touch sensors on your hands.

Other Touch Exercises

1 If you are right-handed, use your left hand for 5–10 minutes every day to write, use keys, switch lights on/off, comb your hair, reach out for things. Left-handed people should use their right hand. This exercise should strengthen the sensory pathways from the hands to the brain.

2 Take your socks off and sit down with your eyes closed. Use the soles of your feet to feel objects like a book, a mug or a shoe. This will help the brain to open up new channels of information.

3 Try the 'Two point threshold exercise'. The two point threshold is the distance by which two very thin rods touching the skin need to be separated before they can be felt as two points rather than one.

You need a partner to perform this exercise. Use two thin rods (non-sharp knitting needles, pencils, etc).

Lie down and close your eyes. Ask your partner to touch you lightly with the tips of the two rods, separated by a distance of 15cm (6 in). You will feel that there are two rods touching you.

Now ask your partner to reduce the distance between the rods, ie bring them slowly closer to each other. Try to guess whether you still feel two rods or one.

Depending on the part of the body being touched by the rods, the distance at which you will stop feeling the two rods and you will only feel one will vary. The average distance if touched in the calf is about 4cm (2in) and if touched on the fingers 0.5cm ($^1/_2$ in).

This exercise trains the skin sensors and the nerves carrying information to the brain to be more sensitive to touch. It also trains the brain to be more aware of touch stimulation.

4 Pottery-making is an excellent way to improve your sense of touch, co-ordination and arm balance. Playing the piano or typing also help in this respect.

Other Senses

You may think that after dealing with the fifth and final sense, your work is over. Wrong! Contrary to popular belief, our body is equipped with more than five ways of sensing information. We have sensors able to pick up signals relating to temperature, vibration, head and limb position, muscle tension, pain and balance. All of these senses become less efficient with age, but there are some ways to help slow down the decline.

To Develop the Sense of Temperature

Younger people are able to feel temperature changes of 1°C but, with the passage of time, we become unable to feel temperature changes even up to 3 or 4°C. This is one of the reasons why some older people develop hypothermia in cold weather. They are unable to feel the drop of the temperature and they think that the environment is still warm.

It may be helpful to pay attention to the temperature of your environment every so often. Guess the temperature of your house or the temperature out in the garden and then see if you were right by confirming it with a home thermometer.

Exercise

Close your eyes and ask your partner to give you two coins, one cold and one previously warmed in your partner's hand. By feeling the two coins you need to guess which is which.

To Develop the Sense of Vibration

A reduction in the sense of vibration may not be very important to some people. Nevertheless, a good sense of vibration can be useful sometimes, for example during driving to sense steering-wheel abnormalities or a reduction in tyre air pressure.

Exercises

With your eyes closed, touch a washing machine while it is on and feel the vibrations. Do the same with a working fridge. For a few seconds, just feel and think about the vibration.

If you have a tuning fork or something similar, you can use it to feel its vibrations on different parts of your body, over bony areas, preferably with a partner and with your eyes closed.

For Co-ordination

Extend your right hand all the way to your right, with your index finger pointing out. Now touch the tip of your nose with the tip of your right index finger. The purpose of the exercise is to lightly touch your nose on the very tip without correcting yourself and without slowing your finger down just before it approaches your nose.

Repeat five times in quick succession.

Repeat the same with your eyes closed and notice how difficult it immediately becomes.

Do the same with your left index finger.

This is scientifically called the finger-nose test(!) and it is used to detect some brain abnormalities such as brain damage in mild stroke.

Diadochokinesis

This helps to improve your sense of joint position and the co-ordination of muscles.

With your left hand rub your stomach while at the same time pat your forehead with your right hand. Try not to confuse the two actions.

Repeat the same using your other side.

Although this exercise is frequently used as a joke, it is in fact a very good way of improving co-ordination.

Another (easier) variety of this is to have your left palm facing the floor and right palm facing the ceiling. Now turn the left palm up and the right palm down. Repeat the same action quickly for five seconds. Stop and immediately change over the sequence.

153

For Dexterity

With your right thumb touch the tips of each of your fingers on your right hand in quick sequence. Repeat many times as fast as you can.

When you feel more confident, do the same with your left thumb (ie, touch the fingertips of your left hand).

After a while, repeat the same exercise using both hands at the same time. Repeat with your eyes closed.

Now do the same but do one movement with the right hand first, one with the left, then the right and so on, alternating the movements in fast succession. Repeat with your eyes closed.

This exercise improves the sense of touch and dexterity.

Position Exercises

Exercise 1

Sit or lie down somewhere quiet. Relax and close your eyes. Wait for a few minutes without making even the slightest move. Then guess, with your partner as an observer if you wish, the exact position of your limbs. For example, in what direction is your right leg pointing, how bent is your left elbow, where is your head turned towards, etc.

This exercise will improve your awareness relating to the body position and, although it may not sound immediately relevant, it can provide valuable clues to help you maintain your sense of position.

Exercise 2

If you have a rotating chair such as a desk chair, sit on it without touching anywhere, with your eyes closed. Ask a partner to turn it slightly and guess which direction you are facing.

This exercise is used to develop the sense of direction and to improve awareness of situations involving direction.

Tips for improving the sense of balance

- Avoid bending down and then getting up quickly.

- Avoid lying or sitting down for long periods.

- Walk on a straight line with a book balanced on your head.

- If you are taking any medication, ask about any side effects which may affect your balance. (There are several medicines which can help restore the sense of balance – ask your doctor.)

- Try balancing a long stick upright on one finger, like circus acrobats do, or symbolically, try balancing a walking stick.

- Practise t'ai chi exercises (*see* pp 100–102).

- Do any form of physical exercise.

Sense Imagery

The technique of 'sense imagery' is used to help consolidate information already stored in the brain.

> Recall a face that you know really well. Then spend a few minutes thinking about its particular characteristics and try to re-create the face in your mind. Instead of using a face you may think of:

1 Well-known scenery, such as your house, your garden or your neighbourhood.

2 Tones of voice, such as the voice of a person well known to you. You should really make an effort to think of the tone. Or you might choose a familiar voice calling you by your name, the shouts of the traders in the market, the noise of an aeroplane …

3 Think of the smell of some common objects such as your perfume or your house, and others such as freshly cut grass, eggs and bacon, and surgical spirit.

4 Can you recall, in turn, the taste of: bread, ketchup, salt, sugar, beer, vinegar? Spend a few seconds with each one until you manage to recreate the sensation.

5 Visualize yourself moving around the house, walking, exercising, dancing, driving.

6 Imagine what it is like to stroke a pet, to feel a hot radiator, running water, soft material, etc.

> All of the above should be done with an effort to really visualize the particular sense and to remember the quality of the item.

> This exercise can be done anywhere – while travelling as a passenger, waiting for a bus, sitting somewhere quiet – to fill in time, but not while driving a car or when walking, or in any other situations which need your full attention.

All of these exercises fortify the sensory pathways to the brain, invigorate the power of imagination and facilitate the registration of new sense-related information deep in the memory banks.

The Benefits of Sense Exercises

If our senses are preserved in good condition we are able to avoid many unwanted, sometimes dangerous situations. We may:

- escape road traffic accidents by keeping our hearing and vision in top form

- prevent nutritional problems by having a reliable sense of taste

- avoid accidents by smelling leaking gas, petrol or smoke

- reduce the risk of heatstroke or hypothermia by being more aware of temperature changes

- avoid the risk of tripping over by keeping our sense of balance as normal as possible

- avoid social isolation by making it easier to communicate with other people

Conclusion

As you make an effort to do physical exercises for your body, so you should also make the effort to do sense and brain exercises for your mind. These mental and sensory exercises should be performed regularly every day or at least every other day. If you don't feel comfortable with a particular exercise, it is not necessary to persist with it, but find others which you do like. Use different exercises every day to keep yourself interested.

As part of your daily exercise plan, allow at least 15 minutes for doing physical exercises and 10–15 minutes for brain and sensory exercises. It can take a few weeks of practice for the exercises to feel comfortable and it may be a while before the refreshing effects become apparent. The effects will be more marked if you really let yourself go and have confidence in the exercises without inhibitions or interruptions. The more frequently you do each exercise, the better the chances of a positive result.

Remember, though, that these mental exercises may not be suitable for everybody. It is always worth checking with your doctor first.

The exercises will be more effective when they are done as part of a general anti-aging routine including suitable nutrition, proper physical exercise and the special supplements which are described later (*see* chapter 10).

Now, with the senses and brain taken care of, let's turn our attention to appearances. You are as old as you feel, but you are also as old as you look.

CHAPTER 7

Keeping Up Appearances

Facing Up to Reality
Is this you?

A man:

- in need of an overhaul
- with a 'groovy' face (ie, too many grooves in it)
- whose hair is leaving his head and growing in his nose and ears
- who is feeling that everybody looks so young these days ...

A woman:

- who is mature or maturing
- obsessed with three things: conceal, moisturize, diet
- who is finding a new wrinkle every day
- who is feeling that everybody looks so young these days ...

If it is, read on. If it isn't, read on anyway, it'll be you soon.

The way we look inspires the way we feel. It also influences immensely how other people think of us. People may say that 'wearing the habit doesn't make you into a vicar', but I think that appearances matter tremendously nowadays.

Father Time cannot, by himself, make you look good unless you help, and help a lot. To see how you are affected by the ravages of time, answer the following questions:

1 Do you have thin skin?

2 Is your skin usually dry?

3 Is your hair falling out fast?

4 Do you think that you have more wrinkles on your face than most other people of your age?

5 Do you sunbathe (on a sun-bed, by the sea, in the garden)?

6 Do you smoke?

7 Does your partner or do other people around you smoke cigarettes?

8 Do you avoid taking antioxidant supplements?

9 Do you drink fewer than eight glasses of fluid (water, tea, juice, etc) a day?

If you answered 'Yes' to more than one question, your appearance is probably affected by aging.

Fortunately, there are many ways in which you can recapture your looks. In this chapter I will explore some of these.

Looking Good

The Aged Skin

Our skin is constantly renewing itself throughout life, but this renewal rate slows down with age. Normally, the skin is supported by collagen and elastin molecules, but these begin to break down and stiffen over the years. The water content of the skin also evaporates. The result is that the skin starts to lose its full, rounded shape and in some places it becomes thin and fragile and bruises easily. The pores increase in size and hair may sprout where it is not supposed to. Blemishes may appear out of nowhere.

An amazing 90 per cent of all the signs of aging on the skin are due to sun damage and not to the aging process itself. The ozone layer which surrounds the Earth like a cocoon filters out most of the harmful ultraviolet (UV) radiation from the sun. Somehow, we have managed to blast enormous holes in this layer, allowing substantial amounts of UV radiation to pass through. These holes are a predicament of the millennium generation. As they get bigger we will experience more radiation damage and in a few years the signs of skin aging will become much more pronounced on many people.

UV radiation causes:

- toughness and yellowing of the skin
- worsening of moles, some of which may change into cancer
- collagen damage, resulting in loose and baggy skin
- age spots and freckles
- certain skin abnormalities which may turn into cancer

  suppression of the immune system

Don't bother about distinguishing between the UVA and UVB varieties of sun rays. Avoid the lot, as far as you can.

Damage due to UV radiation, free radicals and other toxins is made worse by a variety of factors:

a Smoking, which not only damages the skin through the toxic ingredients of tobacco, but also worsens wrinkles by the constant squinting during smoking.

b Too much alcohol or environmental pollution. Avoid exposure if you can and consider using antioxidants in creams or in tablet form.

c The menopause, which affects the skin by making it thinner and by reducing its water content. Women who are on HRT have fewer wrinkles than women of the same age who are not on HRT. Isoflavones could also have a positive effect on skin aging, but not many trials have so far been conducted on this.

Skin Protection

It is possible to avoid or delay some of the signs of aging, but it is best to start early in life and not leave it too late.

Moisturizers are one of the top protectors against age-related skin damage. Many creams contain not only moisturizers but also an array of antioxidants, vitamins and ultraviolet light filters designed to protect the skin against sun damage. Other preparations contain also collagen, aloe vera or other herbal extracts, just to be on the safe side.

Anti-Aging Creams

It is not clear whether creams containing antioxidants and other factors have a worthwhile effect on the skin. The main problem is that it is very difficult for these substances to penetrate the outer layer of the skin. New technologies are aiming to overcome this by using a variety of methods. One method, for example, uses liposomes, which are synthetic fats, to give the preparation extra penetrating power.

In a typical trial, a cream containing antioxidants delivered by liposomes was given to 160 women aged up to 60 for 18 months. Their wrinkles were assessed before and after the treatment and it was found that there was a significant improvement in those who used the cream. Not only did the cream prevent the formation of new wrinkles, but it reduced the size of existing ones. It also slowed down the rate of skin thinning.

Skin Facts

- Our body sheds about 18kg of dead skin cells in an average lifetime.

- Household dust is mainly dead skin cells.

- Using soap excessively can damage the skin.

- Dry skin is made worse by air conditioning or by central heating.

> ## Five ways to reduce skin aging
>
> 1 Avoid frequent washing with soap, which breaks down the protective fats on the skin.
>
> 2 Too much, or even any, sunbathing is definitely out. Don't even think about sun-beds. If you have to go out in the sun, use suitable sun-screens and cover your head and arms.
>
> 3 Avoid using face powder excessively as this dries up the skin and exacerbates the effects of aging.
>
> 4 Invest in a good anti-aging cream (though have faith in it only if it's recommended by other people who have tried it).
>
> 5 Follow the motto of every skin specialist: 'If it's dry, wet it. If it's wet, dry it.'

Creams containing vitamin C have a good effect on facial skin according to a recent trial. This type of cream is effective in reducing sagging and fine lines under the eyes and improving skin tone.

Despite the positive results of these and other trials, not all scientists are convinced that applying antioxidant creams onto the skin actually works, however. Many claim that the skin is unable to absorb some of these antioxidants in sufficient quantities and, even if it does, the antioxidants will not be able to deploy their beneficial effect where this is needed. A small quantity may be absorbed by the skin and some benefits are possible but, if anything, it may be a better bet to take the antioxidants by mouth, to make them work from the inside.

Scientists are also doubtful about creams containing collagen. Many scientists can't agree whether the type of collagen used in these creams can be absorbed by the skin, whether it can find its way to where it is needed and whether it blends in properly with the skin. Many believe that the benefits of these creams are not due to the collagen content but to the moisturizer which is usually added.

When there is a disagreement about a product (and I mean any products, including supplements and drugs, not just creams), I sometimes advise people to try the product for themselves for a while, under supervision. There isn't any other way of testing a product, because even if something has been studied extensively, it may still not work in your particular case. Alternatively, a product may be rejected by the entire scientific community and yet may work wonders for you.

Beware of creams which claim that they have been 'clinically' or 'dermatologically' tested. If you think about it, this means nothing. All creams are tested clinically or dermatologically (meaning 'on somebody's skin'). It doesn't mean that the result is positive. Maybe the product has been tested on one person or on one rabbit only. Saying that the product has been clinically tested creates an impression, a façade, that the product is safe and effective. This may or may not be true.

Also, some manufacturers claim that their own particular brand reduces the appearance of wrinkles by so many per cent. What does this mean? How can one say for sure that wrinkles improve or worsen during a short period and put this into scientifically endorsed percentages?

During my research for writing this book, I contacted a couple of the top cosmetic firms in the UK, asking for scientific information backing their newest anti-aging product. I don't want to spend my time running after solicitors, so I won't mention any names, but those of you in the know will probably realize which I mean. They were very polite and co-operative, but as soon as I told them that I wanted hard (OK, even soft) scientific evidence that their product had been studied and that it did whatever it was advertised as being able to do, they backed down. Not one has been able to send me any scientific papers. Not one was confident that their product would stand up to scrutiny. This makes me very suspicious. If these firms are reluctant to release background information to an open-minded medical practitioner, is it because their product doesn't actually work?

I don't reject all creams out of hand, but I am asking you to read between the lines and not be taken in by pseudo-scientific talk. Use your common sense, try products out, investigate others and try again. Don't pay too much attention to advertisements or claims, but use something which you feel confident with. Smile. A good smile is worth 1,000 creams.

The Treatment of Wrinkles

There are many ways for people who are aging to deal with droopy skin and wrinkles. One example is dermabrasion, where the skin is rubbed away with an abrasive device made of sand or diamonds, or by laser, and then allowed to heal. After healing, a new layer of skin is formed, which looks younger than before. This operation (sometimes needing a general anaesthetic) can be used either together with a facelift or on its own to smoothen out skin irregularities.

Another method, chemical face-peel, works on the same principle. The practitioner uses phenolic acid or strong concentrations of alpha hydroxy acids (AHA), sometimes under local anaesthestic, to bring about a controlled superficial burn which heals after about a week to reveal a younger-looking skin.

AHAs are also included in creams aiming to reduce the effects of skin aging. They come from natural sources and have a stronger effect than moisturizers, but a weaker effect than Retin A. The regular use of creams containing AHAs encourages the exfoliation of dead skin cells.

The natural supporting tissue of the skin consists mainly of collagen fibres, which lose their effectiveness with age, resulting in wrinkles, so one effective skin treatment is injecting purified bovine collagen into the wrinkles to smooth them out. The problem is that this foreign collagen is inactivated by the body, so further treatment is necessary every 3–12 months. New materials are being tested, including Gortex.

Other operations for the aging face include the well-known facelift, technically called 'rhytidectomy', which literally means 'the pulling out of wrinkles'. This involves tightening of skin through incisions near the ears and the hairline. It stamps out any loose and inelastic skin, but doesn't have much effect on the lines of the lips.

Creams containing strong agents such as Retin A are also used to obliterate wrinkles. Retinol, retinyl, Retin A and similar sounding names are all chemicals related to vitamin A. Retinol is a milder variant than Retin A and is used frequently in many types of creams. Retin A was developed in order to treat bad acne but was found to have a super effect on reducing wrinkles and other signs of sun-damaged skin. It is best used under medical supervision, because it may cause skin allergies, mouth ulcers or lip sores. Stop using Retin A and you will be back to square one – wrinkles may reappear.

A new retinoid, tazarotene, was found to reduce wrinkles, skin roughness and age spots in a small but properly performed scientific trial. It looks promising.

All of these treatments have both advantages and disadvantages. In my experience, none of them has proved very popular with the public at large. Celebrities and other people who depend on their appearance do use these methods regularly, however.

Many other treatments have been tried in an effort to 'anti-age' the skin. These include:

a Botulin toxin (botox). This paralyses and relaxes the muscles of the face and reduces squinting. The injection needs to be repeated every few months.

b Electrical treatment with CACI (computer aided cosmetology instrument). This is a non-surgical facelift which tones the muscles.

c Oxygen therapy. This therapy, in theory to improve the oxygen supply to the skin of the face, is becoming very popular. But does it make matters worse in the long-term by increasing free radical damage?

d Thymus extracts to stimulate cell regeneration.

e Laser treatment to literally zap blemishes away.

f Muscle exercises of the face and mouth.

During a television programme on aging, I met a participant who looked as if she was in her thirties. She was in fact 60 years old and she was an expert on face exercises. I was most impressed, although scientifically there should be no reason why the skin is affected by exercise. It is more likely that the desired effects are caused by:

• the strengthening of the muscles underneath the skin

• the reduction of squinting

• correction of bad facial posture

• an improvement in general confidence

• the likelihood that a person who uses face exercises also uses other ways of skin regeneration, so some of the effects may be due to these

The Treatment of Age Spots

Senile purpura, aka 'age spots', are brown marks on the skin. We all get them as we grow older. The spots are due to sun damage and arise on skin which has been exposed to the sun for many years, such as on the hands, throat or upper chest. The French call these spots 'the medals of cemetery'.

Sun-screens, antioxidant creams and camouflage products have all been used to deal with the spots. Selenium supplements may offer extra antioxidant protection, as may aloe vera gel or natural progesterone creams.

If the skin on your hands betrays your age, you may prefer to either hide it by wearing gloves or paint your nails with vibrant colours to direct attention away from the hands to the nails.

General Treatments

- Here are some ideas for general treatments for the skin:

- Use steaming water and a few drops of lavender, thyme or peppermint as facial steam therapy to stimulate the skin, or use fennel to heal minor skin infections.

- Mix a few drops of your favourite essential oil to two or three teaspoonfuls of base oil. Use to moisturize the skin.

- To help tone the skin, use nettle, marigold or rosehip compresses. Apply these on the face and throat or neck. Alternatively, use dandelion root infusions.

- For a face mask, mix finely ground oatmeal with rosewater to make a paste and add a few drops of chamomile oil or lavender oil. Apply on your face and around the eyes, and leave to dry for 30 minutes. If you want to treat small veins on the skin, use geranium, rosemary or cypress oils in your paste.

- Using an oil such as saffron, massage your face, using your index and middle fingers to make small circular movements on the skin. A massage can tone the skin, improve circulation and help get rid of toxic material. Take care not to massage or brush your skin too hard.

Rejuvenex Creams

This range of creams includes certain basic ingredients: RNA and DNA extracts, vitamins A, C and E, natural moisturizers, aloe vera, collagen, ginseng and UV blockers. A variation on the basic cream includes, in addition to all of the above, a melatonin/DHEA complex with liposome delivery for maximum anti-aging effect. The manufacturers claim that the cream is made in such a way to maximize skin absorption of melatonin and DHEA. They believe that melatonin used on the skin protects it from harmful UV radiation and from free radicals in general. DHEA is thought to protect the skin by binding to toxins before these are able to damage the skin DNA. This cream is available from the Life Extension Foundation (*see* 'Resources').

Hair

Normal hair grows continually for about three years and then has a rest period of about three months. Bad diet, unhealthy lifestyle and the effects of normal aging can throw this cycle out of control. With age, hair has a tendency to become thinner and shorter.

On average, there are 200,000 hair follicles on the human scalp. Some balding men may not believe this, but it's true. A proportion of these follicles may be active while others may be in the rest cycle.

Normally we lose up to 150 hairs a day, but this doesn't make any overall difference because new hair grows to replace them. If the loss is faster than the growth, then hair loss will become obvious. Certain people may notice a change in the rate of hair loss through the seasons and this is natural, although the loss may be very light.

There is a hair-raising number of causes of hair loss, but the commonest are just two: chronic telogen effluvium and genetic/hormonal reasons.

Chronic Telogen Effluvium

This usually manifests as an accelerated loss of hair from all over the scalp rather than from any specific area. Certain nutritional deficiencies may make this type of hair loss heavier. I'm going to mention only two, iron deficiency and lysine deficiency.

Sometimes iron deficiency in the body may not be severe enough to cause anaemia but may cause hair loss. This deficiency may be picked up by a blood test which measures ferritin, an indicator of the iron stores in the body. Taking iron supplements, though, is not advised unless recommended by a doctor. This is because iron stimulates the excess production of free radicals, causing more damage to the body. It is best to eat foods which are high in iron or take iron supplements for short periods only.

Another nutritional factor which has been implicated in hair loss is the amino acid lysine. People who avoid meat in their diet may be prone to this deficiency. In experiments, women who took extra lysine supplements experienced an increase in hair growth.

Genetic Hair Loss

This is impressively called 'androgen-dependent alopecia' and is related to a genetic mechanism which, after a certain age, causes an imbalance of the male hormones (androgens). This results in hair loss and thinning of the hair. This imbalance doesn't only affect men. Up to one in three women who experience hair loss are thought to be affected by this condition. Specialist treatment with hormones may improve hair growth in some patients.

Other Causes of Hair Loss

A few other causes of hair loss are:

  a Hypothyroidism (low thyroid hormone, affecting up to
  2 per cent of women).

  b *Alopecia areata*, which is hair loss in patches. The causes
  are not known and there is no effective cure, but hair may
  regrow on its own.

  c The menopause may affect hair growth, perhaps due to an
  age-related imbalance of the female hormones.

  d Infections and other illnesses may cause hair loss which
  does not become evident until several weeks after the
  illness. In this instance, hair will regrow normally.

Treatments

Treatments using drugs which affect hair growth have made their mark over the years. Minoxidil, a drug used to treat severe high blood pressure, has made a difference to many balding men. It is taken in

General Advice for Healthy Hair

- First comb and then brush your hair. Comb your hair before going to bed. Start combing from the end of the hair and work your way deeper towards the scalp.

- Use mild shampoos which are suitable for your own particular hair condition and don't wash your hair too often.

- Grey hair needs extra conditioning as it is more porous. Use sage oil to help darken the colour. Whether you decide to use an obvious or subtle colour to cover your greying hair will depend on your personality, extravagance and flair.

tablet form and also used in hair lotions. Another drug, finasteride, has also been used. Finasteride works wonders in reducing swelling of the prostate but was also found to be effective in reducing baldness, up to a point. Both drugs need a doctor's prescription. Don't expect miracle results.

169

A treatment you can try out yourself is to massage the scalp with lavender and rosemary. Massage using your thumb and first two fingers, starting from the front towards the back. Make sure that the hair is well oiled.

An old-fashioned remedy to stimulate the circulation, and thereby hair growth, is to massage the dry scalp with your fingers twice a day. Others say that massaging and rubbing may damage and break the hair.

Some people worry too much about hair loss which, in the end, doesn't cause any significant baldness. I remember some years ago, I saw a dismayed middle-aged woman who was suffering from hair loss. To convince me that her case was genuine, she had brought with her a large plastic bag in which she had meticulously collected all of her hair which had fallen out over the previous months. There was enough to fill a pillow, yet the hair on her head looked reasonably healthy. She had psychological problems which manifested as excessive and unnecessary worry about normal hair loss.

If you are a balding man, as I am, you may find it liberating to come out in the open and cut your remaining hair very short or shave it completely. Personally, I don't see any point in growing hair from the sides to cover the bald patch on the top, making it obvious to everybody that you have something to hide. I may be wrong.

Nails

Our nails are also affected by age. The ridges along the nails become more pronounced and the nails themselves may become brittle or sometimes harder. To prevent both, use almond oil to moisturize the nail bed.

High-protein food such as egg yolk, nuts and seeds, sunflower or sesame seed oil or protein in powder form will benefit the nails. Horsetail herb extracts, gelatine and brewer's yeast are also used to improve their condition. In general, bad nutrition will adversely affect the nails.

Diseases affecting the nails include:

- psoriasis
- fungal infections
- certain chronic heart and lung problems

Some people claim that they have discovered a miracle cure for crumbling and aged fingernails. Prepare some warm water in a bowl and add two or three cloves of finely chopped garlic. Soak your fingernails for 10–15 minutes every few days. This is great if you can stand the smell.

Part III

CHAPTER 8

Complementary Alternatives

One day our old friend Nustreddin Hodja borrowed his neighbour's donkey to do some work in the fields. After a while, the neighbour came to ask for his donkey back. The Hodja apologized: 'I am sorry, my friend, but your donkey died and I buried it in the fields.' The neighbour, saddened, was ready to leave when the donkey, which was alive and well in the Hodja's garden, brayed loudly. 'Aha,' bellowed the neighbour, 'it is alive, I can hear it!' 'You insult me, my friend,' said the Hodja. 'What kind of man are you to doubt me, an intelligent human being, and choose to believe a dumb animal instead?'

I think that many doctors want us to do the same, in other words believe them and not pay attention to what is obvious. They may say, rightly, that there isn't enough scientific proof to back the claims of complementary medicine. But the truth is that there are millions of people who have tried complementary treatments and found these to be effective. So should we believe the hearsay evidence or what science tells us to believe?

There are dozens of different complementary treatments aimed at treating one health problem or another. In the following discussion I am going to highlight only those therapies which have a particular role to play in aging and in age-related diseases. This discussion is only an introduction, just enough to stimulate your interest and to show you that there is always a way out of suffering. If you are interested in one therapy in particular and wish to find out more details, I suggest you consult relevant books describing the therapy.

What is the difference between alternative and complementary medicine? In practice, the two terms are used similarly. In theory, alternative practitioners such as osteopaths and chiropractors are suitably qualified and are allowed to take clinical care of a patient. Complementary practitioners, on the other hand, are not allowed to take clinical care of the patient themselves but are supposed to offer treatments which complement traditional medicine.

My own first experience in complementary medicine was back in 1984. I enrolled for a weekend course for doctors wishing to learn the basics of acupuncture. There were only three students: two young family doctors and myself. The course, one of the first for doctors in the UK at the time I believe, was run by an Asian doctor from his house, with his children carting in refreshments during breaks.

I could hardly make out what was being said because of the teacher's accent, but he had the foresight to provide a surprising amount of written material in impeccable English for support. I learned of strange meridians which were completely contrary to conventional anatomy, something about two small one-eyed fish encroaching and complementing each other (it was the schematic representation of yin and yang) and a little of exotic health philosophies. For all I know, the course may still be running today.

This was my first contact with non-conventional medicine and it was an eye-opener indeed. Since then I have been trying to reconcile complementary and traditional medicine, to find a common ground, explanations and scientific rationale behind each complementary treatment. This has not been at all easy, but it has certainly been worthwhile.

During the past few years, there has been a more favourable attitude towards complementary medicine among medical professionals. Over 40 per cent of general Western doctors now use complementary treatment and more than 70 per cent make referrals to complementary practitioners.

In Britain, the Foundation for Integrated Medicine was set up a few years ago, following an initiative by the Prince of Wales. Integrated medicine aims to bring together conventional and complementary therapies and practitioners in an attempt to widen the treatment choices for patients. The Foundation for Integrated Medicine takes a serious view of the different practices available and their potential. Eminent professionals from both sides of the healthcare establishment are being brought together to explore and study common pathways to good health.

There is, however, a general reluctance among conventional practitioners to accept some complementary treatments. This is due to several factors. Certain complementary treatments, for example, may indeed not have any effect on health or may be practised by unqualified or unscrupulous practitioners. Also, many, if not all, treatments use ideas foreign to the prevailing medical establishment, giving rise to disbelief among conventional scientists.

It may be that the basic ideas are still the same, but different words are used to describe the same process. I have discussed this with both conventional and complementary practitioners and we have come up with a short list which brings together orthodox and alternative terminology. Here it is:

Complementary Terms and their Conventional Equivalent

a A 'tonic' is something that stimulates protein synthesis, anabolic.

b 'Cleanse the system' means to stimulate immunity, to eliminate dead or foreign material.

c 'The flow of energy' is the circulation of blood and lymphatic fluid, as well as the reactions of chemical energy within the cell.

d 'Eliminate toxins' is the stimulation of the liver and kidney to metabolize and secrete chemical substances.

e 'Balance of energy' is physiological homoeostasis.

f 'Cosmic energy' is fresh air, sunshine and invisible particles like electrons and neutrinos.

g 'Yin and yang' are positive and negative, which need to be balanced to avoid over- or under-stimulation of homoeostasis. Examples are excessive or insufficient production of hormones, hyper- and hypoglycaemia in diabetes, etc.

One of the main benefits of complementary medicine is that it offers a wider choice of treatments, helping patients to take matters into their own hands. Also, these treatments have generally fewer side effects than conventional treatments.

On the other hand, you shouldn't use complementary treatments indiscriminately without proper advice. If you have an illness, involve both your doctor and your qualified complementary practitioner in the treatment and let each know what you are up to.

If you feel confident, you could try the treatments yourself at home, if suitable, but it is best not to try to diagnose any problems yourself because you may use the wrong treatment and cause more damage. If your doctor has given you a prescription for a particular drug, don't just stop taking this when you begin a new complementary treatment.

The following treatments are some of the most common complementary therapies available. These are based on a wide view of health which sees the individual as a whole and are not focused on particular diseases only.

Acupuncture

In common with many other complementary treatments, acupuncture is a very old system of healing. It involves stimulation of certain points along well defined lines of the body, called meridians. The stimulation can be done with needles, sometimes boosted by the burning of a material called moxa.

Variations of traditional acupuncture are:

- electro-acupuncture using electrical needle stimulators
- laser acupuncture
- ear acupuncture

Acupuncture is perhaps the most widely studied of all complementary treatments. In the Western variety, the practitioner uses one needle at a time for some seconds. In the traditional Chinese variety many needles are used at the same time. These need to be twisted regularly by the practitioner. The actual procedure doesn't usually hurt, and the needles are fine and disposable so the risk of infection is minimized.

Treatment is usually decided after an initial detailed consultation with the practitioner. You may be examined in a different way from the way in which your conventional doctor examines you. For example, the practitioner will feel for six different pulses on your wrist, not just one.

The basic principle of acupuncture is that energy flows along body meridians, and the positive and negative energies need to be balanced. These energies are yin and yang. The needles are used to increase the flow of invisible energy in order to balance the two.

The meridians don't correspond to conventional anatomy, but scientists think that acupuncture may work by stimulating the body's release of natural chemicals such as endorphins. These increase the feeling of well-being, are tough on pain and may have other lesser-known advantages.

Acupuncture may be useful in the treatment of:

- arthritis
- muscle pain
- anxiety
- depression
- high blood pressure
- certain skin conditions

177

In addition, small-scale trials have shown that acupuncture may improve some of the symptoms of the menopause, such as hot flushes, and it has also been used to help smokers quit the weed.

Acupuncture practitioners believe that most medical conditions may respond to acupuncture. This is because they believe that most conditions are caused by energy imbalance.

Acupuncture treatment should show results within six sessions and, as is usual with some complementary treatments, the symptoms may initially get slightly worse before they improve.

Many conventional doctors practise acupuncture at their premises. Ask at your local medical centre for addresses of practitioners.

Alexander Technique

Based on the premise that an illness will improve by good posture, this technique endeavours to reduce the muscular tension which progressively builds up in the body. It aims to increase awareness of:

- posture
- position of the limbs
- position of individual muscles (proprioception)

This technique was devised by an Australian actor, Frederick Alexander, about 100 years ago and has been gaining supporters ever since.

In a study of disability due to Parkinson's disease, seven patients were treated with the technique. After treatment, they reported feeling less depressed and had less difficulty with daily movements.

The procedure itself involves making certain movements while sitting or lying on a couch, with the teacher advising on how to avoid muscular tension and how to overcome your natural resistance to movement. The teacher also shows you how to use correct posture and how to avoid incorrect movements. You will be advised on how to maintain a correct posture throughout the day. Sessions usually last for about 45 minutes to one hour.

Self-Help Alexander Technique Exercises

a Stand in front of a mirror and look at your posture. You need to keep your body in a straight line, as if you had a straight iron bar running from your head to your feet. Try to maintain that posture during your daily activities. Stand naturally and without exaggerating your posture.

b Lie on your back on the floor, somewhere quiet, with your hands resting on your stomach. Gently bend your knees, keeping them together and as you do that, try to think of the tension in the different parts of your body. Take time to think that the tension is disappearing and that you feel more relaxed.

Alexander Technique can be used for sciatica, neck pain, stress or anxiety, depression, insomnia, chronic illnesses such as osteoarthritis and rheumatoid arthritis. A correct posture can also help prevent age-related lung problems by maximizing the capacity of the lungs and by fine-tuning the breathing movements.

Aromatherapy

This is a holistic type of therapy which makes use of the healing powers of the scent of plants. Oils derived from herbs were used in many great ancient cultures such as China, India and Egypt, and interest in the subject was revived in the 1930s.

Aromatherapy is thought to work by:

a rousing the sense of smell, which in turn activates particular areas of the brain.

b absorption through the skin. The scented molecules from the oils then home in to the brain via the bloodstream. They act on parts of the nervous system to stimulate other chemicals and hormones. Researchers are still trying to clarify these effects but the general scientific idea is sound.

179

When deciding on an oil for yourself, make sure to choose oils that are pure, ie not mixed with alcohol. The oils are extracted from different parts of the plant and many can evaporate. Some need to be kept in dark bottles to avoid sun damage. There are more than 300 different oils in use.

A practitioner will examine you, discuss your general lifestyle and then discuss with you a choice of oils to use during treatment. The actual treatment may involve massage, inhalation or compresses.

You need to be careful with aromatherapy if you have high blood pressure or asthma, because some treatments may make it worse. Keep the oil away from your eyes and don't apply it neat on your skin unless specifically directed to do so. Geranium and orange oils in particular may irritate the skin. On the other hand, tea tree oil can be applied directly on to the skin to treat small areas of infection, such as spots.

Aromatherapy Recipes

For General Health

> 5 drops of tea tree
>
> 1 drop of cedarwood
>
> 3–4 drops of eucalyptus
>
> 1–2 drops of lemon
>
> diluted in 4tsp of carrier oil

Use this in any of the ways below.

My Wife's Aromatherapy Travelling Aid

This is excellent for motion sickness, upsetting aeroplane noises and unpleasant smells. It also aids relaxation and gives a comforting sense of 'home' when visiting strange countries.

Collect fresh lavender flowers after the dew has dried in the morning. Hang them in bunches to dry in the airing cupboard for two weeks. Gently crumble the flowers and a few leaves from the stalks into small cotton bags – 8cm (3in) by 8cm (3in) – and carry these in your travelling bag. When the smell starts to fade, add a few drops of lavender oil or, better still, replace the old lavender material with new.

How to use aromatherapy oils yourself

- during a relaxing or sensuous massage
- in a hot bath or in a refreshing foot bath
- in burners or in candle form
- on soothing compresses using lint
- on your pillow or handkerchief
- in steaming water for inhalations (use three or four drops)

Uses of Aromatherapy

Aromatherapy is an ideal companion to smell exercises. The smell centres and the memory centres of the brain are in close proximity to each other, which explains why a suitable smell can evoke past memories.

Consider trying aromatherapy if you suffer from stress, headaches, asthma, infections or constipation. Oils for specific ailments are:

- geranium, sage, tarragon and fennel for menopausal symptoms
- lavender for low moods, infections and insomnia
- rose for sleep problems and depression
- sandalwood to relieve fluid retention, insomnia or cystitis
- eucalyptus or mint for winter depression and as decongestants
- wood marjoram for muscular pains and joint stiffness
- chamomile for anxiety

More general remedies:

- Cypress and lemon can be used for invigoration, especially for men.
- Rosemary is a diuretic, antiseptic and a mood booster.
- Frankincense can aid sleep and is a decongestant.

Ayurveda

Ayurvedic medicine is an ancient Indian philosophy of health. It aims to re-establish the balance between internal and external energy or *prana*. An imbalance of these two energies is considered to cause disease. A basic principle of Ayurvedic medicine is that the mind influences the body.

The body's own natural energies, which also need to be balanced, are:

a *vata* (air) which controls the muscular system, the nervous system and the bones

b *pitta* (bile), which controls digestion of food, the body's metabolism and the balance of fluids

c *kapha* (phlegm) which controls the growth and development of the cells and tissues

Ayurvedic treatments involve diet, herbs, yoga, massage by specialist practitioners and breathing exercises. Over 15,000 herbs and minerals are used. The emphasis is mainly on prevention.

The first consultation usually takes an hour. The practitioner will examine your pulses, tongue, skin and eyes. You should expect to be questioned about all your private habits, personality and disease history. The practitioner may decide that you need in-patient care (called Panchakarma therapy). This is an energetic form of detoxifying the body from poisons and it takes seven days to work. Laxatives, enemas, steam baths and medicated oils are used during this therapy.

Ayurvedic treatments are particularly effective in the treatment of rheumatism and joint pains, immune system problems, muscle weakness, headaches, infections, memory loss, skin problems, sexual problems (such as impotence, loss of libido), anaemia, cystitis, hair loss or thin hair – quite a long list. Usually Ayurvedic treatments can be used in association with other treatments, both conventional and complementary.

Examples of herbs used in Ayurvedic medicine are:

- *Asparagus racemosus* for boosting immunity and sex drive

- *Asphaltum* for prostate enlargement

- *Azadirachta indica* for diabetes

- *Commiphora mukul* for arthritis

- *Whithania somnifera* for anxiety, stress or sleep problems

The effectiveness of these treatments is based on centuries of practice, but there are not enough modern scientific trials comparing them to conventional treatments.

Which of the following describes you best? (Most people are a combination of two of these.)

- *vata* are people with dry skin, a low voice and quick movements, who are talkative, have a high sex drive and coarse curly hair.

- *pitta* are those who don't like the sun or the heat, have early greying of the hair or baldness, a smelly mouth, prefer sweet and light foods, have a good appetite and warm hands or feet.

- *kapha* are those who don't like the cold, have smooth skin, are energetic, have a high sex drive and a graceful gait, are heavy or obese, have a deep voice and an attractive appearance.

Bach Flower Remedies

This system, devised by Dr Edward Bach in the 1930s, concentrates on the effect of the emotions on healing.

Bach divided the basic personality into seven types, each disposed to a different emotional problem:

- fear

- indecision

- despair

- over-caring for others

- loneliness

- lack of interest

- over-sensitivity

This good doctor then collected several flowers and plants to counter-act the negative effects of these states of mind.

A Bach mixture is prepared in a small quantity of brandy and it is suitable for self-use. The remedies can be applied on the tongue or mixed with mineral spring water.

Flower remedies are believed to work on the mental processes as a whole and aim to balance any negative thoughts or fears.

Examples of treatment are:

- olive for exhaustion and tiredness

- aspen for anxiety

- Rescue Remedy (a mixture of five flowers) for shock

Other conditions amenable to treatment by flower remedies are menopausal problems, arthritis and nausea.

The consultation with the practitioner usually takes about an hour. You will be asked about your general health and about your particular problems. You will be given suitable remedies to take two or three times a day. If, after a couple of months, you feel that your condition has not improved, the practitioner may try a different combination of remedies.

There are no contraindications to using the remedies and they can be used in conjunction with any other complementary therapy. Some practitioners are calling for proper scientific trials to support the use of these remedies.

Biofeedback

The great psychotherapist Carl Jung was one of the first people to use this technique in the early 1900s. During treatment, the patient focuses on a specific area to be treated and tries through a biofeedback device to affect the body's reaction to the problem.

The biofeedback device to which the patient is connected records brainwaves, skin reactions to temperature and muscle activity. The signal can be seen on a screen or it can be a bleeping noise. The patient then uses breathing, feelings, meditation or thoughts to try and alter the signal. The result is shown immediately on the screen, helping the patient to register the success and re-enforcing their thoughts.

For example, in patients suffering from urinary incontinence, it is possible to monitor the muscles and nerves controlling the bladder, flash the result on a computer screen and use the brain in order to affect these responses.

The patient learns to affect the illness by altering the responses to the autonomic nervous system, the part of our nervous system which is normally not under voluntary control. The autonomic nervous system affects blood pressure, pulse, sweating, skin temperature, stomach and bowel movements. That's why you just can't control those embarrassing stomach rumbles during quiet meetings – unless you have biofeedback treatment of course.

Biofeedback is used for:

- pain, such as cancer pain, neuralgia or neck pain
- high blood pressure
- vertigo or tinnitus
- Bell's palsy
- problems with the menopause or diabetes

This treatment has been well researched in over 2,000 scientific projects. The biofeedback device can be used at home in some cases, following initial training at a specialist centre.

Breathing

As already mentioned, Taoist monks believe that breathing less frequently or holding the breath for as long as possible makes them live longer. Practitioners of the Buteyko method of breathing also believe that breathing less often prolongs life span. According to this theory, our breathing is not usually balanced, because we tend to breathe too deeply or irregularly, and this causes a disturbance in the normal gas concentrations in our body. Practitioners of the Buteyko method believe that this imbalance may cause high blood pressure, immune system failure and extensive damage from free radicals. Their suggestions are:

1 Breathe only through your nose (this is more natural and it makes scientific sense because the nasal passages filter the air clean from impurities, warm it to body temperature and stimulate the lung tissues to take up the oxygen better).

2 Try to breathe less deeply and less frequently. In other words, regulate your breathing and slow it down to below

the natural level, which is around 12 times a minute. This reminds me of the breathing frequencies recommended by practitioners of chi kung.

Supporters of this breathing method claim that their patients can feel 20 years younger, but there are no scientific trials to support this.

During a consultation with a Buteyko practitioner, you will be taught how to control and regulate your breathing pattern. This may be done alone with the practitioner or in a group with other patients. Some practitioners offer a money-back guarantee if there has not been any improvement.

Other Breathing Techniques

Apart from this particular breathing method, there are other ways to improve age-related breathing problems. Our lungs get less elastic with age and scientists who have studied these age-related changes consider the loss of lung elasticity as the first sign of aging. This starts at around

---

Three lung exercises to fortify the elastic tissue of your lungs

1 Buy a large box of balloons. Every day blow up a balloon a few times. This makes you breathe against resistance and expands the lung muscles and tissues.

2 Place a few feathers, some fluff or a few hairs on a table about a metre away from you and blow these off if you can. Increase the distance gradually and you will notice that, with time, you will be able to blow double the original distance.

3 Take deep breaths in and out through pursed lips a few times, as deep as you can. This also strengthens the lung muscles.

The above exercises may cause dizziness, so only perform these when you are sitting down. Stop immediately if you feel dizzy or short of breath.

30 years of age. The chest wall becomes more restricted and the diaphragm muscle, which separates the abdominal cavity from the lungs, has to work harder to push air out of the lungs. For healthy people these changes don't cause many problems, but smoking and a history of asthma or chest infections can make matters worse. Increasing air pollution is also to blame.

You can slow this damage right down: contemplate the use of suitable antioxidants, scorn smoking and pollution, and practise regular breathing, yoga or chi kung exercises.

Chiropractic

Chiropractors use their skills to treat conditions like muscle or joint problems, headache, back pain, tinnitus, vertigo and asthma. The chiropractic method was developed in the 19th century and now it has over 60,000 practitioners world-wide.

The practitioners see the spine as a protector of the nervous system and aim to treat misalignment of the spine by maintaining good posture. They focus on manipulation of the joints to keep internal organs in good shape. There is evidence that chiropractic methods work wonders in certain conditions.

Chiropractic treatments are useful in relaxing tight muscles around joints and improving suppleness of movement. They are particularly effective in treating the back or neck problems which are so common after middle age.

During a consultation, the practitioner will ask you about general health matters and will examine your joints to discover any locked or misaligned joints. People suffering from osteoporosis or circulation problems should be treated with extra care. X-rays of particular joints may be taken. The course of treatment lasts from three to six weeks and then a maintenance session every few months may be appropriate.

Certain forms of arthritis may not be suitable for treatment, but otherwise chiropractic may be used in association with any other complementary and conventional treatments.

Flotation

The flotation method of healing was originally devised in the 1950s when scientists wanted to study the reactions of the brain after taking away all external stimulation and performed experiments in eerie 'sensory deprivation chambers'.

Flotation is now used world-wide to banish high blood pressure, tiredness and anxiety. It is also effective in reducing the risk of heart disease. It invigorates the immune system and reduces certain hormones which are connected with stress.

The treatment involves the patient floating in a soundproof tank filled with warm water, wearing ear plugs and eye covers. External stimulation is reduced to the minimum, but it is possible to open the door of the chamber at any moment if you so wish. Aficionados say that it is best to float naked.

During the session, the brain is stimulated to release the natural pain control chemicals endorphins. These are similar to morphine or heroin and help reduce aches and pains and induce a state of happiness and relaxation.

It is best to have supervision during a flotation session if you suffer from claustrophobia, anxiety or depression. Otherwise, no supervision is necessary.

Healing

There is considerable controversy about this form of treatment. Many unscrupulous practitioners have used healing for personal gain only, disregarding the patient's condition. Suitably qualified and experienced practitioners, however, say that if healing is properly performed, it can be useful in many conditions involving pain, depression and anxiety.

The practitioner will ask questions about your medical history and then will scan you using their hands to detect abnormal energy levels surrounding your body. Following this, the treatment may proceed in two different ways: either with the laying on of hands or by distance healing. In this type of treatment, the practitioner's hands are placed about 4–5cm (10–12in) away from the patient's skin. The aim is to try to balance abnormal energy levels and thereby help the organs of the body to function properly.

There have been a few scientific trials evaluating the effects of healing, but these are not enough. It is almost impossible to tell what is an actual improvement due to healing and what is a placebo response (an improvement which is not due to healing, but could have happened anyway).

Healing is not recommended for patients who have heartbeat irregularities or those who have a pacemaker implant.

Herbalism

Meaning 'healing by the use of herbs', herbalism is a popular holistic treatment. Herbal therapies have been used by all cultures throughout the ages. Nowadays, herbal therapies are sometimes used in association with other treatments such as acupuncture or massage. Herbs are used both in prevention and in cure.

One problem with some herbs is that they may contain very strong chemicals similar to those used in conventional medicine. Accordingly, if you are using any conventional drugs, don't use any herbal medicines without medical supervision, because the two may interact and cause side effects.

It is relatively easy to find therapeutic herbs. Some grow in ordinary gardens. The herbs can be used as infusions, in ointments, mixed with food or taken in tablet form. Some examples are:

- arnica for skin healing and circulation (if taken internally it can speed up recovery after surgery)
- comfrey to help the repair process after an operation or a fracture
- echinacea, a very well-known plant remedy, for all types of infections but mostly for colds, flu, thrush or sinusitis
- garlic for reducing cholesterol, blood pressure and heart disease
- lavender for muscle aches and pains
- linden and rosemary for circulation problems

For menopausal problems, there are two different sets of treatments:

1 To boost oestrogen use sage, motherwort or blackcurrant leaves.

2 To boost progesterone use wild yam or chaste berry.

189

Silimarin, the extract of milk thistle (*Silybum maranum*), is used to cleanse the organism from toxins. It protects the liver and stimulates protein synthesis as well as being a potent antioxidant. It is also used to protect the liver against alcohol damage.

Traditional Chinese Herbalism

This type of treatment is becoming popular and better studied following the return of Hong Kong to China. The treatments were outlawed in Hong Kong during the British rule.

Many herbs are used in Traditional Chinese Medicine to treat age-related problems. Here is a list of some of the more important:

- *Angelica sinensis* (dong quai) for menopause and anaemia
- astragalus for immunity and healing
- dan shen (*Radix salvia*, similar to sage) for circulation problems
- ginger for reducing cholesterol and maintaining a healthy heart
- ginseng for general health and stamina
- green tea for those all-important polyphenol antioxidants
- jin yin hua (*Lonicera japonica*) for infections
- sheng di huang to help anxiety, stress and indigestion
- woody mushrooms for general anti-aging

Some Chinese medicines, for example those used for eczema, can have serious side effects such as liver failure. Also, due to lack of proper controls, some preparations may contain fewer active ingredients than expected. If you are trying to treat a medical condition, always ask an experienced practitioner first for proper advice. Only if your condition is very mild can you use common sense and treat it yourself, and even then a little chat with a pharmacist will not be in vain.

Homoeopathy

Many practitioners of homoeopathy are medically qualified and homoeopathy, like all complementary treatments, can be used in association with conventional medicine. It helps the body heal itself. The theory is that it is the person as a whole who needs the treatment and not just the disease.

Homoeopathy was devised in 1796 by a German doctor, Samuel Hahnemann. The treatment involves giving a small dose of special remedies based on the idea that 'like cures like'. Practitioners say that the remedies may have an effect on the energy flow of the body rather than on the particular disease. This is a concept not appreciated by conventional medicine. The remedies come in tablet, powder or liquid form.

The first consultation may last up to two hours. The questioning may include details about your general health, dietary habits, moods and feelings, relationships and other personal details. Tell the practitioner about any other medication you may be taking.

After starting treatment, the symptoms may get slightly worse. Practitioners believe that this is a sign that the treatment is working. It may take some time for the effects to be noticeable, as the treatment works from the inside. Sometimes it may cause rashes, boils or diarrhoea. The homoeopathic explanation for this is that the body is starting to heal itself and all the impurities are pouring out.

The form of treatment depends on whether you are addressing a chronic problem or an acute one. Chronic problems should be treated by specialists, whereas some acute problems can be treated at home.

Suitable homoeopathic treatments exist for Bell's palsy, vertigo, insomnia, mouth and leg ulcers, cystitis, diabetes and bad breath.

Examples of some homoeopathic remedies are:

- sepia, belladonna, graphites or pulsatilla for menopausal problems – these help reduce hot flushes and vaginal dryness but must be prescribed by a qualified practitioner

- cantharis, apis mel, nux vomica and belladonna for cystitis

- rhus tox, bryonia, apis mel, pulsatilla and arnica for arthritis and muscle pains

Regarding the general effectiveness of homoeopathy, a review of 105 scientific trials showed that 81 were positive and 24 were equivocal. These results have been questioned by some scientists, but give you a general idea about the effectiveness of homoeopathy.

Hydrotherapy

In plain English, hydrotherapy means 'treatment with water'. This popular therapy harnesses the healing power of water in several ways. It was enjoyed by the ancient Greeks and Romans in the form of hot and cold baths. It is from these treatments that the idea of the spring of eternal life comes from. This idea has expanded over the centuries to include thermal and mineral spas, as well as the mud baths popular in some European countries.

It is surprising how water can be used in so many different ways. Apart from swimming, hydrotherapy treatments may include alternating hot and cold baths or showers, high pressure hosing with cold water, and hot or cold body wraps. All of these are used mainly to revitalize the circulation.

Research has shown that alternating hot and cold compresses has a powerful effect on the immune system, whereas cold baths help lower the blood pressure. Several mineral spas are famous for treating skin conditions, arthritis, heart problems and many others.

Aquarobics, exercises in swimming pools, are best for arthritis, muscle pains and increasing suppleness. Another variation of hydrotherapy is thalassotherapy, which is treatment with seawater. Jacuzzis or whirlpool baths are also forms of hydrotherapy.

Hypnotherapy

The use of hypnosis in shows and television programmes has taken away the scientific value of this practice, but hypnosis has been used therapeutically for many years. It was first introduced into Europe by Dr Anton Mesmer, who used to 'mesmerize' his patients.

During hypnotherapy sessions, you will learn to reach a state of deep relaxation and subconscious peace. The body's reactions are slowed down, you feel relaxed and your metabolism works more slowly. This in itself is a bonus which reduces the effects of free radicals on the body. You may remember that slow metabolism means a reduced rate of aging.

The session starts with detailed questions about your health. You then need to lie on a couch or a comfortable chair and are told to relax. The practitioner will guide you during this process. When you reach a state of very deep relaxation, the practitioner will explore your subconscious mind in order to treat problem areas. After about 30 to 60 minutes, you will be directed to return your thoughts to everyday life again, as if you are waking up.

The scientific effectiveness of hypnotherapy is not clear. The brain-wave patterns recorded during hypnosis are more or less similar to those recorded during everyday life. It is however approved by some official health bodies (for example it is available on the NHS in Britain) for treatment of certain conditions.

Serious psychological problems are not suitable for this type of treatment, but hypnotherapy is very useful in association with yoga, meditation and chi kung.

193

Laughter Therapy

This therapy is good fun. It can be practised either in a group or on your own. It doesn't take much practice, but you need to be in the right mood and make an effort to fight your inhibitions. The therapy is simple: take a deep breath and laugh out loud. After a while you will really start laughing from your heart.

Scientific research has shown that laughter helps combat excessive stress, supports the immune system, balances the blood pressure, improves well-being and banishes pain. During laughing, the muscles

---

Do-It-Yourself Laughter Therapy

- Have a good laugh in conversation.
- Read a humorous book or listen to a funny tape or film and laugh at even the slightest joke.
- Try to exaggerate laughing if you find something amusing – but don't overdo it!

make enough effort for laughter to be considered a form of aerobic exercise.

Normally, healthy adults laugh or smile about 40–50 times a day on average, whereas a depressed person may laugh or smile fewer than five times. Smiling also helps improve stress and works wonders for your appearance.

Light Therapy

In our modern world, we are starved of light, but our body needs it in order to function properly. Unfortunately, pollution, long working hours and avoidance of direct sunlight reduce substantially the amount of light we receive.

Light therapy is not the same as sun-bed treatments, so there is no need to worry about your skin if you are advised to have light therapy. It is used to treat hormonal imbalances, including menopausal problems, sexual problems and poor immunity, also to boost the vitamin D content of the body, to improve morale and to reduce the effects of depression. Skin conditions may also respond to this treatment, particularly eczema and psoriasis.

During treatment, you will lie on a bed facing a light source, which is usually just above you. The session may last for 45 minutes. The eyes don't have to be covered. On the contrary, the treatment aims to feed light to your eyes in order to stimulate the brain to release essential hormones. You may need to take off your clothes if you are being treated for osteoporosis, in order to expose your body to the vitamin D-boosting effects of light.

People suffering from SAD (seasonally affective disorder or winter depression) may find that having light therapy at home during the dark winter months is the only solution to their condition.

Light therapy sessions need to be continued every week until the problem improves. Then maintenance sessions every few months may be necessary.

Magnetism

The principle of magnetism is the same as that of acupuncture, but without the needles: it is used to balance the flow of energy. Magnetic therapy sees our bodies as something over and above a biochemical machine. The magnet creates a field similar to that of the Earth's magnetic field, so it is therefore 'natural'.

The supporters of magnetic therapy say that our Earth's magnetic field has been altered by all sorts of electronic devices – satellites, mobile phones, etc – so we need to use additional devices to top magnetism up. Researchers have also come up with the possibility of a 'magnetic deficiency syndrome' which is due to the overpowering of the natural magnetism by modern devices. If you have muscle stiffness, aches and pains, headache, dizziness, constipation or tiredness, you may well be suffering from MDS.

Magnets can be used in several different ways: in a mattress or pillow, as armbands, as used in acupuncture in the place of needles. In magnetic mattresses, a series of magnets are placed in certain positions to create a field which wraps the body like a cocoon. This is thought to improve circulation and literally energize the body. There is no electricity involved, as only magnetic energy is used.

Apart from the symptoms listed above, magnetism is also used to treat:

- arthritis
- insomnia
- high blood pressure
- macular degeneration
- other chronic conditions

There are even claims that it retards the aging process by unblocking the flow of energy, helping blood and lymph circulate smoothly throughout the body. This encourages the delivery of nutrients to the cells and the elimination of toxins.

The treatment stimulates bone tissue to heal itself after fractures and is also effective in cases of osteoporosis. The magnetic field can penetrate the skin and acts on the broken bone to stimulate the osteoblasts, the cells which create new bone. It encourages the migration of calcium into the bone, regulates the flow of ions and affects the performance of certain enzymes. It also activates the healing processes in cases of soft tissue damage.

All this is not endorsed by mainstream medicine. Nevertheless, magnetic devices are slowly becoming popular and there are several companies advertising their products in health magazines. A few scientific articles on magnetism have begun making a timid appearance in established scientific journals.

Massage

A method of treatment in use for over 5,000 years, therapeutic massage is mentioned by Hippocrates (fifth century BC) and has been discussed by other medical men through the ages. The need for physical contact certainly plays a vital role in maintaining good health. We tend to touch and be touched less as we grow older and this can contribute to feelings of loneliness, irritability and anxiety.

There are different types of massage. *Marma* massage is an Ayurvedic type of massage, using 107 *marma* points on the body. Lymphatic massage gently stimulates the flow of lymph and *tuina* is a type of Chinese massage. All of these have a relaxing effect on the brain.

Apart from the improvement of mental conditions, massage has physical benefits as well: it helps maintain a fine sense of touch, it lowers high blood pressure and, in certain forms, it subdues the pain and stiffness of arthritis.

Self-Massage

a Use your fingertips to massage the muscles of your face in small, gentle, circular motions.

b Use your fingertips and thumb to massage your hands, palms and wrists to avoid impaired mobility and joint problems.

c Gently massage yourself, using your thumbs, starting from the back of the head, then moving down to your neck and shoulders. Then repeat the whole procedure.

If you have a partner, you can use aromatherapy oils for back, shoulder or abdominal massage.

Massage energizes the nerve endings, including the touch and pressure sensors. It enlivens sluggish blood circulation to the skin and invigorates the production of collagen. Deeper massage stimulates the muscle tissues and eases blood flow to the muscles. It helps improve their tone and it activates the lymphatic system, stimulating better elimination of toxins. Remember that fewer toxins means slower aging.

Music Therapy

If you want to stimulate your memories and revitalize your endorphins, then music therapy is ideal. Its big plus is that it can be done in the comfort of your own home. There are, however, also special centres teaching music therapy.

At home, listen to a piece of music for a while and meditate: What does it remind you of? Think about this scene and try to remember all the small details. Take time to listen to the music and not merely hear it in the background.

As well as listening to music, playing an instrument is not only therapeutic, but also stimulates your brain to keep up with the learning .

A Musical Exercise

Two or three times a month, or more frequently if you wish, listen to music that is completely different from your usual taste. Tune your radio into anything unusual to you, perhaps children's music, heavy rock, the latest pop songs, opera, rap, ska, ethnic music, foreign folk music, and so on. Visualize what the composer or the singer is trying to pass on to the listener. It is a better exercise for the brain if you don't have a clue about the words but still make the effort to understand the general meaning of the song.

Naturopathy

Hippocrates, in the fifth century BC, was one of the first proponents of naturopathy. He used the healing powers of nature together with natural medicines and healthy food, believing that if properly cared for, the body has the power to heal itself.

Modern naturopathy uses:

- suitable vitamins and minerals
- fresh mountain or seaside air
- sunlight
- mud packs
- mineral baths

to eliminate toxic material from the body and to support the immune system. Exercise is also used along with other natural treatments.

Naturopaths believe that fever or inflammation are signs that the body is trying to heal itself and these should not be suppressed.

Conventional medicine accepts some of the naturopathic treatments such as exercise, diet and relaxation, but is more reluctant to accept others.

If you decide to see a practitioner they will want to have a complete picture of your physical and mental health. They may want to examine your eyes, sweat, hair or muscle strength. The treatment could be catabolic, ie involve cleansing the system and getting rid of poisons with fasting, or anabolic, ie involve boosting and strengthening the metabolism with nutritional supplements, exercise and relaxation. Sometimes, the symptoms may worsen initially when the cleansing of the toxins takes place.

Naturopathic treatments are also used specifically in aging to promote general good health and an active brain, and to deal with conditions such as arthritis, depression, asthma, bronchitis, atherosclerosis and stomach ulcers.

Try it for yourself – follow a natural diet, go out into the fresh air to do breathing exercises, drink up to eight glasses of water a day to help eliminate toxic material, use health supplements wisely when needed. Use a brush or a loofah to scrub and stimulate the skin during a bracing shower or bath.

Practitioners may recommend mud or steam therapy, or oxygen facial treatments to rejuvenate the skin. The latter treatment is becoming popular with women who want to recapture their youthful skin. During oxygen treatment, oxygen molecules which are trapped in particles of oil are used to feed and refresh the skin. Those who use this treatment claim that it reduces fine lines and wrinkles. Skin experts are still debating whether it actually works. In theory, providing extra oxygen to the skin increases free radical damage and, unless antioxidants are included in the treatment, more damage will be caused.

Reflexology

Reflexology or 'zone therapy', as it is also called, aims to heal the body through contact with the feet. It is another ancient method of healing, having been used for thousands of years in the East.

Practitioners have created maps of the body on the soles of the feet. Broadly, the toes correspond to the head and brain, the middle of the foot corresponds to the abdomen and the heel corresponds to the coccyx and genital areas. The practitioner will examine the state of the feet and identify the problem. Remember, however, that regulatory organizations, such as the Association of Reflexologists in the UK, forbid their members to offer a medical diagnosis.

When the area to be treated is identified on the foot map, this is massaged to help improve the blood and lymphatic circulation to the

---

How to give a reflexology massage

Gently massage each toe using your thumb.

Then, with your thumb and index finger, flex, extend and move each toe sideways gently.

Next massage the metatarsal area of the foot. This area is the bony part immediately before the toes.

Finally, apply pressure with your thumbs on the solar plexus area. This is the area on the sole of the foot between the big toe and the second toe below the large pad where the arch of the foot starts.

corresponding area of the body. Alternatively, the practitioner may apply pressure, using the thumbs, on certain areas of the feet. This stimulates the natural healing power of the body and promotes a better transmission of healing messages via the nerves.

Reflexology is used for general aches and pains, back pain, depression, sleeping difficulties, loss of libido, restless legs, menopausal problems and Parkinson's disease. It may also tip the balance in your favour if you want to stop smoking or reduce your alcohol intake. Side effects of the treatment may be diarrhoea or an increased frequency of urination.

Reflexology is also good for feet, which are usually neglected in anti-aging care. In fact, aging can cause several problems with the feet such as ulcers, bunions, nail abnormalities, local circulation problems and bone pains. Referral to a chiropodist or other specialist may then become necessary.

Conclusion

These are some complementary therapies which have relevance to aging. I hope that I have given you enough information to help you decide which treatment may be suitable for your particular situation. If you do decide to follow a certain treatment, it may be necessary to find out more information about it. Aim to do some sessions with a qualified practitioner before you try home exercises or treatments. The decision whether to use established, well-researched treatments or new alternative ones should be made after careful consideration of the effects and side effects of each. Have a frank, open-minded discussion with a doctor who is willing to listen.

CHAPTER 9

Age-Related Problems

There are several diseases which thrive on the biological changes which happen to all of us during aging. In addition to these, some other diseases are caused (or made worse) by unhealthy lifestyle, by the modern way of living or by other preventable factors. The following discussion will help you just to scratch the surface of some of these diseases. It is not meant to replace the professional help of a healthcare practitioner. Nothing you read in books could do that. The best way to defeat any illness is to work in partnership with your practitioners, both conventional and complementary.

Alzheimer's Senile Dementia

This awful disease affects half a million people in the UK and 11 million in the USA and Western Europe. One in 20 people over the age of 65 has dementia and this narrows down to one in five over the age of 80.

Dementia is a progressive worsening of the mental faculties which devastates cognition, intelligence and memory. It is due to certain changes in the brain, including a build-up of damaging and unnecessary chemical substances inside the brain cells. Some scientists see Alzheimer's dementia as a natural consequence of aging (ie, we will all get it if we live long enough), whereas others see it as a separate and independent disease which sooner or later will be cured. Scientific opinion constantly swings from one point of view to the other.

People who have had a poor education and therefore did not exercise their brain enough face an increased risk of developing Alzheimer's dementia, according to a study published in the *British Medical Journal*.

There is no known cure for Alzheimer's dementia, despite some claims to the contrary. Certain other cases of dementia, however, are not due to age degeneration alone but to preventable causes, like artery disease ('multi-infarct dementia'), vitamin B12 deficiency ('megaloblastic madness'), alcohol abuse or thyroid problems ('myxoedema madness').

Patients suffering from dementia may be unable to remember events which happened some days or weeks ago. During the early stages, they may still remember events which happened many years ago. Eventually, though, these memories go as well.

Memory problems may be caused not only by the processes of dementia, but also by other factors. One example is atrial fibrillation, which is a form of irregular heartbeat very common in later life. Italian researchers have discovered that atrial fibrillation makes brain problems worse because it causes tiny blood clots which go on to block the small arteries in the brain. The researchers recommend regular checks with a doctor who would be able to diagnose atrial fibrillation and then prescribe anti-clotting drugs, such as aspirin, to prevent further damage.

Apart from memory loss, other problems seen frequently in dementia include:

- depression
- no interest in personal hygiene
- confusion
- reduced learning ability or loss of concentration
- restlessness
- incontinence

Certain treatments aim to replace the missing acetylcholine or the other chemical messengers in the brain. These use drugs such as Aricept and Excelon, but unfortunately they are not always effective.

There is, however, some evidence that certain supplements have a positive effect on dementia. A study published in the *Journal of the American Medical Association* showed that one third of patients suffering from Alzheimer's dementia showed some improvement after being treated with ginkgo biloba. For the effects to become apparent the patients had to take ginkgo for several months. Several other studies also support this conclusion.

Experiments looking at the action of the co-enzyme Q10 in rats showed that it stimulated the activity of their brains and increased the use of energy by one third. When a toxin was given to the rats, the brains of those who were treated with Q10 did not suffer any damage, suggesting that Q10 is a strong brain cell protector.

In an attempt to reduce the effects of dementia, researchers have used reminiscence therapy, reality orientation and remotivation therapies in groups of patients. Those who received the treatment showed a significant improvement of their mental power. This research suggests that stimulating the brain is essential in slowing down the effects of dementia.

Complementary treatments for dementia aim to lessen the burden of the disease, but do not affect its progress. Treatments include:

- massage for mental and physical relaxation
- nutritional therapy with suitable natural and organic ingredients to fortify the body
- music therapy to revive lost memories and to stimulate the brain

An alternative strategy, which aims to prevent or reduce the effects of dementia and memory loss, includes:

- following a low fat diet
- using a combination of co-enzyme Q10 with vitamins E and B
- extra phosphatidyl serine, vinpocetine and ginkgo biloba, plus pregnenolone, DHEA and selegiline
- mind/body exercises, including breathing, relaxation and brain exercises

A few doctors also recommend RN13 and SAMe on top of all of the above for good measure. For more details on these drugs see chapter 10. This strategy has been advised by some experts in dementia but the majority of conventional doctors don't endorse it.

Anaemia

When I was a junior medical officer, I heard the best explanation as to what anaemia is. A very old illiterate woman from a village was admitted with anaemia to our ultra-modern eastern Mediterranean hospital. She couldn't understand what she was suffering from. We were keen to explain about haemoglobin, oxygen in the blood and red blood cells, but in vain. Finally, the consultant pompously arrived and in a split second he thundered: 'You've got anaemia, granny. Your blood has turned into water.' She understood immediately and agreed to proceed with the treatment.

Anaemia is usually caused by iron deficiency (which may also cause the nails and hair to be brittle), but there are many other causes. The result may be:

- dizziness
- fainting
- paleness of the inside of the eyelids
- tiredness
- loss of appetite

One cause of anaemia is persistent blood loss, as in heavy menstrual periods or chronic bleeding from the stomach or bowels. The risk of bleeding from the stomach in older people can be reduced by exercising. Brisk walking three times a week was proven to reduce the risk of bleeding in a study of 8,000 patients aged over 67 years. Very vigorous exercise does not have any added benefits.

Conventional doctors aim to find and correct the exact cause of the anaemia. It may then be necessary for the patient to take iron supplements in tablet or injection form, or other supplements such as vitamin B12, folic acid, vitamin C and zinc.

Perhaps the only complementary treatment for anaemia is nutritional therapy. If the anaemia is mild, it may be enough to treat it by eating food with a high iron content instead of taking pills, though check with your doctor first. Food high in iron includes:

- red meat

- beans

- brewer's yeast such as Vegemite/Marmite

- soya

- dandelion, watercress and parsley (these can be used in salads or in the diet in general)

Angina and Heart Disease

Atherosclerosis (*see* below) can cause narrowing of the arteries in the heart, which in turn may cause heart disease. Heart disease could be:

a angina, which is pain in the chest due to too little oxygen supply to the heart muscle

b heart attacks (myocardial infarction)

c heart failure, with shortness of breath and swelling of the legs

There are several types of conventional treatment which are very effective in treating heart disease. The ones commonly used include GTN sprays or tablets, beta blockers and calcium blockers. Newer types of drugs are being discovered all the time but these are usually aimed at more severe cases of the disease.

Surgery for the heart is also very effective. This could be in the form of:

a angioplasty, using a balloon or laser to unblock a narrow artery

b a by-pass operation using healthy veins from the leg to by-pass the diseased arteries in the heart muscle

Apart from treatments for established heart disease, there are several approaches for preventing any problems and reducing the risk in susceptible individuals. These include the usual: take exercise, stop smoking and avoid fat. There are also many suitable dietary and nutritional supplements available.

Garlic

Garlic is hailed as one of the best of these. It has been used for thousands of years as a general stimulant and health-sustaining plant. It is most suitable in reducing cholesterol, lowering high blood pressure and generally protecting against heart disease. Garlic contains the chemicals alliin and alliinase, which are stored separately within the garlic plant. Crushing, chewing or digesting garlic releases these two substances, which react together to form garlic's active chemical, allicin.

Garlichas many benefits, but most importantly it:

- lowers cholesterol and triglycerides
- energizes the mechanisms which break down blood clots
- normalizes the blood pressure
- improves general well-being
- eases the flow of blood through the small arteries of the tissues

Use garlic in cooking, but if you decide to try garlic supplements make sure you choose preparations which deliver enough allicin. This should be standardized in order to provide the same quantity of alliin and alliinase every time. Cultivation of the garlic plant is also important. Chinese garlic is considered to be stronger than garlic from other countries. Follow the directions on the package because garlic tablets may need to be taken three times a day in order to maintain the active ingredients in the blood.

The odour of garlic is due to the formation of allicin. If you wish to avoid smelling of it, choose preparations which don't allow the mixing of the two ingredients until the tablet is well down in the bowel, so the odour can't escape from the mouth. That is the theory. In practice, though, somebody with a good nose may still be able to pick up the scent.

General facts on garlic (real or alleged)

- One clove of garlic contains 1–4 calories.
- Garlic can help reduce infections.
- It is a good antioxidant.
- It boosts blood circulation to the nail bed.
- It eases digestion.
- It can help ward off mosquitoes.
- If rubbed on the teeth, it can improve toothache.
- It can make warts disappear.

Q10

Another supplement which has a preventative role in heart disease is co-enzyme Q10. Q10 is an antioxidant, it improves oxygen metabolism, strengthens the heart muscle and enriches the process of energy production by the mitochondria, which are the power-houses of cells. In a trial of patients who just had a heart attack, Q10 was found to be effective against angina, irregular heartbeat and heart failure.

Chelation Treatment

A non-conventional treatment for atherosclerosis and heart disease is chelation therapy. This is not officially approved in the US or in the UK, but it is used in these countries nevertheless. Chelation therapy may also help osteoporosis.

This controversial treatment involves using binding agents which neutralize several chemicals implicated in causing health problems. Other ingredients of the chelation mixture are vitamins, minerals or phosphatidyl choline, which can also be used on their own.

The treatment can be given in tablet or more commonly in injection form, via a drip. Not only is it not endorsed by mainstream cardiologists, they don't even want to talk about it. But chelation practitioners claim dramatic results. They say that the treatment has been used on nearly one million patients by over 1,000 physicians world-wide.

Homocysteine

The amino acid homocysteine has been blamed for playing a serious part in causing heart disease, stroke and thrombosis. High concentrations of homocysteine act as a poison and destroy certain chemicals in the cell. Homocysteine is as important as smoking and high cholesterol in causing damage to the arteries, blockage of the blood circulation and worsening of atherosclerosis.

Lack of exercise, too much alcohol and an unhealthy diet can drive levels of homocysteine sky high. Excessive homocysteine can be neutralized, however, by SAMe (*see* chapter 10), vitamin B12, vitamin B6 and folate. There are a few hospitals offering blood tests for detecting homocysteine and these tests will become much more widespread in the near future.

Complementary Treatments

Complementary treatments used in heart disease are:

- acupuncture, which may help improve the heart muscle and reduce pain

- hawthorn to strengthen the heart muscle, lower blood pressure, prevent palpitations and improve angina pain (hawthorn contains flavonoids and comes in capsule or liquid form at doses of 200mg standardized extract)

- Ayurvedic medicine, with several different treatments

- chi kung, which if practised regularly is excellent at reducing blood pressure and helping the blood circulation

As you can see, there are several treatments aiming to relieve the symptoms of heart disease. None is perfect, but a carefully selected combination may make the sufferer's life worth living again.

Anxiety

We are all familiar with anxiety. Although it can affect people of any age, it becomes more common and perhaps more severe in later life. The symptoms of anxiety are:

- a general feeling of uneasiness

- irritability

- tiredness

- shakiness

- palpitations or breathlessness

- bowel problems

- difficulty in sleeping

Conventionally, anxiety can be treated with drugs, counselling or a combination of both. Other specialized techniques are used in more severe forms of anxiety.

Help for less serious anxiety includes the following complementary therapies:

- massage to reduce the tension in the muscles

- aromatherapy to soothe the nerves and increase well-being

- touch therapy (the laying on of hands)

- hypnotherapy, particularly self-hypnosis, to help control stressful situations

- homoeopathic remedies (gelsemium, phosphorus or arsenic to be taken after expert advice)

- naturopathy to stabilize the blood sugar levels

Many people use honey mixed in a hot drink for its sedative properties. It is necessary to avoid too much coffee or tea if you suffer from anxiety, because caffeine highlights the symptoms of the condition.

Arthritis

Over 80 per cent of people aged 50 and above have some form of arthritis. The most common type is osteoarthritis. There are other less common types, for example, rheumatoid arthritis, gouty arthritis and psoriatic arthritis. These are not generally as related to the aging process as osteoarthritis.

Osteoarthritis is an age-related disease, but it is also made worse by over-using a particular joint or by previous injury to the joint. It is a degenerative disease, meaning that it gets worse with time, but in some people this progression may be very slow. Osteoarthritis most commonly affects the knees, hips, neck and hands, but it can affect any joint.

The healthy joint is made of three main parts:

1 cartilage, a gelatinous substance around the end of the bone

2 synovial fluid, which lubricates the joint and helps the ends of the bones move without friction

3 ligaments, which hold the joint together

With age, all of these constituents may become affected in one way or another, causing pain, stiffness and deformity of the joint.

Arthritis may be common, but it doesn't mean that you have to put up with it. Preventing it is difficult but there are some sensible steps I can recommend:

a Shun obesity, which puts excess pressure on the joints, causing early wear and tear.

b Consume extra supplies of omega-3 fatty acids in the form of fish oils, which play an active part in prevention.

c Pursue a generally healthy lifestyle and eat plenty of dark-coloured fruit and vegetables.

d Consider nutritional supplements (antioxidants or similar).

Once the arthritis is established it can still be treated. Reasonably effective conventional treatments are:

a pain-killers and NSAIDs (non-steroidal anti-inflammatory drugs) which reduce the inflammation within the joint but may cause stomach bleeding (also to be avoided in asthma or blood clotting conditions)

b steroid injections

c physiotherapy

d surgery, as a last resort

The pain of arthritis can be reduced by a cream containing capsaicin, an extract from chilli peppers. Capsaicin has been used for many centuries in Mexico and is now used by conventional doctors as a topical analgesic. It blocks the transmission of pain signals to the brain and it may be worth a try.

Recently, doctors have tried injections of hyaluronic acid (brand names are Hyalgan or Sinvisc) into the joint to help stimulate the sinovial fluid. Hyaluronic acid has been found particularly effective in arthritis of the knee. One of the main drawbacks is that, for best results, the injections need to be repeated up to 10 times a year. This treatment is available from doctors who have had training in the technique.

There are quite a few complementary treatments for arthritis:

- acupuncture for pain and for relaxing the muscles around the joint

- osteopathic and chiropractic treatment using manipulation to relax the muscles and to help the joint move easily

- naturopathy, involving cutting down on processed food and using more fish oils, grain and fresh fruit (co-enzyme Q10, flavonoids, pantothenic acid, vitamin E and C are also used, with some effect)

- herbal treatments including willow and devil's claw for inflammation, elderflower extracts (antioxidants) and bittersweet

- homoeopathy with arnica and rhus tox

- *Boswellia serrata*, a herb known to Ayurvedic practitioners, which contains the anti-inflammatory substance boswellin and has been proven to reduce pain and swelling of the joints and improve the range of movement

Hydrotherapy, using cold water, can also reduce heat and joint swelling. In a recent study, researchers found that hydrotherapy was very effective in the treatment of arthritis. It improved joint tenderness and extended the range of joint movement. Hydrotherapy can be used at home for mild arthritis, or at special centres such as hospital physiotherapy centres or even local swimming pools, where it may be possible to enrol in special classes.

You can try some water exercises in a warm swimming pool. Do some stretching of the arms and legs, some arm and shoulder rotation, and walking on the spot in the water, or gently massage the affected joint while still in the water.

Complementary treatments for arthritis don't end there. New Zealand green-lipped mussel extract has been known to have an effect on arthritis, including the rheumatoid variety. Maoris living in the coastal areas of New Zealand have a low incidence of arthritis due, it is believed, to their admirable habit of consuming large quantities of these mussels.

In an experiment, patients were given the extract daily for about three months, and they reported an improvement in the degree of pain, a reduction in morning stiffness, and a strengthening of their power to grip. In this trial, the mussel extract reduced joint swelling by an amazing 90 per cent as compared to a reduction of 60 per cent by

---

Exercises to Help Arthritis

Below are some examples of exercises for arthritis sufferers which aim to avoid stiffness, improve mobility of the joint and strengthen the muscles around it:

- **For the Neck**
  Turn your head very gently all the way to the left. Keep it as far as it can go for a few seconds and then move back to the straight position. Then do the same to the right. Repeat five times.

- **For Shoulder Flexibility**
  Lean over a chair using one arm to support you. Make circular movements with your other arm to work on the stiff shoulder joint, first clockwise then anti-clockwise.

- **For the Knee**
  Sit on the floor with your affected knee straight. Place a rolled towel under your heel to support it. Tighten the muscles of the knee while pushing your heel away from you. Aim to touch the floor with the back of your knee. Hold for three or four seconds, relax and repeat a few times.

Brufen (Nurofen) and a mere 40 per cent by aspirin. Sceptical doctors demand more trials before they are convinced.

The extract is not thought to cause problems to those who are allergic to fish because it is chemically stabilized. Its promising benefits are thought to be due, in part, to the richness of omega-3 fatty acids and glucosamine in the mussels.

Two other nutritional supplements which aim to reduce the symptoms of arthritis are glucosamine and chondroitin. Glucosamine alone is used by many arthritis sufferers as well as by those affected by sports injuries, spine degeneration or slipped disc, after a medical consultation to diagnose the problem first.

Glucosamine may also be combined with chondroitin. This combination helps repair collagen within the joint. Normally, there is a constant breakdown and reconstruction of the tissues within the joint. This speeds up with the passage of time and the process of destruction is not balanced by the process of repair. Providing the raw materials such as chondroitin and glucosamine may help balance the process of reconstruction of the joint.

Controversial drugs used by some people who have arthritis include SAMe (which is thought to stimulate the production of new cartilage by the special cells in the joint called chondrocytes), DHEA and pregnenolone (*see* chapter 10).

I once saw a patient who swore that thrashing himself with stinging nettles a few times a week cured his arthritis completely. This is a painful treatment, but similar therapies in the past included using bee stings, burning with hot irons and other ways of causing pain so that the attention of the sufferer was diverted from the painful joint. Or, perhaps, the treatment stimulates the production of natural pain-killing substances such as endorphins, which are the body's own heroin fix. The stinging nettle extract blocks some components of the inflamation process.

Atherosclerosis

Atherosclerosis, meaning 'hardening of the arteries', is blamed for almost every illness: angina, heart attacks, stroke, impotence, pain in the legs during walking, dizziness and memory problems.

Atherosclerosis may start in childhood, with a build-up of

cholesterol and other fatty deposits within the wall of the arteries. This build-up continues slowly over the years, causing loss of elasticity and furring (calcification) of the arteries, like the inside of a kettle, with eventual blockage of the blood flow. The process is speeded up in smokers, in overweight people and in those who have excessive stress or high cholesterol in their blood.

Cold weather makes the blood clot more easily. This means that in the winter, people who have atherosclerosis have a higher risk of suffering a heart attack, stroke or thrombosis. If you are at risk, you should take cold weather seriously and try to keep warm whatever you do.

Treatment for atherosclerosis is by:

- drugs or diet to lower cholesterol
- aspirin
- control of the blood pressure
- surgery in serious cases

214

Aspirin eases the flow of blood through the arteries by reducing its stickiness, making the blood less likely to clot. It can reduce the symptoms of angina and the risk of stroke and heart disease. Bear in mind that one side effect of taking aspirin is bleeding in the stomach in sensitive individuals.

Omega-3 fatty acids help reduce cholesterol and improve stickiness of the blood. These are found not only in oily fish, but also in olive oil, flax seed oil and perilla oil. Omega-3 oils help relieve almost all problems associated with atherosclerosis. Flax seed oil can be used in salads or on boiled potatoes and in capsule form. Perilla or canola oil are available in liquid form from natural food stores.

Exercise is to atherosclerosis what water is to fire. Regular exercise dampens the effects of atherosclerosis and it is one of the strongest weapons in our fight against this disease. Exercise doesn't need to be performed in the gym in order to be effective. Regular home exercises can provide enough muscle strength and stamina too.

Regular exercise increases the activity of clot-busting enzymes in the body, such as tPA (tissue plasminogen activator). This enzyme is given as a life-saving treatment to heart attack victims to reduce clotting of the blood.

Researchers are currently exploring the benefits of vitamin K on the arteries. Vitamin K is essential for healthy bones, clean arteries and for balancing the clotting of blood. This vitamin throws a spanner in the works of certain mechanisms responsible for atherosclerosis. Too low a concentration of vitamin K in the blood is related to a high risk of atherosclerosis. Some scientists also say that vitamin K has a positive role to play in preventing Alzheimer's dementia.

To complicate matters, though, many older people have low vitamin K concentration in their blood. The reason for this is not known.

Vitamin K is usually found in leafy vegetables but antibiotics may reduce it in the gut. It is also available in tablet form but not widely used as a supplement yet.

One complementary treatment for atherosclerosis is naturopathy. This recommends general lifestyle improvements, a high fibre diet, stress reduction and exercise. The diet should contain extra fruit and salads for antioxidants, as well as oily fish to boost the intake of omega-3 fatty acids.

215

Smoking and Atherosclerosis

You already know that cigarette smoking is a risk factor for atherosclerosis, contributing to angina, heart attacks, stroke and other problems with circulation. It does, of course, increase the risk of many other illnesses such as cancer, skin aging and lung infections.

Statistics show that over half of smokers don't reach the age of 65. Not only this, but the number of people who die from smoking-related illnesses in the UK is equivalent to a large jet crashing every day.

If you want to stop smoking, nicotine replacement products are a reasonable starting point but you need to be careful not to swap smoking a cigarette for taking nicotine in other forms. The purpose of nicotine replacement is to wean you slowly off cigarettes and nicotine.

Herbal supplements which have been tried for kicking the habit include lemon, eucalyptus, dandelion and rosemary, all used as infusions or through formal aromatherapy sessions.

Other complementary therapies are used by an increasing number of smokers who want to stop. These are:

- relaxation
- yoga or t'ai chi

- meditation

- hypnotherapy

- acupuncture

- nutritional modification

Does your lifestyle make you prone to atherosclerosis? Ask yourself:

1 How much exercise do you take each week?

2 Do you avoid salt in your diet? Do you avoid additives?

3 Do you usually add sugar to your drinks?

4 Do you usually eat fried food?

5 Do you drink more than two cups of coffee every day?

6 How much red meat do you eat?

7 Have you had a medical check up recently?

8 Are you overweight?

9 Do you smoke?

Comments

The benefits of exercise on the heart and on the prevention of osteoporosis are well known. Researchers also say that exercise helps maintain a robust brain function. Research is currently under way to substantiate claims that exercise improves, prevents or even reverses some of the symptoms of Parkinson's disease.

Your eating habits are important in avoiding atherosclerosis. You know about the adverse effects of a diet high in salt, sugar and fat. The caffeine contained in coffee, chocolate, tea and some colas can be addictive and even two cups of coffee a day can cause caffeine dependency. Eat lean red meat only once a week, choose chicken or fish and choose to eat vegetarian sometimes.

Our efforts to maintain health should include regular medical checkups to detect early signs of disease which may strike at any time. These medical checkups should be repeated regularly in order to be effective.

Five ways to help you stop or reduce smoking

1 Hold the cigarette in your hand for as long as possible before lighting up, or hold a cigarette imitator.

2 Smoke the cigarette only half-way through and then throw it away.

3 To reduce cravings, take deep breaths, go for a walk in the fresh air, drink extra quantities of water or fruit juice, suck a low sugar mint, brush your teeth using strong-scented toothpaste.

4 Try not to inhale every single time.

5 Use (but not abuse) a nicotine replacement treatment.

Being overweight carries a risk of heart disease, diabetes and some forms of cancer, to name a few. Try to maintain an ideal weight, best suited to your age group and to your own lifestyle. If you are a smoker, it would be well worth trying out the tips above.

Bronchitis

This is infection of the lungs, which is common in smokers, asthmatics or frail older people. It causes a cough, difficulty in breathing, the production of infected sputum and general debility or weakness. Conventional treatments are antibiotics, oxygen and inhalers, which are usually effective.

Other treatments for bronchitis or for any type of chest infection include:

- hypnotherapy to relax the muscles and decrease the need for medication

- herbs to reduce sensitivity to allergens: hyssop, euphorbia and coltsfoot

- homoeopathy to deal with a particular allergen

- nutritional therapy to boost immunity, using garlic and oily fish, or echinacea supplements

- aromatherapy using tea tree oil, eucalyptus or thyme inhalations

- hydrotherapy with steam

- massage to dislodge the phlegm from the lungs

Bereavement

Although not strictly a medical problem, bereavement can be an important cause of anxiety and worry as we grow older. The possibility of losing a loved one increases with age and sooner or later everybody will experience the devastation of a death.

Often people don't realize that there are different stages of grief. They are not sure of their feelings and they may believe that they are experiencing strange symptoms or unique emotions.

In fact there are four stages that we all go through following a loss:

1 First there is disbelief and shock. This is a natural reaction designed to lessen the impact of loss.

2 Then comes grief, with pining, yearning, feelings of guilt, anger at the injustice of the loss and remembering the old times.

3 This is followed by depression, as the full reality of the loss begins to sink in, often causing loss of self-confidence and loss of identity.

4 Finally there is recovery and acceptance.

These phases last for different times in different people, but they are more or less always present.

As you grow older, be prepared for the loss of bereavement. Think about the future and don't take anything for granted. Make it easy for yourself by learning to do things you don't usually get involved in: cooking, doing the housework, learning new skills, doing the household bills.

For the bereaved, sharing the fears and grief with others or attending counselling sessions can also help. Many people rediscover the healing powers of spiritual and religious experiences during bereavement.

Complementary treatments to help lessen the impact of bereavement are:

- homoeopathy, using ignatia immediately after the loss and natrum mur for long-term problems

- flower remedies, using pear blossom and honeysuckle to reduce grief

- hypnotherapy to help come to terms with the loss, emphasize the good points of the dead person and to reduce all the negative images of the fatal disease

Cancer

Contrary to what you may think, the 'big C' doesn't stand for 'Cancer' anymore, but for 'Brave, Intrepid, Gallant and Confident'. Although cancer is still one of the most ruthless killers of our time, we are now learning to fight back.

Tumours can develop in any part of the body which has cells able to grow and divide. The growth of the tumour can be slow or fast and the tumour is called 'malignant' if it is not under the control of the organism, ie it is uncontrollable. Malignant cells are able to invade and destroy nearby tissues or migrate along the bloodstream and lymphatic canals to reach organs such as the brain, lungs or bones.

For a cancer to start in the first place, it is necessary to have an agent (a carcinogen) which stimulates the cells to become malignant. Carcinogens are chemicals found in polluted air, in cigarette smoke and in certain foods. Certain viruses are also carcinogens. Once the malignant change has taken place, the cancer starts growing and it is encouraged by other agents which promote its growth, or by free radicals and a variety of other dastardly chemicals.

In many people, cancer will grow so slowly that it stays undetected for several years, perhaps for life. This happens, for example, in the case of prostate cancer in some older men. Perhaps you yourself have cancer now without realizing it and hopefully you will never find out. But if you want to avoid cancer it makes sense to try to do everything in your power to defeat it before it takes a foothold.

To control cancer growth, our body has several defences:

- antioxidants to help reduce free radicals
- the immune system to attack the growth and contain it
- DNA repair mechanisms to avoid further growth
- eliminating mechanisms to get rid of toxins and poisons

The immune system, in particular, attacks cancer in several ways. It exterminates cancerous cells, cuts off the nutrient supply to the growth and marks cancerous cells so that they will be picked up again by the immune system at a later stage if the growth reappears.

The tumour also needs a good blood supply in order to develop. Substances which cut off the blood supply to newly developing tumours are thought to be efficient in shrinking them or killing them off completely. Examples are the isoflavones which inhibit angiogenesis (the formation of new blood capillaries). Isoflavones have other functions, too, being antioxidants and immune boosters. There are products on the market which contain suitable quantities of isoflavones and lignans, important dietary phytoestrogens which are normally found in soya, seeds, cereals and grains. Some of these come in tablet or powder form but, lately, they have also been combined in food/cereal bars.

Scientists believe that up to 80 per cent of bowel and breast cancer may be preventable by following a suitable diet. Risk factors are the old foes: smoking, lack of exercise, being overweight and drinking alcohol to excess.

Breast Cancer Facts

- One in 12 women will have breast cancer and half of these will die from the disease.
- Men can also develop breast cancer, but this happens about 100 times less frequently than in women.
- Breast cancer often affects women over 60 and early menopause increases the risk.
- One in 20 women with breast cancer has a close relative who had the disease.

Conventional treatment once cancer has been diagnosed is with drugs, intravenous or locally applied chemotherapy, radiotherapy and surgery. Complementary treatments are best used in association with conventional ones following medical advice. These are:

- aromatherapy with chamomile for relieving anxiety and worry
- reflexology for pain and nausea
- healing with the laying on of hands
- acupuncture for pain and nausea
- a good diet with antioxidants
- meditation and visualization for strengthening immunity
- astragalus, echinacea or aloe vera

Aloe vera has been used by many sufferers to help reduce the effects of cancer. It is difficult, however, to find many scientific research projects supporting these claims. Because the development of cancer depends on the health and efficiency of the immune system, and because aloe vera can boost the immune system, theoretically it can also affect the development of cancer. It can also fight infections which are frequent in patients suffering from cancer. It is not known whether it can prevent cancer from appearing, as some of its supporters claim.

A UK pioneer in the use of complementary treatments in cancer is the Bristol Cancer Help Centre, which offers a complete range of treatments and help in all areas of fighting cancer. For more details *see* 'Resources'.

Red Meat and Cancer

A survey of 3,660 people showed that there was no association between red meat consumption and cancer. Other research results show similar findings, to the point where some nutritionists have stopped recommending avoidance of lean red meat.

Carnosine (*see* chapter 10) which is present in red meat, is actually thought to reduce the risk of cancer. Another constituent of red meat, CLA (conjugated linoleic acid) is also thought to help prevent cancer. This is a fatty acid, which is also found in cheese, and it is claimed that it plays a vital part in preventing breast, prostate and bowel cancer. Red meat doesn't contain as much CLA as it used to, because of changes to feeding routines in cows. It does, nevertheless, contain some beneficial amounts of it.

Apart from helping in cancer, CLA is also thought to help reduce body fat, increase muscle mass, support certain constituents of the immune system, lower cholesterol and reduce the risk of atherosclerosis. Most commercial CLA is obtained from a chemical process involving sunflower oil. Recently, CLA has been added to preparations to help reduce fat under the skin and dimples of the skin. Research is in the early stages and more is needed before doctors are convinced one way or another.

Prayer

Several cancer sufferers have reported an improvement in their condition following prayer. The use of prayer for its healing powers goes back millennia, but the first semi-scientific experiment to study its effects was performed towards the end of the 19th century by Sir Francis Galton. He wanted to find out whether prayer had any effect on the life span. At that time, people prayed regularly for the well-being of their monarch and Galton thought that the mental power of so many people might actually make monarchs live longer. When he finished his studies he was somewhat disappointed not to find any difference in longevity. He thought that the reason for this was that monarchs in the past were living a particularly stressful and dangerous life so the benefits of the prayers were wiped out.

Since then there have been other experiments into the effects of prayer. Recently, researchers asked a group of priests to pray for particular patients who were in the intensive therapy unit of a hospital. The patients had absolutely no idea that someone was praying for them and the doctors didn't know which patient was receiving the prayer until after the trial. In the final results, the patients who had been prayed for recovered much faster than those who had not.

Some scientists dismiss these results as merely statistical mispresentation of the truth, but prayer has been scientifically studied and found to have benefits for the body. It is not only for religious individuals, but it is for everybody, a basic human need. It may help the brain to produce immune-boosting chemicals and substances to help fight cancer or to release pain-killing endorphins. Prayer is another form of meditation, but deeper and perhaps stronger.

Cataract

This is yet another disease related to aging. It is a gradual clouding over of the lens of the eye, causing loss of vision. The damage is caused by free radicals or by too much ultraviolet light from the sun affecting the proteins in the lens. Due to the particular anatomy of the lens, damaged proteins aren't easily repaired or eliminated, remaining inside the lens for life and causing the cloudy areas.

It has been discovered that people who have high levels of the antioxidant carotenoids in their blood have a low incidence of cataract. This suggests that by consuming more carotenoids such as beta carotene, lutein and zeaxanthin from spinach, broccoli and tomatoes, the chances of developing cataract may, just may, be reduced.

Conventional advice on preventing cataract includes wearing sunglasses, consuming high-concentration antioxidants and using low doses of aspirin.

In established cases, surgery may be used to restore vision. Complementary treatments are not very successful but include:

- acupressure on the bone below the eye
- the Bates method of exercising and re-educating the eye muscles
- Ayurvedic treatments

You are perhaps familiar with the Australian advice for anybody who goes out in the sun:

- slip (on a shirt)
- slap (on a hat)
- slop (on a good sun-protection lotion)

But this doesn't cover sun damage to the eyes, so I would add:

- sling (on your sunglasses). You are now well protected.

CVA

Stroke, or CVA (cerebrovascular accident), happens when the brain is damaged by an abnormal blood flow. This may be caused by the blockage of an artery in the brain or by haemorrhage, a tumour or an injury.

Prevention of stroke is possible up to a point by following a healthy lifestyle with an emphasis on the avoidance of atherosclerosis as well as on controlling high blood pressure and cholesterol.

Treatment of established stroke is a complicated business, depending on the degree of damage, whether it is affecting the dominant or non-dominant side of the body, whether there is confusion, difficulty in swallowing or in articulating words and so on. There are many new treatments including medical treatments, rehabilitation, physiotherapy and surgery, all aiming to restore as much lost function as possible. Several experimental drugs are being studied, so there is hope on the horizon.

Complementary treatments used in stroke are:

- massage, including Ayurvedic *marma* massage to help co-ordinate the body and mind

- acupuncture to rebalance the energy in the body

- hydrotherapy to strengthen the muscles

- meditation or healing to restore the circulation of blood and the damaged nervous system

- herbal treatments with lavender and damiana

All of these treatments help relax the muscles around the affected area to try and make movements more active.

My advice to patients who have had a stroke is: don't give up. Ever. There is always something you haven't tried yet which may make a difference to your condition.

Cystitis

Cystitis is infection of the urinary bladder. It is common in women of any age due to the shortness of the urethra making it easy for bacteria to reach the bladder from the outside. Cystitis affects men, too, particularly those who have prostate problems. Approximately one in 10 of all patients seen by a general family doctor is suffering from urinary infections.

If you are a sufferer, antibiotics are your best bet. These usually clear the infection in a few days but many people prefer to use plant remedies instead. Preparations containing extracts of bearberry leaves (arctostaphylos uva-ursi), dandelion, echinacea, cranberry and others are promoted as being effective. On the other hand, I have met a small minority of patients whose infection worsened after taking cranberry juice or extracts. This should remind you that not all so-called 'natural' remedies are harmless.

Other complementary treatments for cystitis are:

- acupuncture to reduce 'damp heat' which is thought to cause the burning and pain on urination

- homoeopathy both for short- and long-term problems, with cantharis or staphysagria

- hydrotherapy with baths to the lower part of the body

225

Depression

In general, depression is on the increase all over the world. It is particularly common in older people and this is because problems such as chronic pain, bereavement, loneliness, social isolation and the side effects of drugs are common in this age group. Women around the time of the menopause are more likely to be affected.

Depression should not be confused with temporary feelings of sadness which are a normal part of everyday life, though it may be difficult for a non-specialist to separate actual clinical depression from everyday low mood. Over 10 million Americans have depression without even knowing about it.

Apart from low mood and frequent crying, depression also causes:

- loss of interest in personal care
- low concentration
- loss of motivation
- low self-esteem
- sleep problems
- tiredness
- aches and pains
- headaches

There are several prescription drugs which can treat depression quite effectively. Modern drugs have fewer side effects than some older treatments. Fluoxetine (Prozac) has received a lot of publicity, but newer drugs are equally effective. Complementary treatments are also effective in some cases.

St John's Wort

One of the most widely used herbal remedies is St John's wort. This is obtained from the flowers and leaves of the plant *Hypericum perforatum*. It has been used for over 2,000 years to treat melancholy and sadness and takes its name because it flowers in the summer around the birthday of St John the Baptist, 24 June. It has been studied in several research projects. In one experiment, after four weeks of treatment it was shown to be effective in improving depression, low mood and nervous tension.

The ingredients of the plant are flavonoids, tannins, anthocyanidins and hypericin. Hypericin is the best-known active ingredient and it is presented as a standardized extract (an extract which is constant in every tablet or capsule of the product). Sometimes this standardized extract is called by its scientific designation LI 160. Look for this designation on the package if you are using this supplement. Choose preparations providing 300mcg of hypericin (LI 160). This should be taken three times daily for four weeks for the best results. There are also once-a-day tablets on the market containing a total dose of 900mcg.

Hypericum extracts increase certain chemical messengers in the brain which are necessary for regulating the emotions and for other brain activities. These chemicals are serotonin, norepinephrine and GABA.

In Germany, St John's wort is sold more frequently than the prescription antidepressant Prozac. It may be better tolerated by depressed older people because the conventional antidepressant drugs are more likely to cause side effects in this age group. It is not, however, recommended in serious cases of depression where there are suicidal tendencies.

A rare but potentially dramatic side effect of St John's wort is a rash after exposure to sunlight. The rash improves when the treatment is stopped.

St John's wort exists in homoeopathic form, where the active ingredient is diluted many times until the final preparation contains only a very small amount of the active component. In this case, the extract is used for different ailments such as pain relief. It is not suitable for treating depression.

St John's wort is also used in dried form to make tea. This can help depression but is not as effective as the standardized extract.

Hypericum also improves sleep problems, lack of drive and tiredness, and speeds up reaction time. It has been studied in cases of SAD (winter depression), for which it was found to be effective.

In a study of 114 people aged up to 78 years who were given St John's wort three times a day for five weeks, it was found that it improved psychological symptoms and mental well-being. In particular, it reduced nervousness, tiredness and anxiety.

In other experiments, St John's wort was found to have fewer side effects than the antidepressant amitriptyline and to be equally as effective. It's mode of action may be similar to certain other antidepressants.

Some doctors prefer to use St John's wort instead of ordinary antidepressants precisely because of the lack of side effects. Others are not happy with the current evidence and call for more trials to establish for certain that St John's wort is effective and has fewer side effects. I don't recommend taking this supplement without a doctor's advice, because it may mask serious underlying depression which needs specialist treatment. If you want to give it a try, have a chat with your doctor first.

227

Other Treatments

Other effective and not-so-effective treatments for depression are:

- a good diet, avoiding alcohol or too much sugar and including food rich in B vitamins (lentils, seeds, fish, bananas, rice)

- counselling and other psychological help, together with drugs or supplements

- herbs: rosemary, vervain, oatstraw and gentian, all used as teas

- the homoeopathic remedies aurum, ignatia and pulsatilla

- laughter therapy

- flotation therapy

A controversial supplement is hydroxytryptophan (5-HTP). This is used to boost the chemical messenger serotonin in the brain and it has few side effects. The recommended dose is 50mg three times a day. This supplement is easily available from health food stores, but take it under medical supervision only.

The supplements SAMe and GH3 (*see* chapter 10) are used by patients from some European countries (not the UK) for treating depression.

Dentures and Teeth

Aging affects the tissues around the teeth, as well the different constituents of the gums. Prevention of tooth problems is essential and this involves regular toothcare, checkups with the dentist and avoiding too much sugar.

Vitamin K can help prevent tooth decay because it stimulates the teeth and bone tissue to calcify. For strong gums use antiseptic or anti-inflammatory herbs such as aloe vera, echinacea, citrus seed extract and gotu kola extract.

The ubiquitous co-enzyme Q10 is used to treat gingivitis and reduce bleeding, swelling and pain in the gums. In one experiment, 24 patients who had severe gum problems were studied. Half of these took Q10 and the other half took a dummy treatment. Of the

Q10 group, nine improved dramatically whereas only three of the placebo group improved somewhat. Q10 should be used in association with good general dental hygiene and advice from a dentist.

Dentures also need to be taken care of, with a meticulous daily cleaning routine. One frequent problem affecting older people is dentures which don't fit properly. The bones of the face change throughout life and this means that those wearing dentures should have them checked and changed as necessary. Otherwise difficulty in chewing, infection around the mouth and malnutrition could result.

Diabetes Mellitus

This is also called 'late-onset diabetes' or 'non-insulin dependent diabetes mellitus' (NIDDM). Despite this name, diabetes in later life may eventually need insulin.

Patients with diabetes don't have enough insulin, the hormone which helps burn down the sugars in our body. The small amount of insulin which remains in the blood is not able to work properly, leaving large quantities of unused sugar going round the bloodstream. Too much sugar destroys our proteins in a process called 'cross-linking' (*see also* chapter 10).

The numbers of new cases of diabetes increase with age. On many occasions there is a genetic predisposition to this disease. Eating too much refined sugar is also thought to make diabetes more likely in certain sensitive people.

Diabetes can cause:

- retinopathy (damage to the retina of the eye causing visual problems)
- kidney damage
- leg ulcers
- impotence
- increased risk of thrush

To reduce the danger of developing diabetes, it is best to avoid excess sugar throughout life, particularly if you have a close older relative who has diabetes. Shed any excess weight.

Conventional treatments include tablets which urge the pancreas to release insulin or which make insulin work in harmony with the cells. When these treatments fail, insulin injections are used.

Controversial treatments for preventing diabetes include the drugs aminoguanidine and the hormone DHEA. Chromium picolinate supplements have also been tried (but ask your doctor before starting these if you are already a diabetic), as have garlic and nettle root teas.

Glaucoma

Glaucoma is a disease of the eye which usually develops after the age of 40. Normally, fluid inside our eyes (called aqueous humour) is constantly produced and then drained, but sometimes the production becomes excessive or the drainage becomes blocked, resulting in a build-up of fluid. The pressure inside the eye rises, causing damage to the optic nerve which carries visual images from the eye to the brain.

A particular type of glaucoma, called 'chronic open angle', is common but doesn't cause any symptoms initially. Only an optician with a special device can detect it.

On the other hand, another variety of glaucoma, called 'acute closed-angle', is caused by a sudden blockage in the eye, resulting in sudden pain and dramatic loss of vision. This type of glaucoma can be repaired, but the treatment needs to continue for life.

Approximately one in 100 people aged over 40 suffer from glaucoma and yet half of these people don't even know that they have it. But early diagnosis and treatment can avoid problems which could lead to blindness.

People at high risk for glaucoma are those who:

- are over 40 years old
- have high blood pressure or heart disease
- have diabetes
- are severely short-sighted
- have a close relative with glaucoma

The diagnosis of glaucoma is made by tonometry, which measures the pressure of the fluid inside the eye (the 'intra-ocular pressure'). Another way of diagnosing glaucoma is by studying the appearance of the inside of the eye using a special torch called the ophthalmoscope, or by evaluating the vision using special charts.

The medical treatment of glaucoma involves different kinds of eye drops. This includes drops to slow down the production of fluid inside the eye or to unblock its drainage. Examples of these are:

- beta blocker drops to reduce the amount of fluid (though these are not suitable for those who have asthma or heart failure)

- adrenaline drops to help drain the fluid (though these can cause burning and irritation)

- pilocarpine drops, which improve the flow of fluid by opening the drainage canal

- prostaglandin analogues and carbonic anhydrase inhibitors, newer drugs used in association with the above

231

About half of those who have glaucoma need to take more than one type of eye drop and sometimes it may be difficult to distinguish between the different bottles. Luckily, there are special preparations of drops which contain two of the necessary ingredients together in a single eye drop to save the trouble of having to remember to use all the necessary drops.

Surgery for glaucoma is performed either by using lasers or by conventional methods:

a Laser surgery, called laser trabeculoplasty, involves drilling about 50–100 holes inside the eye to help drain the fluid, but drops may still be needed after the operation. More than half of the patients develop the symptoms again within two years of the operation.

b Conventional surgery is similar, creating a small hole in the eye using a suitable scalpel.

These procedures may correct the pressure of the fluid but can't reverse the existing damage to the optic nerve.

Complementary therapies for glaucoma are:

- nutritional treatment with antioxidants

- homoeopathic eye drops

- cranial manipulation by an osteopath

These therapies are not always effective but are used by some patients nevertheless.

Immunity

There are many ways to stimulate your immune system and keep it in good shape. Whole books have been written about this subject, so here I am going to summarize the most important things you can do yourself.

Apart from a suitable diet which nourishes the immune system (*see* chapter 4) there are also nutritional supplements which may play a part. Some of these immunological boosters may make a difference in cases of cancer, infection or inflammation but have no effect on healthy people. So you would need to choose wisely between those immune boosters thought to be especially effective in prevention and those which are only effective in cure.

One example of the former is a special type of amino acid called dimethylglycine (DMG). It helps tissues use oxygen better and is a general immunity stimulant. DMG is normally produced by the human body, but not in large enough quantities. As it is not usually found in foods, some scientists recommend taking extra supplements of it.

DMG modulates both the immune cells and immune proteins to help prevent diseases such as cancer and viral infections. It can be given by mouth and this is an advantage over some other immune stimulants which need to be given by injection. As a dietary supplement it has been found to be safe and without side effects. The enthusiasm of its supporters isn't shared by many conventional doctors who think that this supplement is not at all effective.

Another immune stimulant is the plant *Aloe vera*. This grows in hot climates and it has been used for many centuries to treat a variety of illnesses. Low amounts of aloe extracts are also used in creams for beautifying the skin and in shampoos for healthy hair. For maximum effects it is best to take it by mouth in tablet or liquid form.

Aloe has anti-inflammatory effects, helping wounds heal faster, so it is sometimes used by patients after surgery. In this case, it stimulates the repair cells of the body to replace cells damaged by the operation.

One of the main benefits of aloe is stimulation of the macrophages. These are a particular type of immune cells which circulate round the body picking up foreign material, engulfing it and digesting it. Aloe helps maximize this process by prodding sleepy macrophages into waking up and eating more dead material. It also allegedly prevents the development of allergies and helps in reducing some of the effects of cancer.

Finally, two other plant remedies which are thought to boost immunity are cat's claw and olive tree extracts. Cat's claw was originally found in the South American rainforest. It has anti-inflammatory properties and is also an antioxidant. Its extracts are used in cases of infection or inflammation to support several components of the immune system.

Olive tree extract counteracts the effects of several infective diseases. It encourages the immune system to fight infection and kills the bacteria and viruses which cause common infections such as thrush, flu, bronchitis and cystitis.

Other complementary treatments to brighten up sluggish immunity include:

- massage to stimulate the flow of lymph in order to remove waste material

- meditation

- the use of thymic proteins which aim to replace the age-related loss of vital immune chemicals

As usual, many conventional doctors don't endorse any of these supplements or methods because they are unsure about their effectiveness. Scientific studies on the effects of the above treatments are very few, if any, and sometimes give equivocal results. However, many patients – who are the people that matter – are pleased with the treatments.

Incontinence

Urinary incontinence means an involuntary leaking of urine, which can happen at any time, not only just after urination. It is a very common problem which affects mainly women, though men can also be affected, especially if they have prostate problems or infections.

Most sufferers are too embarrassed to ask their doctor for advice, while others think that leaking a bit of urine is a normal sign of aging. Research shows that a staggering 75 to 80 per cent of sufferers are not keen to discuss this problem with their partner. Yes, their partner, let alone their doctor or nurse.

The problem can affect people of any age but it becomes more common after the age of 40. In women it may be related to previous trauma to the urethra during pregnancy, or in both men and women it may be due to infections or to urogenital aging – the changes which accompany the menopause.

Traditionally, urinary incontinence has been divided into three different forms:

1 Stress incontinence, the leaking of urine during coughing, laughing, sneezing or jumping.

2 Urge incontinence, also called 'unstable bladder'. This is an urgent feeling of wanting to go to the toilet without managing it in time, with loss of urine on the way there. This is due to a disturbance of the nerve signals which tell the bladder when to empty.

3 Dribble incontinence, which is when the bladder doesn't empty completely and the leftover urine leaks afterwards (leaking only one or two drops after urination isn't usually a cause for concern). Dribble incontinence may happen when there is an obstruction of the bladder such as an enlarged prostate, constipation or a tumour.

These different types of incontinence may co-exist, making it difficult to establish exactly which type the patient suffers from.

Women who smoke are 30 per cent more likely to suffer from urinary incontinence than non-smokers. Also, smoker's cough makes matters worse by putting pressure on the bladder and causing leaking of urine.

234

Five ways to reduce the effects of incontinence

1 Try regular exercises of the bladder.

2 Avoid smoking, alcohol and too much coffee.

3 Follow a high fibre diet to reduce the effects of constipation.

4 Discuss it with your doctor if you are taking any diuretics (water tablets) or nutritional supplements.

5 Try complementary treatments: cypress oil or horsetail, the homoeopathic remedy pulsatilla, and biofeedback to retrain the muscles which control the bladder.

Special easy-to-perform exercises may be used in order to strengthen the muscles around the bladder. Bladder training aims to increase the capacity of the bladder so that it can hold more urine for longer. Time yourself and try, if you can, to empty your bladder every four hours and not as soon as you feel the urge to go.

235

The traditional advice to stop yourself midstream and then start again has been criticized as interfering with the normal emptying mechanisms of the bladder and is not recommended by some authorities.

Prescription drugs for incontinence are becoming more effective and have fewer side effects nowadays. The drugs aim to improve the muscle strength of the bladder or to regulate the nerves which tell the bladder when to empty. Injection of collagen-supporting material into the muscles of the bladder has been tried with some success and research of this technique is continuing.

Intermittent catheterization is a special technique using a plastic urinary catheter which the patient inserts in their urethra to drain the urine. This may be used a few times a day. The catheter is removed each time.

As you can see, there are several treatments for incontinence, but you must first see your doctor to discuss which one is the best for you. Don't leave matters too late and don't suffer in silence – it's completely unnecessary.

Insomnia

Insomnia is a dissatisfaction with the amount or quality of sleep, not merely sleeplessness. Half of people aged 40–55 can't sleep properly at night, either suffering from an inability to fall asleep, waking up frequently or waking up too early in the morning. If you are younger or older than this age group you may also be affected, but less frequently. We all suffer from sleeplessness every now and then but this is normal. Insomnia is when this inability to sleep affects our everyday life and we feel uncomfortable and disturbed by it.

In a study of 2,000 British family doctors, almost half admitted that they had no formal training in sleep disorders and the rest had fewer than five hours of training in sleep problems. It is estimated that insomnia costs the US economy an astonishing $100 billion a year.

People who catnap during the day and then don't sleep at night may still be getting the normal total amount of sleep they need in 24 hours. Sleeping during the day has been discouraged by many doctors, but others think that it may be related to normal sleep–wake rhythms, so it is natural to catnap.

A recent survey has shown that young men who suffer from insomnia are more likely to suffer from depression when older. There is no information regarding women as yet.

Seven tips to help avoid insomnia

1 Be active during the day, as it helps you sleep at night.

2 Avoid coffee or tea before bedtime.

3 Don't go to bed either hungry or full.

4 Have a warm milky drink in the evening.

5 Rise at the same time every day.

6 Consider changing your mattress or pillow.

7 Don't go to bed just to snack, sip tea, sit and talk or spend time watching television. There are only three reasons why you should be in bed: sleep, sex or sickness.

As we grow older, the time we spend in bed increases whereas the time we are actually asleep shrinks. This is because the number and length of awakenings increases.

Just counting the causes of insomnia can make you sleepy:

- depression
- anxiety or excitement
- pain
- money worries or other stress
- a cold or noisy bedroom
- constipation
- uncomfortable bed or pillows
- restless legs
- cramps
- urinary problems
- coughing
- indigestion
- the side effects of drugs

The standard treatment of insomnia is with drugs, the commonest being the benzodiazepines such as Temazepam, Diazepam and Nitrazepam. These help millions of sufferers. While many don't experience any side effects, others may suffer from daytime drowsiness or feel groggy in the morning. Newer drugs have even fewer side effects. Other conventional treatments include counselling or treatment of a particular cause of insomnia.

The complementary treatments are:

- the extract of valerian plant (*Valerina officinalis*) available in tablet or liquid form
- aromatherapy treatments with chamomile, sage, lavender or marjoram on the pillow or to inhale before bedtime
- infusions of chamomile, melissa, passionflower and hyssop

- the homoeopathic remedies coffea, aconite or nux vomica
- melatonin
- naturopathic treatments with healthy diet and exercise, warm baths, massage
- Chinese herbs such as poria or fleeceflower
- flotation therapy

Snoring

Some 40 per cent of middle-aged people (both men and women) snore. Being overweight, consuming too much alcohol and suffering from nasal problems make snoring worse.

One of the causes of snoring is obstructive sleep apnoea. This is a condition causing difficulty in breathing during sleep which makes the sufferer wake up hundreds of times during the night, often without realizing it, and then feel tired and sleepy during the day. An operation on the soft palate or treatment with oxygen throughout the night usually helps this problem.

Herbal snoring remedies aim to lubricate the throat with oils, such as eucalyptus, almond and olive oils.

Macular Degeneration

Age-related macular degeneration (ARMD) causes millions of cases of visual impairment every year world-wide. It affects one in four Americans between the ages of 65 and 75, and it is estimated that incidence of ARMD will increase by 400 per cent in the next 30 years. It is the commonest cause of partial blindness in Europe. Even if you consider yourself 'young', you still need to take steps now to prevent ARMD in the future.

The macula is a part of the retina, the light-sensitive layer of the eye which picks up visual images. It is responsible for the central part of our vision, which explains why people with ARMD may have dark spots in the centre of their vision.

For some unknown reason, women are twice as likely as men to develop ARMD. People over the age of 70, those who have been exposed to sunlight for long periods and heavy smokers are more at risk than the general population. People who have blue or green eyes have a high risk of developing ARMD.

ARMD comes in two types: the 'dry' form and the 'wet' form. The 'dry' form is the more common of the two and in this the loss of vision is gradual. In the 'wet' form, the macula is flooded with liquid from swollen and leaking arteries from under the retina. This may cause sudden loss of vision but no pain.

People who have macular degeneration may have difficulty seeing the centre of an image while the peripheral vision remains normal. This can cause difficulty in:

- reading

- watching television

- writing

- anything else which requires detailed vision

Fortunately, macular degeneration doesn't usually cause complete blindness.

The causes of macular degeneration are not clear. It is connected to age – as people live longer, the likelihood of ARMD increases. Damage caused by free radicals and by sun radiation has been blamed, at least partially.

Laser treatment can be effective in some cases of macular degeneration but it isn't always satisfactory in the long term. A diet containing high levels of antioxidants has been suggested by some authorities, both to prevent and to treat the condition. Cataract is another eye disease which may be amenable to treatment with antioxidants and it

239

A DIY Test for ARMD

Ask somebody to draw a series of straight lines 1cm ($^{1}/_{2}$in) apart. These should be criss-crossed by another set of horizontal lines each 1cm apart, at right angles to the first set, like a net. Look at the centre of this net covering one eye at a time. If the lines appear blurred, bent or twisted, then something may be wrong and you need to see a specialist for further tests.

may be worth taking supplements to deal with both diseases.

Suitable supplements are the vitamins C, E and beta carotene, the minerals selenium and zinc, and ginkgo biloba and bilberry extracts, which improve blood circulation in the retina. Also recommended are isoflavones, lycopene and lutein. Some doctors endorse the use of up to 25,000 units of beta carotene a day to help slow down the appearance of ARMD. Lutein, in particular, has been touted as a good preventor of the disease. Foods high in lutein are corn, broccoli, spinach and tomato sauce.

As with the case of cataract, protecting your eyes from strong sunshine is recommended. If you want to be safe, then slip, slap, slop, sling.

An experimental treatment which claims a good success rate in treating ARMD is a technique called 'apheresis filtration'. This makes use of special biological filters to clear from the blood abnormal proteins and other impurities which are thought to be involved in macular degeneration. This technique is available in a handful of centres in the USA, but other centres in Europe and elsewhere plan to offer this facility if more research confirms the initial benefits.

The Menopause

This is the second and most interesting stage of life. In a woman the menstrual flow stops and the woman becomes infertile, due to a failure of the ovaries to produce sufficient quantities of oestrogen and proges-terone. This usually happens at around 45–50 years of age. There is considerable debate as to whether men go through a similar process called the 'andropause', which is essentially the male menopause, when there is a similar decrease of the male hormones.

Whatever the case, the symptoms of this stage of life are much more obvious in women. Lack of oestrogen causes an increased risk of osteoporosis and heart disease, as well as symptoms such as:

- hot flushes
- cold sweats
- dry vagina
- nervousness, tiredness or depression

- headache
- difficulty in sleeping

All of the above symptoms may last anything from a few months to several years, but they are not always present and many women sail through the menopause without too much trouble. If a woman wants to avoid experiencing the symptoms of the menopause she has the choice of different HRT (hormone replacement therapy) treatments.

Some women mistakenly believe that the menopause signals the end of their femininity and the beginning of old age. In fact, being feminine does not depend on whether a woman can bear children or not or whether she has a menstrual period. Most women who have had a hysterectomy (ie, stopped having periods and can't have children) feel that they become even more feminine than before for one reason or another. Optimists see the menopause as the beginning of a long period of enjoyment which may last for another 40 or 50 years.

Researchers from the University of Plymouth showed that many women in their sixties reported feeling better than they did in their forties. After the menopause, their quality of life improved and they had a better sense of well-being.

There are, however, medical problems associated with the menopause and these need to be sorted out. A common problem is urogenital aging, the menopause-related changes affecting the vagina and bladder. After the menopause, the likelihood of urinary incontinence, bladder infection and loss of libido increases. A study of 2,000 British women between the ages of 55 and 85 found that about half of them reported having been affected by these symptoms. Most of them chose to suffer in silence, being too embarrassed to seek advice from their doctor. Others were completely unaware that suitable treatment existed.

Treatment of urogenital aging is usually with HRT or other treatments which are aimed at balancing the oestrogen in the body. These are described below.

Two other medical problems associated with the menopause are muscle pains and weight gain:

1 The loss of collagen which happens after the menopause can cause muscle pains, a condition called 'menopausal

myalgia'. This is easily improved after treatment with HRT (either conventional or natural) lasting from 6 to 12 months.

2 Some women may find that they put on excess weight during the menopause and this is due to the hormonal changes. This may be normal and natural up to a point. Oestrogen is stored inside fatty cells and this may be nature's way of preserving the hormones for a time of need. Women who put on a bit of weight during the menopause shouldn't despair but should understand that they are carrying their own supply of HRT inside their fatty cells.

Hormone Replacement Therapy

HRT with oestrogen and progesterone aims to replace the hormones which are lacking at the menopause. It can be taken in the form of tablets, skin patches, creams or implants. The risk of cancer of the breast or of the womb is very small indeed and the benefits outweigh the risks.

The treatment needs to be taken for at least five years for the full benefits and it should be continued for 10 years and over. The protective effect wanes after stopping HRT and returns to zero after five years of stopping it.

Regular checkups with the doctor will help minimize the risks. Not all women can go on HRT and the doctor will be able to give advise on this. HRT is given not only for the prevention of osteoporosis or to treat the hot flushes, dry vagina and other troublesome symptoms of the menopause, but also to protect against heart disease, dementia and skin aging.

The majority of women who go on HRT stop taking it after a year. Reasons for this include fear of side effects, abnormal periods or putting on extra weight. Many prefer to take HRT which doesn't cause monthly bleeding and there are such products on the market.

Common side effects of HRT are:

- headaches
- excessive vaginal bleeding

- weight gain

- breast tenderness

- abdominal problems, nausea and indigestion

- skin rash or leg cramps

Natural HRT

It is possible to use natural alternatives to HRT, for example natural progesterone or plant oestrogens. These should preferably be used under medical supervision and not taken together with conventional HRT.

I have seen several women who have treated themselves with natural HRT, believing it to be safe, but who had disturbing side effects from it instead. These side effects are sometimes similar to those of conventional HRT:

- a return of the menstrual flow, which can be very heavy and prolonged

- worsening of fibroids in the womb

- stomach upsets

There are, however, many benefits of using natural HRT. Natural progesterone helps reduce the effects of depression, menopause symptoms and osteoporosis (the bone-forming cells need progesterone to function properly). It also has an effect on memory and on libido.

The aim of the treatment is to replace as much progesterone as possible without suffering side effects. Progesterone regulates the actions of oestrogen and the two work together for optimum hormonal balance. Some natural progesterone creams include herbal extracts such as ginseng, black cohosh and vitamins for good measure.

Natural progesterone in cream form, once applied on the skin, is quickly absorbed into the bloodstream. It is usually applied on the breasts, arms or face, abdomen or inner thighs.

This type of progesterone is usually obtained by a chemical reaction from the wild yam, although raw, unprocessed wild yam creams may not have strong effects. Yam extracts may not have the capacity to be transformed into actual progesterone by the body so it is preferable to use the ready-made progesterone cream.

Apart from natural progesterone, there are also natural oestrogens called phytoestrogens. These are plant chemical substances related to human oestrogens. Because phytoestrogens have a similar chemical structure to oestrogen hormone, they can bind to the oestrogen receptor on the cell membrane, and so stimulate the cell.

The following plants contain large amounts of phytoestrogens:

- soya

- chickpeas and beans

- arrowood

- lentils

- nuts and clover

Phytoestrogens not only reduce the symptoms of the menopause, but are also good antioxidants and anti-inflammatory factors. One particular group of phytoestrogens is the flavonoid group which contains thousands of different individual substances. The isoflavones are the largest group of flavonoids. They mimic the effects of oestrogen on the body and balance its effects. When there is too much oestrogen, flavonoids block the excess. When there is too little oestrogen, flavonoids raise the levels to normal. They are, in effect, a natural type of SERMs (*see* 'Osteoporosis' below).

A promising benefit of the isoflavones is that they are methyl donors. During normal metabolism isoflavones create these chemicals which are then used for the repair of DNA. Loss of methyl groups by the DNA is considered to contribute to aging. In chapter 10 you will find more details on this process.

It is difficult to consume a diet which is high in isoflavones because the Western diet now contains only 10 per cent of isoflavones compared to our diet of 50 years ago. This is because we consume more fast food and more processed or genetically modified food. Japanese women consume 30 times more isoflavones than Western women and experience only very few menopausal symptoms.

Isoflavones can also lessen the risk of heart disease, reduce cholesterol and improve osteoporosis. In an Australian study, researchers using isoflavone supplements in menopausal women (aged around 50) found that they reduced hardening of the arteries down to what is normal for a 30 year old. Isoflavones help improve blood flow through the arteries, reducing abnormal clotting of the blood in the blood vessels. Some isoflavones also have a healing effect on the prostate.

For a diet high in isoflavones, choose seeds, pulses, grains, deep-coloured vegetables or red wine. Isoflavones are available in tablet, powder or grain-bar form.

Lignans are a chemical group of plant oestrogens with actions similar to soya oestrogens. These are found mainly in flax seed oil. Flax seed oil can be taken in capsules, or the oil can be added to food, but don't use for frying, because the heat damages it.

Complementary Treatments

Complementary treatments for the menopause:

1 Herbs for menopausal symptoms:

- for bloating use tea made from fennel, dandelion or parsley

- for hot flushes use black cohosh or sage

- for vaginal dryness try aloe vera gel or other artificial lubricants inside the vagina

2 Aromatherapy treatments include bergamont, jasmine, geranium or rose oils.

3 Homoeopathic remedies are sepia, pulsatilla and sulphur for mood swings and hot flushes.

4 Light therapy stimulates the brain to produce hormones and other chemicals to boost well-being and to improve circulation. It can also help with hot flushes and vaginal problems.

5 A herbal supplement, dong quai, the extract of the plant *Angelica sinensis*, is used by many women to reduce the symptoms of the menopause. It should not be used alongside conventional HRT. Other benefits of dong quai are an improvement in high blood pressure and blood flow to the brain, a reduction in the frequency of

245

migraines and a reduction in allergies such as food allergies or hayfever. The recommended dose is 1,000mg once or twice a day.

Osteoporosis

This is progressive thinning of the bones which mainly affects women following the menopause. Specifically, it affects one in every four women over the age of 60, but it can affect men too. One man in every nine over the age of 60 has osteoporosis to some extent.

Osteoporosis is a slow disease, developing over several years. It is associated with easy fractures of the bones, mainly of the hip, wrist and spine. In the UK, osteoporosis causes 60,000 hip fractures, 50,000 wrist fractures and 40,000 spinal fractures every year.

Until the age of around 30, our bones store calcium and are able to keep growing and repairing any damage effectively. After this age, we begin to lose calcium from the bones. The rate of this loss can be slowed down or increased depending on certain factors. Young women should consume high-calcium food to store as much calcium as possible before the aging process starts reducing it from the bones.

The spine may be first to be affected, resulting in weakness and the curving of the spine called 'dowager's hump'. It is quite common for older women to complain of back pain for which no reason can be found initially, but on further investigation osteoporosis is diagnosed.

An important reason for the development of osteoporosis in women is the decline of the levels of oestrogen associated with the menopause. Low levels of oestrogen are connected with accelerated drain of calcium from the bone. HRT replaces the oestrogen but there are other factors which may help prevent osteoporosis.

As mentioned above, we all need to build up a plentiful storage of calcium in our bones to start with. This is only possible before the age of 30–35. After this age, the reserves of calcium in the body gradually fall. Weight-bearing exercise, avoiding smoking or alcohol, and a diet high in calcium all help in reducing the rate of calcium loss from the bones.

The risk of developing osteoporosis is higher in women who:

- had their menopause before the age of 45

246

- had a hysterectomy before the age of 40
- have infrequent periods
- are thin, fair-haired and of small stature

The risk is also high in both men and women who:
- take prednisolone or other steroids
- have recently had a bone fracture
- have had chemotherapy
- have a close relative who had the disease
- have experienced loss of height

The diagnosis is confirmed by special X-ray tests. Bone mineral density scans can pinpoint individuals who have a high risk of developing the disease. If you are at risk, you will be given priority for a scan.

There are several ways to check the bone mineral density. One way is to use the DXA scan, also called DEXA (dual energy X-ray absorptiometry). During the scan it will be necessary to have an injection of a very small amount of radioactive material. This will give a final picture of the state of the calcium in your bones as well as predict the risk of future bone fractures.

An easy way of assessing the risk of osteoporosis is to check your hair colour. People who have premature greying of the hair are at higher risk of developing osteoporosis. A New Zealand study found that those who had grey hair before the age of 40 also had abnormal thinning of their bones.

At present, one of the most effective treatments of osteoporosis is HRT. Because of concerns about its side effects, however, particularly concerns about the risk of breast cancer, scientists have developed newer drugs which target only specific organs.

One example is the group of drugs called SERMs (selective estrogen receptor modulators). These attach to the oestrogen receptor on the cell membrane and block the binding of excess oestrogens on the receptor. Raloxifene is one of the first SERMs to be developed. This protects the bone tissue without increasing the risk of breast cancer. The modulators able to balance the levels of oestrogen. If oestrogen is too high, the

SERMs block it. If it is too low they boost it. Treatment with SERMs does not affect the symptoms of menopause such as hot flushes, it only prevents osteoporosis (and perhaps also heart attacks and stroke). More variants are in the pipeline.

Calcium needs to be taken daily, in a dose of over 1,000mg (1g) (some authorities recommend over 1,500mg a day). This should preferably be a combination of calcium-rich food plus supplements. The average diet contains only 600–800mg of calcium a day and this is why it may be necessary to take extra supplements.

Be careful when choosing calcium preparations. Not all calcium is absorbed by the body unless it is in certain chemical configurations. Some people may only be able to absorb one fifth of the calcium they take and most commercial preparations contain insufficient amounts of good quality calcium. Our bodies are usually able to absorb calcium in the elemental form, one variety of which is calcium bis-glycinate, so have this in mind when reading the ingredients on the label. Choose calcium in capsule form because tablets may not break down completely in the gut.

Vitamin D, in the order of over 400 units daily, is needed to help the bones absorb calcium properly and to keep it there. It needs to be taken together with calcium supplements and there are several products on the market offering this combination.

Other drugs used for the treatment of osteoporosis are called bisphosphonates. Examples of these are etidronate (Didronel) and alendronate (Fosamax), which increase the bone strength and reduce the risk of fractures. These are not hormones and they have different side effects. Treatment with bisphosphonates is mainly reserved for established cases of osteoporosis, not for prevention at present.

In a recent trial studying the effects of alendronate on nearly 2,000 women in 34 countries, researchers found that it dramatically boosted the strength of the bone tissue and reduced the risk of fracture.

Osteoporosis in Men

Statistically, one man in every 10 will have at least one fracture due to osteoporosis in his lifetime. The reasons why men develop osteoporosis are not exactly clear but may include:

- calcium loss due to aging in general

- hormonal imbalance, perhaps during the male menopause
- diabetes
- treatment with steroid drugs
- lack of exercise

Osteoporosis in men causes the same symptoms as osteoporosis in women – mostly loss of height and bone fractures. Changes in the shape of the ribcage may restrict the movement of the lungs and cause breathing problems.

Apart from calcium, vitamin D and lifestyle measures, specific treatment for men includes the use of anabolic steroids such as the drug Restandol, in tablet form, which is available through a doctor's prescription. This helps prevent any further bone loss, increases muscle tissue and stimulates the appetite. Etidronate and other bisphosphonates are also used in the treatment of men.

Other Treatments for Osteoporosis

Apart from calcium, mineral supplements include magnesium, boron and zinc, all of which help maintain robust bones. Zinc stimulates the bone-forming cells called osteoblasts to work harder. These mineral supplements should preferably be taken together with calcium preparations.

Lack of exercise is a risk factor for osteoporosis. During exercise, particularly weight-bearing exercise, the bone is stimulated to retain calcium and repair itself well. Good exercises for the prevention of osteoporosis are brisk walking, weight training, moderate gardening, dancing, impact aerobics or general exercises at the gym. Some gyms offer special exercises for osteoporosis.

Weight-bearing exercise is best. If you don't have time to go to the gym, do some basic weight lifting at home using books or tins of food. Try leg and arm exercises involving pushing, pulling or holding against gravity.

Homocysteine, the amino acid implicated in the development of heart disease, is also blamed for causing bone destruction, by blocking the formation and repair of collagen within the bone tissue. Folic acid and vitamin B12 supplements may help prevent this.

Complementary treatments of osteoporosis are:

- yoga (weight-bearing postures)
- Ayurvedic treatments with sesame oil, ginger and sugar
- magnetic therapy to increase bone strength
- light therapy to help the body produce the vitamin D needed for strong bones

Parkinson's Disease

This is a common neurological disease which brings disability to millions of sufferers around the world. It affects one in 400 older people. The symptoms get progressively worse over the years.

The disease is due to damage to certain areas of the brain with a consequent loss of the vital chemical called dopamine. This is a messenger molecule, helping information flow smoothly from one part of the brain to another. The damage can be caused by certain chemicals, aging in general and free radicals in particular, and other unknown reasons.

The symptoms include:

- stiffness of the limbs
- shaking of the hands, head or face
- difficulty in walking and in talking
- depression
- weight loss
- loss of balance

There are several variants of the disease but there is no known cure, although the treatment aims to provide relief from the symptoms.

The majority of conventional drugs strive to restore the missing dopamine by stimulating its production or by preventing its destruction. These drugs are called dopamine agonists. Other drugs are used to reduce some of the signs of the disease – anticholinergic drugs are used to reduce the tremor in particular – but the treatment doesn't always work smoothly.

Selegiline, a drug also marketed under the names Eldepryl or Deprenyl, prevents dopamine from being destroyed too soon and it is used by many patients. Some scientists believe that it may not only improve the symptoms but can also slow down the disease. Others go even further and claim that selegiline may help prevent Parkinson's disease from appearing in the first place and can even help prevent other neurological diseases. They believe that selegiline shields the brain against free radical damage and minimizes the premature death of brain cells. In some experiments it was found to prolong the life span of animals, improve sex drive and memory, and protect against the toxins which may cause Parkinson's.

Supporters of selegiline recommend a dose of 10mg a week, which is well below that used in actual Parkinson's patients. It is only used under medical supervision, but there are no reliable human studies regarding its alleged anti-aging properties.

Most doctors dismiss the view that selegiline has any anti-aging or protecting effects and quote the example of a large trial in which it was found that selegiline may actually increase the death rate.

All of these are theoretical arguments based on the interpretation of statistics from trials. There are, however, some people who do take preventative selegiline, particularly those with close family members who suffered from Parkinson's disease and who want to avoid developing it themselves. Time will show whether they are right.

New technological gadgets are also being used in controlling the symptoms of this disease. Implantable and adjustable devices can be used to control the tremor of Parkinson's almost at will, and also to reduce shakiness due to other causes, for example due to essential tremor. Transplants of small chunks of brain tissue have also been used, with variable success.

A non-traditional treatment of Parkinson's disease used by a small minority of doctors is this regime:

1 Use a combination of Q10, glutathione and riboflavin supplements to reduce free radical damage inside the brain cells. (Glutathione concentration has been found to be low in the brain of Parkinson's disease sufferers, so taking supplements is believed by some doctors to help reverse the damage.)

2 Add deferoxamine supplements to reduce iron in the blood. (Deferoxamine binds to iron and neutralizes it. Too much iron causes an excess of free radicals.)

3 Use selegiline and SAMe for all-round protection.

Parkinson's disease, in fact any degenerative disease, can cause very distressing symptoms and modern medicine is unable to offer treatments which work 100 per cent. As long as this continues to be the case, there will always be patients desperate to try anything to free themselves from the shackles of decay. I hope that unscrupulous practitioners will not take advantage of this.

Complementary practitioners support the use of:

- acupuncture to help with the blood circulation and to balance the body energy

- the long-term use of reflexology

- flower remedies such as poison hemlock to strengthen the nervous system

- massage and exercises to stimulate the nerves and muscles

Prostate Problems

The prostate is a small gland, the size of a walnut, which surrounds the male urethra, the tube that carries urine from the bladder to the outside. The tissues of the prostate are made of fibre, muscle and cells producing fluids. The gland is under the control of several hormones and growth factors which, in a healthy man, are all fine-tuned to keep the gland healthy. Sometimes, particularly in later life, this fine-tuning becomes unbalanced, causing prostatic disease.

Benign prostatic hyperplasia (BPH) is an age-related enlargement of the prostate affecting up to 75 per cent of all men over the age of 50. It may cause obstruction of the flow of urine, giving rise to:

- having to wake up a few times at night to go to the toilet

- dribbling of urine

- a poor stream

- a feeling of incomplete emptying of the bladder

Do you have prostate problems? Answer these questions to find out

1 Do you wake up at night more than once to urinate?

2 During urination do you frequently notice stops and starts beyond your control?

3 After you finish passing urine, do you still have dripping of urine for over two or three seconds?

4 Do you frequently notice a lot of spraying during passing urine?

If you answer 'Yes' to any of these questions, you need to see a doctor for investigation, because you may have an enlarged prostate.

The cells making up the enlarged prostate are benign, meaning that they don't have the capacity to migrate and cause tumours in other parts of the body. With time, however, they may indeed turn malignant, causing cancer of the prostate, which carries the risk of spreading to the bones, lungs or brain.

Some scientists believe that all older men have a minute number of cancerous cells in their prostate. This mini-cancer remains undetected and doesn't cause any problems, because it grows extremely slowly.

Treatment of BPH is with drugs, nutritional supplements or surgery. The surgical operations commonly used are transurethral resection of the prostate (TURP) or laser treatment.

Men who undergo an operation of the prostate should know that this carries a 50 per cent risk of sexual side effects. These include reduced orgasm or impotence, as well as urinary infections or incontinence. Doctors don't always discuss these problems with the patient according to research published a couple of years ago in the *British Medical Journal*. Surgery is only used, however, in more severe cases of prostatic disease.

In mild cases of BPH, drugs are used to improve the symptoms. There is a variety of suitable drugs. Some, like those called a1-blockers, relax the muscles within the prostate gland, so improving the flow of urine. Others, such as finasteride (Proscar), reduce the size of the prostate but can take up to three months to work and may have side effects such as impotence and loss of libido.

Herbal Supplements

Apart from strong prescription drugs, there are also several herbal supplements which aim to reduce the symptoms of BPH.

Saw Palmetto

One of these is the extract of the plant *Serenoa repens* or *Serenoa serrulata*. It is also called the American dwarf palm tree or saw palmetto (Permixon). In several experiments it was found to reduce inflammation of the prostate and improve the symptoms of prostate enlargement. It reduces the number of times the sufferer has to get up to pass urine during the night.

A German study of over 2,000 older men found that saw palmetto stimulates the emptying of the bladder and increases a general feeling of well-being.

One of the ways saw palmetto works has only recently been clarified. It blocks the enzyme called 5a-reductase, which helps convert testosterone to dihydrotestosterone. Dihydrotestosterone is a molecule which binds to prostate cells, causing them to grow and resulting in BPH or eventually cancer of the prostate. So, by blocking the enzyme, this conversion doesn't take place and the prostate cells are not stimulated to grow dangerously out of control. This implies that saw palmetto takes time to work (30–45 days) and needs to be taken for long periods to maintain the blockage of the enzyme. If saw palmetto is stopped, then theoretically the reaction will be free to go ahead.

The side effects, stomach upset or indigestion, are rare. The recommended dose is 160mg twice a day and this is suitable for mild to moderate cases of BPH.

Some trials comparing saw palmetto with the prescription drug Proscar found that apart from causing more side effects, Proscar was 20 per cent less efficient than saw palmetto in improving the symptoms. Other trials found the two treatments to be equal. Yet others found no benefits for saw palmetto. These are early results and more trials are needed for confirmation. If you are taking any medication for prostate problems, don't change it without a doctor's advice.

African Plum (*Pygeum africanum*)

Other plant extracts used in prostate problems are African plum and nettle root extracts. These are sometimes used together in different products which are currently on the market.

African plum extract is taken from the bark of the African plum tree. It is believed to be active against swelling of the prostate and several trials are currently under way to confirm or reject this.

Nettle Root (*Urtica dioica*)

Too much unbalanced oestrogen has been associated with increased growth of the prostate. Nettle root has been found in some experiments to block the formation of new oestrogen molecules in several ways, plus block the binding of existing oestrogen to the prostate cells. So, its mechanism of action is different from saw palmetto and scientists recommend taking both together to experience the full effects. Some experts recommend taking it only if you are at risk from prostate disease and not otherwise.

255

There are several preparations using extracts of nettle root, but very few scientific trials to support its use. In one trial using a six-month combination treatment with saw palmetto and nettle root there was a mild improvement of prostate problems as compared to no treatment at all. The researchers suggest that the combination needs to be taken for at least one year for the full effects to be seen.

African Star Grass

Finally, African star grass (*Hypoxis rooperi*) improves flow of urine and helps empty the bladder effectively. It also improves the quality of life in BPH sufferers. In one trial, the improvement was maintained for 12 months after stopping the treatment.

Other researchers, although noting that patients felt better while on the supplements, were unable to find any changes in the prostate which could be measured scientifically. More trials are needed to prove this one way or another.

Other Treatments

Additional treatments for BPH are:

- homoeopathic treatment with apis mel, belladonna and pulsatilla tablets

- hydrotherapy, involving showering the lower abdomen, alternating three minutes with hot water and one minute with cold water

- nutritional measures, using the plant chemicals isoflavones and lignans (found mainly in soya), as research shows that these may be able to balance the hormones which affect the prostate and block excessive production of hormones which stimulate the prostate to grow

Cancer of the Prostate

Prostate cancer is the second most common form of cancer in men after lung cancer. As life expectancy increases and men live longer, the cases of prostate cancer will also increase. Asians (who consume large quantities of soya) are 100 times less likely to develop prostate cancer than Western men.

A few scientists think that the isoflavone genistein blocks prostate cancer cells from developing and it may both prevent and treat prostate cancer. Also, saw palmetto reduces the rate of growth in prostate cells, and may be a useful treatment in prostate cancer, in association with other treatments. Isoflavones specifically aimed at reducing prostatic disease are available in tablet or capsule form.

Patients with BPH should have regular PSA (prostatic specific antigen) tests. PSA is a marker for worsening of the disease or for detecting cancer of the prostate.

Conventional treatments are not very effective in prolonging the survival of the prostate cancer patient, but can reduce the severity of the symptoms. The treatment includes surgery, radiotherapy and hormonal manipulation with hormone blockers.

Sex and Aging

Unfortunately, age-related illnesses affect several areas of sexual health, causing a variety of problems such as impotence, loss of libido and urogenital aging. It is possible, though, to by-pass many of these problems by knowing about the ways in which aging affects us.

Normal age-related sexual changes in men aged:

30 The level of the hormone testosterone is at its peak.

40 The quantity of semen production starts to decrease.

50 The time necessary for arousal is prolonged. The likelihood of impotence increases.

60 Ejaculation is not achieved on every single sexual encounter. The time for recovery after an ejaculation increases.

70 An erection fades quickly after an encounter.

Normal age-related sexual changes in women aged:

30 All sexual functions are at their peak.

40 Arousal takes longer, so foreplay becomes even more necessary.

50 The vagina gets thinner and less able to cushion the rubbing effects. Orgasm may become less intense.

60 The time taken to achieve orgasm is prolonged. Infections and pain on intercourse become more likely.

70 The clitoris shrinks and may become less sensitive.

Many older people have managed to overcome their sexual problems. Researchers say that 6 in every 10 men and 1 in 3 women over the age of 80 are sexually active.

Problems Affecting Men

Testosterone is a steroid hormone which plays a part in maintaining masculinity. It is called the male hormone but it also has a role to play in women. An age-related decline of the levels of testosterone in the blood can contribute to osteoporosis and heart disease and sexual problems such as impotence and floundering libido.

Low testosterone is also associated with tiredness, depression and a reduction of facial hair.

The production of this hormone varies during the day. It is higher in the morning and low in the evening. Some men have a more noticeable loss of testosterone than others, so it is difficult to establish what is a normal level and what is abnormal. Some doctors use testosterone replacement therapy to prevent angina and heart attacks, to improve mental function and to help treat impotence.

Lack of testosterone may be a natural effect of age, sometimes called the andropause or male menopause, and doctors believe that replacements of testosterone are necessary to overcome this. Other doctors don't believe that the male menopause exists.

Libido is the desire to have sex, whereas potency is the ability to achieve an erection. Testosterone affects both of these functions, but it is possible for one to exist without the other. Impotence, the inability to achieve and maintain an erection for sufficient time to have a sexual experience, is affected not only by testosterone but also by:

- atherosclerosis and circulation problems of the blood to the penis

- diabetes

- drugs

- psychological problems including stress, depression or anxiety

- operations on the prostate

This problem affects 20 million Americans and many more millions world-wide. The arrival of Viagra has only scratched the surface, but there are many other treatments, some more effective than others. These include:

- implant devices, placed within the tissues of the penis and stimulated on demand

- a vacuum pump device

- rings applied at the base of the penis to trap blood inside and prevent it from escaping

- injections in the penis with chemicals to aid blood flow

- pellets which are applied inside the urethra to stimulate the tissues and maximize the flow of blood

- herbal supplements such as ginkgo biloba and yohimbine

Yohimbine is the extract of the West African yohimbe tree. It increases the flow of blood to the penis and has a role to play in boosting flagging libido. Side effects include dizziness, headaches and nervousness. In practice, it is only somewhat effective in one in three users.

Another herbal supplement used in impotence is ptychopetalum olacoides (*Muira puama*). This is a Brazilian shrub, the extracts of which have been used by the Amazonian Indians for centuries as an aphrodisiac and to aid erection. Standardized extract of this shrub has been used in a trial involving over 2,000 people in Paris. Its manufacturers recommend taking three to six tablets a day for several days, as it works long term and not on the spot. As usual, there is only a very small number of trials supporting the use of this supplement.

Other complementary treatments for impotence are:

- hypnotherapy to boost confidence and to reduce anxiety

- touch therapy (healing) to reduce feelings of stress and to make positive use of energy

- chi kung, also to balance the energy within the body

- breathing exercises with shallow breathing (the Buteyko method)

Problems Affecting Women

Age-related sexual problems which affect women are:

- urogenital aging causing dry vagina, pain on intercourse and infections

- loss of sensitivity or excessive sensitivity of the clitoris

- lack of sexual desire

- breast pain or over-sensitivity

The main treatment of these problems is with HRT and this and other treatments have already been discussed under 'Menopause' above.

I think it is important to note that some people may be affected only partially, and from several of these problems at the same time, without knowing which one in particular is causing the most disturbance. If you think you have any problems with your sexual health, have a chat with an expert and see if you can pinpoint the exact cause. Only then will you be in a position to consider suitable treatment. Don't take any treatments blindly.

Varicose Veins and Foot Problems

Varicose Veins

People who stand for long periods are more likely to develop varicose veins. Sometimes pregnancy and tight stockings can make them worse. The problem is that varicose veins are not only unsightly for some but can also cause pain and discoloration of the affected area.

Varicose veins develop easily in the legs, but can also appear in the veins of the anus (the familiar haemorrhoids) or the veins of the oesophagus (the gullet) in some patients with severe liver problems.

Several treatments have been suggested but the most effective are injections with special material or an operation to remove the affected vein. Special elastic support stockings may help delay the progress of the problem. Other treatments are:

- horse chestnut supplements, which contain the astringent chemical aescin

- massage with cypress oil

- alternating cold and hot baths

- hazel or cotu kola herbal teas or supplements

Externally applied marigold has been used by some sufferers. Homoeopathic treatments are carbo veg, hamamelis and pulsatilla. Nutritional supplements include antioxidants and lecithin. Suitable exercises are swimming and yoga (headstand position).

Five ways to avoid varicose veins

1 Avoid tight socks or stockings.

2 If you can, keep your feet up when you sit down.

3 Avoid crossing your legs when sitting.

4 Take regular breaks from long periods of standing on your feet.

5 Perform regular foot exercises such as circling your toes and ankles.

Feet

By the time we are 75 years old, we will have walked the equivalent of four times around the world. The size and shape of your feet change with the passage of time, so it is important to get your feet measured properly before buying any new shoes.

To reduce the risk of any problems, use moisturizers regularly, avoid having too long or too short toenails and visit the chiropodist early if you notice anything abnormal.

Massage your feet with marjoram and black pepper oil or add these to a warm foot bath. Use more garlic, cayenne pepper and ginger in cooking, as these are thought to power-up blood circulation to the feet.

Problems with the Feet

Bunions

These are painful bone deformities affecting the big toe joint. On some occasions, keeping the big toe straight using a small splint may help delay their appearance. Use a bunion shield, available from chemist shops. In serious cases, the only treatment is an operation to straighten the bone.

Chilblains

To avoid chilblains, keep your feet warm and dry. Use ginkgo biloba supplements and avoid smoking. See a doctor if your chilblains are severe.

Exercises for Tired Feet

- While holding on to a table or chair, stand on tiptoe for a few seconds and repeat 5–10 times.

- Rotate your foot as if you are drawing a circle with your big toe. Do this clockwise and then anticlockwise a few times.

- Mobilize your foot first up and then down as if pressing on a pedal.

Diabetic Foot Problems

If you are a diabetic, take your feet very seriously indeed. Examine them regularly and if you see anything unusual, seek advice immediately. I have seen diabetic patients who had to be kept in hospital for months following infection of the foot. Some of these did not escape an amputation.

Vertigo and Tinnitus

Benign positional vertigo (BPV) is a common variety of vertigo which brings suffering to millions of people. There are many other forms of vertigo, some due to high blood pressure, atherosclerosis, the side effects of certain drugs, ear disease and so on.

Tinnitus causes noises in the ears, and as many as one in three people over the age of 60 is affected. The noises are due to abnormalities of the hearing nerves and may be associated with hearing loss or with vertigo. The causes of tinnitus are head injuries, ear wax, age-related damage to the nerves, certain antibiotics, aspirin and quinine.

The sense of balance can be worsened in older women who smoke, according to a US study. This is thought to be due to the narrowing effects of nicotine on the arteries of the inner ear.

Many treatments have been tried for vertigo, some by complementary practitioners. Herbal supplements include ginkgo biloba and the extract of periwinkle, vinpocetine.

Five complementary ways to avoid vertigo

1 Avoid caffeine, alcohol and salt.

2 Use ginger or lemon balm.

3 Have a course of acupuncture.

4 Try Ayurvedic treatment with sesame oil.

5 If vertigo is caused by low blood pressure, use cold baths and eat food rich in wholegrains.

Recovery from vertigo may be delayed by immobility. On the other hand, it can be helped by exercises.

The exercises given here are best performed under expert supervision because they may not suit the particular type of vertigo you suffer from. Some examples are:

- walking backwards with the head bent sideways
- head movements such as bending and rotation
- bending forwards
- walking in a circle
- walking in a straight line while throwing and catching a ball with a partner

Relaxation and psychological advice are necessary to deal with any panic attacks and worry related to vertigo.

Regarding tinnitus, one way to deal with the problem is to use noise generators like hearing aids to create a pleasant noise which masks the unpleasant tinnitus. Other treatments include manipulation of the spine by a chiropractor, ginkgo biloba supplements and prescription drugs from the doctor.

Conclusion

I believe that choosing a combination of conventional and complementary treatments may be the best way to reduce the effects of certain age-related problems. Following only one path may not be enough. You need to expand your choices and explore different treatments.

Let your healthcare practitioner guide you through the confusing jungle of health choices, but remember that you alone will carry the burden of this expedition. Only you will suffer or benefit from any discoveries during your trip. Will you find the elixir of youth? For more on the latest discoveries, turn to the following chapter.

CHAPTER 10

Elixirs of Youth

In this chapter I return to the question of the elixir of youth. Does it exist? What is it? The elixir of youth is a potion, tablet or injection which is used in the hope that it will prevent or reverse aging. It has existed in the past, it exists now and it will exist in the future. The only problem is, it hasn't as yet been effective.

Many people are nevertheless taking anti-aging drugs and nutritional supplements in general (antioxidants, brain boosters, vitamins and other 'natural' products). There is raging debate about this. Here are some of the arguments for and against using nutritional supplements and alternative anti-aging drugs.

Arguments for:

1 These treatments offer a much wider choice to an interested and open-minded individual.

2 Generally, they have fewer side effects than some conventional therapies.

3 They empower us to help ourselves instead of relying on others (such as doctors or pharmaceutical companies).

4 It is true that there is no full scientific proof as to their effectiveness yet, but we choose to give them the benefit of the doubt. Anyway, the interest in scientific research into these drugs is growing and looks promising.

5 The treatments offer us hope and expand our horizons.

6 By exploring these treatments we become an integral part of the new millennium health culture, taking an ambitious and active part in the world around us and experiencing what our era has to offer.

7 Those who take these supplements become more motivated to lead a healthier lifestyle in general, as directed by conventional medicine.

Arguments against:

1 Some treatments are replacing hormones or chemicals which are supposed to be low in aging. A fall in the levels of a hormone may not necessarily be abnormal but could be an essential part of growing old. Giving extra treatments may unbalance this natural state of affairs.

2 Does the supplement contain sufficient active ingredients? Is the pill properly absorbed in the gut? If it is absorbed, does it reach the parts of the body it is supposed to? Does it bind to the right receptors to be able to have any effects? During aging, the cell receptors become distorted, making it difficult for drugs to reach the inside of the cell.

3 Some chemicals are finely balanced inside the cell. Having more of one will decrease another. For example, taking extra antioxidants could make the body slow down the production of its own natural antioxidants in order to balance this influx of external supplements.

4 Many of the effects claimed for supplements or drugs are only hearsay. There is not enough scientific evidence that any of them actually work. Some evidence exists but it is very feeble. These trials can be criticized for not being conducted properly or for being biased towards the sponsoring drug company, which may have an interest in the final result.

5 Therapies and supplements are expensive, they need to be used long term and some are not properly regulated. Is the expense worth the benefit?

6 There are many unscrupulous practitioners and manufacturers around, making the treatments sound like quackery. Some supplements have been found to have a small effect on mice and rats, and the manufacturers expand this to say that the supplement has a good or definite effect on humans, which is not the same thing at all. Mice are not men.

7 A 'natural' product is not necessarily a safe product. Some can have nasty side effects. ginkgo can make you dizzy, others cause allergic reactions to the sunlight, isoflavones may unleash menstrual bleeding and certain Chinese herbs may poison your liver.

8 Is it worth worrying too much about pills and supplements or is it best to enjoy your life now, within reason? What is the point of living longer if you have to spend the rest of your life worrying about taking pills?

I am sure that, if you think about it, you can find many more arguments for or against taking non-conventional supplements. In fact, do this as a brain exercise.

In any case, the effort goes on and researchers are continually putting on the market natural or synthetic products which could qualify as elixirs of youth. Some of these are described below. I mention these drugs for information only and this doesn't mean that I endorse their use, unless I specifically highlight this. Don't spend time reading this directory from beginning to end, just concentrate on those products which may be of interest to you. You can always come back and look more products up at a later stage.

If you decide to take any of the following, you should consult a medical practitioner who is fully aware of the effects of the particular drug. Unfortunately, it is difficult to find practitioners who would be willing to prescribe these drugs and it may also be difficult for your physician to locate a supplier.

Under aminoguanidine, carnosine and SAMe, I address certain essential mechanisms of aging which I haven't had the chance to mention before. So it's more biology for you ...

Acetyl-L-Carnitine (ALC)

(This is not to be confused with carnosine (*see* below), which is a substantially different chemical.)

This is a particular type of amino acid which makes the brain buzz with energy. It is thought to prevent neurological damage, improve mental performance and emotions, and ease circulation. Its supporters claim, rightly or wrongly, that ALC can help protect cells against the effects of aging in general.

Side effects include nausea, headache and dizziness at the beginning of treatment.

Aminoguanidine

During normal aging, sugar molecules in the body react violently with proteins, causing them to malfunction. This process is called glycosylation (or glycation) of proteins. The chemical leftover products from this lethal encounter are called AGEs (advanced glycation end-products).

Glycosylation causes cross-linking of collagen, enzymes and other proteins as well as damage to the DNA. Cross-linking is an abnormal process during which proteins attach to each other as if they have been plastered with glue, becoming stiff and unnaturally twisted. Generally, these abnormal proteins are immediately removed from the body, but with age this removal becomes sluggish as the body wears out, allowing abnormal proteins to pile up.

Cross-linked proteins are found in diabetes, Alzheimer's dementia and in many other diseases of aging. For example, AGEs are blamed for causing:

- cataract
- abnormal blood clotting
- stiffening of the collagen which supports the skin
- destruction of the immune system
- kidney problems
- damage to the arteries

Too many AGEs in the blood is a sign that the rate of aging is speeding up beyond control. AGEs make you age.

Certain chemicals can put a stop to the production of AGEs. One of these is aminoguanidine, another is carnosine (*see* below). Treatment with aminoguanidine is believed by some specialists to stop aging before it even starts.

Aminoguanidine has certainly been used to prevent cataract, arthritis, osteoporosis, wrinkles and other age-related illnesses. It has also been used by diabetics to try and reduce the damage related to too much glucose in the blood. It doesn't reverse existing damage, but does prevent further cross-linking.

I have been to several respectable meetings where scientists from the UK and the US presented studies supporting the benefits of aminoguanidine. Other scientists just don't want to know.

Carnosine

Carnosine is a naturally occurring dipeptide (b-alanyl-L-histidine). In simple terms, it is made up of two amino acids, the building blocks of proteins. It is naturally present in the brain, nerves, muscle tissue and in the lens of the eye.

Researchers from the University of London have been studying the effects of carnosine as a supplement for several years and have arrived at consistent results. There have been previous studies by Japanese and Russian researchers, but interest started growing recently after British and Australian researchers published results about carnosine's near-miraculous anti-aging properties.

Carnosine lengthens the life span of human cells in the laboratory. It has antioxidant properties and zaps toxic ions and other poisons. It shields tissues against radiation damage, excites the immune system and speeds up wound healing. The use of carnosine stabilizes and strengthens the membrane of our cells, which is beneficial. In laboratory animals it has been shown to prevent or reverse cataract.

I have already discussed the cross-linking of proteins (*see* above). Carnosine blocks several chemical pathways leading to cross-linking and so reduces the production of AGEs, saving our body from, what else, carnAGE.

So, carnosine can protect us against free radical damage and against AGEs. But there are other toxins which can cause age-related damage. One of these is aldehyde and its by-products. Experiments have repeatedly shown that carnosine protects the tissues from the effects of these rogue products.

Why is carnosine different from other anti-aging 'miracle cures'? Because it takes part in three different battles to neutralize toxins:

1 Free radicals

2 AGEs

3 Aldehyde products

Vitamin C, vitamin E and other commonly used antioxidants barely manage to fight free radicals. Damage caused by AGEs and by aldehyde remains unaffected.

Even if we concentrate only on the battle against free radicals, carnosine is still superior to ordinary antioxidants. To understand why, it is necessary to appreciate that we have several lines of defence against free radicals. Commonly used antioxidants, fighting alongside carnosine, are effective only as a first line of defence. Once this line is overrun, antioxidants have no effect.

The second line of defence is to neutralize the several dangerous by-products of the first reaction. That is where carnosine comes in again for the second time, because it is able to blast these by-products away.

Aging has been associated with many different causes and stages of damage. Because carnosine has many different actions, it works at the very heart of age-related reactions, from the inside. It is fair to say that all of these actions have been extensively studied in the laboratory only, and not fully in humans as yet. Initial results are very encouraging though. People who have used carnosine say that their muscles feel firmer and their face looks younger. In theory, carnosine is potentially useful in the treatment of Alzheimer's dementia, cancer and inflammation, as well as cataract, arteriosclerosis and kidney disease due to diabetes.

In animals, the amount of carnosine in the muscle tissue indicates how long the animal will live. The higher the concentration, the longer the life span. Will the same be proven true for humans? Watch this space.

High amounts of carnosine are found in lean red meat and chicken. Carnosine supplements exist in capsule form. These supplements are made by bringing together the two amino acids in special laboratories to create exactly the same natural product as the one found in muscle. The product is not taken from the muscles or brains of dead cows or anything similar.

Centrophenoxine

This is a specific brain booster. It tops up oxygen and the energy supply to the brain, and stimulates the brain to use this energy more efficiently. It also protects the brain cells from damage due to environmental pollution.

Centrophenoxine plays a part in reducing the age-related pigment lipofuscin, which mounts up in the brain with age. Centrophenoxine also improves the production of antioxidants in the brain and activates protein construction inside the brain cells. It has been used in both demented and normal older people to repair learning abilities.

All of these effects have been observed in experiments on laboratory animals and only a few studies have been conducted on humans. The long-term side effects have not been studied.

271

DHEA

The hormone DHEA (dehydroepiandrosterone) is one of the hottest anti-aging drugs on the market. It is normally produced by the adrenal glands (which are near the kidneys) and has been extensively studied both in laboratory animals and in humans.

The levels of DHEA in our blood fall progressively from around 25 years of age. The loss may be speeded up in some people but nobody knows why this happens. Taking extra supplements can replace the lost DHEA in the blood and this is associated with an improvement in several areas of the body. Many conventional scientists, however, don't agree that DHEA has any worthwhile effects and say that it shouldn't be used at all. Do have this in mind during the following discussion.

Those who support the use of DHEA say that its benefits are nothing short of miraculous:

- improvement of mental well-being
- expansion of memory function
- loss of excess weight

- recapture of lost sexual function
- reduction of the risk of heart disease, cancer and diabetes

Specifically, DHEA reduces the concentration of viruses in the blood and energizes the thymus gland which in turn stimulates the immune system. It facilitates the use of glucose by the liver, reduces the appetite for fatty food and creates a feeling of fullness by affecting the hunger centres in the brain. However, most people who take DHEA report that they only experience some of these benefits, not all.

Other effects of DHEA are that:

- It reduces cholesterol and it was also found to be low in patients who had a heart attack or dementia.

- It may be used together with conventional HRT for better treatment of the menopause.

- It prevents damage to the nerve cells, although high doses may cause a worsening of memory, so a balance needs to be found.

- Some studies showed that it prolongs the life span of mice by 50 per cent and recent studies also found that, in men over the age of 50, it reduces general mortality from all causes.

In a study using 1,600mg of DHEA a day, a group of lucky women who were assigned to receive the active DHEA and not a placebo lost one third of their body fat and gained muscle tissue equivalent to a more youthful level. This is 'rejuvenation' in my book.

A deficiency of DHEA is found in certain cancers, including stomach, bladder and breast cancer. On the other hand, excessive use of DHEA is associated with an increased risk of prostate problems and cancer of the ovaries.

There are no clear guidelines about the dose. Most people take 50mg a day, but some people take anything from 25 to a whopping 2,500mg a day. A doctor will check the PSA (prostatic specific antigen) in men to make sure that there are no problems with the prostate and do a baseline saliva or blood test to find out what the level of DHEA is in order to have a starting value.

After taking the DHEA pills, it will be necessary to check the saliva or blood in 4–6 weeks to see whether the dose is adequate and increase or decrease it accordingly. It is then essential to repeat the tests every 4–6 months.

In addition, taking antioxidants will reduce damage to the liver, which eliminates the leftover products of DHEA. Men will be advised to also take saw palmetto and check their prostate function every year.

Problems with DHEA are:

- increased hair growth in both men and women

- a return of the menstrual period in post-menopausal women

- a danger of prostate cancer in men

- many others, which a specialist would be able to discuss with you

Gamma Hydroxy Butyric Acid (GHB)

This very controversial product has been described by some as the real elixir of life and by others as a dangerous chemical causing GHB – Grievous Harm to the Body.

A few eminent scientists believe that GHB is one of the top five anti-aging drugs. Its legal status fluctuates between different countries and different states. Its supporters claim it has a 40-year record of safe use. GHB should only be obtained from a medical practitioner who is familiar with this product.

Possible benefits of GHB are that it:

- cocoons the tissues against damage from lack of oxygen

- balances the metabolism

- protects the brain against several poisons

- has an antioxidant action

- aids better sleep

- is a releaser of growth hormone (*see* below)

Gerovital (GH3, KH3)

I know a few doctors and scientists who swear by the effectiveness of this drug. Only a few. Gerovital was one of the best-known anti-aging drugs in the '50s and '60s, and its main ingredient is the local anaesthetic procaine. You can get Gerovital by injection, but more recently it has also been made available in tablets.

Over the years there have been many claims about the effectiveness of this drug. Doctors who are enthusiastic about using GH3 report that it improves blood pressure, arthritis, energy, memory, depression and most other problems associated with aging. Only a handful of scientific studies have been performed outside Romania's Ana Aslan Institute, however. Those studies were mostly negative or gave equivocal results.

Although there has been a lot of publicity about this drug in the past, today most scientists don't endorse its use. Several patients, though, have tried this product under medical supervision and found it to be very effective.

274

Ginkgo biloba

The extract of the maidenhair tree (*ginkgo biloba*) is used by millions of people across the world. Its main properties include:

- an improvement in the circulation of the blood in the small capillaries of the extremities

- an antioxidant effect

- improvement of crumbling mental prowess

Age-related mental problems can be anything from forgetfulness to lack of attention, dizziness, tiredness, sleep disturbances, restlessness and anxiety. ginkgo is thought to alleviate most of these symptoms.

Scientifically studied and endorsed benefits of ginkgo:

- It improves the processing of information.

- It expands the attention span and concentration.

- It stimulates visual memories.

- It promotes mental well-being.

- It blocks the platelet-activating factor which is produced when the organism reacts to inhaled pollutants, so it reduces inflammation in the lungs and improves asthma.

- It improves intermittent claudication (pain on walking due to blocked arteries).

- One of its ingredients, bilobalide, protects the nerve cells from damage.

- It is effective in reducing tinnitus (noises in the ears) in some patients.

In an experiment using 240mg extract of ginkgo, the brain performance of mild to moderate Alzheimer's dementia patients improved. Attention and memory improvement was evident after taking ginkgo for six months to a year. Also, ginkgo improved social functioning and general brain performance in doses of 120mg.

If you decide to try ginkgo, your practitioner may recommend that you take it for at least four weeks for the effects to become apparent, but it is best to take it long term.

Side effects are rare but real: headache, dizziness, skin rash and menstrual period abnormalities.

When choosing a ginkgo preparation aim for one which contains at least 120mg of standardized extract (not raw leaf), with 24 per cent flavone glycosides, 6 per cent ginkgolides and bilobalide. There are different strengths available on the market. The prices vary enormously and the cheapest brand isn't necessarily the best, because it may not provide enough ginkgo for any worthwhile effects. Choose wisely.

Growth Hormone

After the age of 20 the level of growth hormone (GH) begins to wane in our body. By the age of 70 it has dwindled to less than one fifth of the youthful level.

The benefits of GH supplementation include bulkier muscles, shrivelling of body fat, improved skin thickness and powerful bones. In addition, it improves sexual function and immunity.

The side effects of treatment with GH can be severe, but with suitable adjustment of the dose these should improve. Some common side effects are:

- fluid retention
- carpal tunnel syndrome
- diabetes
- headaches
- high blood pressure

GH is only available by injection from a few specialist clinics. See under Baxamed or Optimal Health Clinics in the 'Resources' section.

Secretagogues

Because of the expense involved in using genetically engineered GH, scientists have tried to use cheaper substances which stimulate the body to boost its own natural GH production. These products are called secretagogues. You are going to hear more about these during the next few years.

Some of these newer products are based on herbal extracts or amino acid sequences (peptides). Amino acids used as secretagogues are arginine, ornithine, lysine, glutamine and tryptophan. These are best used in combination for maximum effects, not just on their own.

Another releaser of growth hormone is the chemical GHB (*see* above) which, in an experiment, was found to increase the level of growth hormone 16 times in a single hour.

The effectiveness of the secretagogues is still being scrutinized. This is an area of intense research at present and there are already several secretagogues on the market. Some laboratories have even produced homoeopathic GH, claiming that their product has a string of benefits: improvement of joint pains, night sweats, skin dryness, immune function and muscle strength.

Hydergine

This is another brain booster which is supposed to revitalize worn-out brains. It has been approved by the Food and Drug Administration in the USA for use on people over the age of 60 with mental incapacity.

Hydergine has many effects on the brain but an important one is protection against damage from toxins and free radicals. This is relevant because the oxygen we breathe reacts with the fatty parts of the cell membrane during a chemical process called peroxidation, If there is excessive production of free radicals, peroxidation gets out of control, causing damage to the cell membrane, which crumbles like a shattered eggshell. Hydergine prevents this from happening. It also stimulates the production of new nerve endings (dendrites) which facilitates better communication between the brain cells.

Hydergine is used both to treat and prevent dementia. Higher doses are more effective and there are no serious side effects, but it can cause mild stomach upset and nausea. The treatment is claimed to be most effective in early dementia. It is not possible to reverse advanced dementia because the brain has already been damaged.

Hydergine is a prescription-only drug. The majority of US, Australian and British doctors haven't even heard of it, though, and are therefore probably unable to prescribe it.

Melatonin

This stuff certainly got its 15 minutes of fame, though I have heard experts on aging say that melatonin inspires more claims than scientific data and more sarcasm than discussion. Yet melatonin is still one of the best-selling anti-aging drugs.

The biological modulator melatonin is produced by the pineal gland in the brain. The concentration of melatonin is high during darkness and low during daylight. Generally, production of melatonin wanes with age and this may be one of the reasons why older people suffer more frequently from insomnia.

Supporters of melatonin claim that it helps in immunity problems, cancer and depression. Low melatonin levels and increased breast cancer risk do go hand in hand. Melatonin stops oestrogen binding to the receptors on the cell membrane and that is the reason why it is thought to reduce the risk of breast cancer.

The only widely known effects of melatonin are two:

a an improvement in sleep

b control of jet lag

Supporters also claim that melatonin is an antioxidant and a general anti-aging factor, but while there has been some positive research in mice, this has not yet been proven in humans.

The average dose is 1–3mg at bedtime. My personal experience with melatonin is that it didn't touch my jet lag on several occasions, so I am reluctant to believe that it will have any other effects on me.

Phosphatidyl Choline and Serine (PC and PS)

Phospholipids are a group of chemical substances including phosphatidyl coline (PC) and its cousin, phospatidyl serine (PS). In the scientific sense, PC is the same as lecithin. In practice, though, you may see the two terms used differently. The commonly available lecithin may contain very low amounts of PC. If you are taking lecithin, make sure that it contains at least 30 per cent PC. I am going to stick to this distinction during the following discussion.

Lecithin is a complex phytochemical found in plant oils. It removes lipids from the skin while at the same time it moisturizes and maintains a smooth skin complexion. Lecithin is used to protect the brain cells from damage and in this way it may boost memory and brain function.

Sources of lecithin include corn, rice, soya beans, wheatgerm and peanuts. It is also available in tablet form from health shops.

Phosphatidyl choline is found in the kidneys, the brain and in soya. PC is necessary for the production of the chemical acetylcholine which provides the spark to the nerve endings, helping to carry messages from one nerve to another. Generally, it helps improve memory and clears the thinking process, breaks down excess cholesterol and helps in the absorption of vitamins D, E and K. Claims that PC can boost immunity, reduce the risk of cancer and may help reduce the accumulation of fatty tissue under the eyes have also been made but there is not much research supporting these.

Phosphatidyl serine is a naturally occurring chemical. It can improve learning and remembering and boosts concentration and alertness. It improves the memory for names and faces, lengthens the attention span, normalizes the sleep pattern and expands the reaction time.

There have been several trials studying the effects of PS. In some trials it was found that it can make the brain up to 12 years younger (for example, a 64-year-old regular user has the mental abilities of a 52 year old). The effects begin about three weeks after starting the tablets.

PS protects the brain cell membrane and the different cell constituents. It helps in transporting the messages across the nerves and promotes the production of nerve growth factors which are necessary for repair and growth of the nerve cells. It may make a difference in people who find that memory information cannot flow quickly from one part of the brain to another and who frequently end up saying 'er' or 'um' as a result.

Soya products are good sources of phospholipids in general but provide only a small amount of PS. High quantities of PS are found in the brains of pigs, sheep and calves, but these products are not consumed as widely as in the past. So, scientists suggest taking supplements in tablet form at an average dose of 300mg a day. PS tablets are prepared from soya beans by a chemical reaction rather than from animals.

PS is considered to be safe, without any significant side effects apart from vivid dreams and nightmares, and also difficulty in falling asleep, so it is best taken in the morning. It can be used together with ginkgo biloba for maximum benefit for those who worry about their memory.

Piracetam

There are over 30 trade names for this drug and this shows how popular it is. Piracetam is the world's best-selling brain booster, promoted as being effective in improving memory, intelligence, creativity and learning. It is also thought to be an antioxidant and a stimulant of the brain metabolism, helping the smooth flow of information throughout the brain.

Chemically, piracetam is related to certain amino acids. It has been used in the treatment of dementia to improve the process of cognition. Several other benefits have been claimed. Side effects are headaches and stomach upset, but these are rare.

Piracetam is not officially approved in the USA, Canada, the UK or Australia, but some doctors can prescribe it in special situations. Piracetam and similar varieties such as piramiracetam and oxiracetam are officially used in some European countries.

Pregnenolone

This hormone is produced from cholesterol and acts as a blueprint for the formation of several other hormones such as DHEA, progesterone, testosterone and oestrogen. It is used as a general anti-aging drug and to improve memory and brain cell protection, also as a stress reduction drug. It improves depression and mood and has also been used in arthritis with some success.

Pregnenolone concentrations in the human brain plummet to about 5 per cent of normal by the age of 90. Supplementation aims to bring the levels back to youthful concentrations.

During treatment, saliva or blood tests are recommended to monitor the concentration of pregnenolone in the body. The dose is anything between 10mg and 50mg, with some people recommending 200mg a day. This highlights the uncertainty surrounding this drug.

The majority of doctors are not aware of the effects of this product and are therefore unable to comment on its possible effectiveness.

Regeneresen (RN13)

RN13 is an anti-aging 'designer drug'. It contains RNA (ribonucleic acid), which is responsible for manufacturing proteins using a blueprint from its cousin, DNA. Some people believe that RNA can help regenerate aging organs. It has been studied in several research projects.

The material is collected from cattle tissue or cattle foetuses. Organs such as the heart, lungs and muscle contain their own type of RNA, so, it is claimed, when additional RNA is injected into the body it should help stimulate regeneration of those particular organs. If a patient has liver failure, for example, the treatment would make use of liver RNA.

In one small trial using RN13 on older people, it was found to improve osteoporosis, brain function, the ability to walk and energy levels.

RN13 contains 13 different types of RNA from the liver, brain, ovaries, testes, kidney, heart and others. It is mainly given by injection, but also exists in capsule form.

SAMe

S-Adenosyl L Methionine (SAMe) is one of the most promising anti-aging drugs on the horizon. It is a special type of modified amino acid and works at the microscopic level inside cells, affecting the DNA and proteins.

SAMe is normally produced in our body and this production is under the influence of an internal biological clock. Production is highest in the evening, in harmony with the production of melatonin by the pineal gland. Older people (and older mice) show a decrease of the levels of SAMe in their blood, a decrease which worsens with the passage of time.

Initial studies suggest that SAMe may be effective in preventing:

- heart disease
- liver problems
- arthritis
- osteoporosis

It works by donating essential chemicals called 'methyl groups' to proteins which desperately need these groups in order to survive.

Methyls are chemical substances necessary for the production and repair of DNA and proteins. Methyl groups are also needed to transform several molecules to their active form. Methylation is when a methyl group is attached to a target molecule such as a protein or DNA. So, because SAMe has extra supplies of methyl groups, it donates some of these to the DNA or proteins in need.

The DNA molecule needs to be methylated regularly to stay in good form. Gradually, with age, this process slows down, but it is not clear whether this is the actual cause or just a side effect of aging. Cells which live for a long time and which multiply many times have extremely lively methylation. Maintaining your DNA methylation is essential if you want to avoid cancer, immune diseases and aging.

The amino acid homocysteine plays a part in the process of methylation. Homocysteine, a toxic by-product of the amino acid methionine, is blamed for playing a serious part in causing heart disease, dementia, and inflammation (*see* 'Angina and Heart Disease', chapter 9). It is set to become one of the great risk factors for heart disease, together with cholesterol, cigarette smoke and obesity. It is not very smart to let large amounts of homocysteine linger in your body, but homocysteine may be inactivated and transformed back into the harmless methionine by using methyl groups.

Alternatively, homocysteine can be inactivated and eventually transformed into the very useful antioxidant glutathione. Usually helpful in this respect are the key nutrients vitamin B12, folic acid and zinc as well as SAMe.

At present, SAMe is used only as an anti-depressant, but it has potential for general anti-aging use. The dose for depression is anything between 200 and 1,600mg a day. It is not known what the ideal dose is for anti-aging purposes but, in any case, using SAMe is expensive. One authority recommends 800mg a day, which costs in the region of £100 ($160) a month at present. SAMe in injection form costs around £112 ($180) a month. With more research and better understanding of its manufacturing processes, the price is expected to fall dramatically.

The side effects are rare and include indigestion, nausea and over-stimulation of the nervous system.

SAMe has mainly been studied in Italy and there are no reliable studies proving the full anti-aging effects of SAMe in humans. This is because this idea is a relatively new one. Several projects are under way at present, but there are no definite results as yet. Theoretically, use of SAMe makes sense and it offers a new direction, an opportunity to fight the aging process from a new angle.

Vinpocetine

The extract of periwinkle plant, vinpocetine, is one of the latest smart drugs to hit the USA. Vinpocetine was originally researched by Hungarian doctors and was found to reduce memory problems, dizziness and the effects of stroke. It helps the brain use glucose and oxygen more easily and boosts some of the chemicals necessary for normal transmission of information. It also helps the brain retain information. It protects the nerve and brain cells from damage due to oxygen starvation and eases the blood flow by reducing its stickiness.

There have been over 100 trials on the effects of vinpocetine and most of these show some benefits. In one report, which studied 3,000 patients who took the supplement, 70 per cent said that they experienced 'some improvement'. No side effects were observed.

Vinpocetine is used in the treatment of dizziness, vertigo, anxiety, difficulty in sleeping and transient ischaemic attacks (TIAs), as well as with memory problems. It may also help in cases of macular degeneration, glaucoma and hearing problems.

The suggested use is one or two 5mg tablets three times a day, but this should be continued for at least a year for maximum results.

Summary

The current state of affairs is this: gerontologists believe that aging is affected by free radicals, AGEs, other toxins and defective methylation.

1 Antioxidants deal with only the free radicals.

2 Carnosine affects free radicals, AGEs and some other toxins.

3 SAMe affects only methylation.

So, taking only one of these supplements leaves other areas uncovered.

If you want to deal with aging as we understand it today, it makes sense to ask a knowledgeable medical practitioner to consider prescribing all of these products to cover yourself from all angles.

The Definitive Elixir of Youth

- In theory, if I had to recommend an all-inclusive, the ultimate, anti-aging elixir, fit for the millennium generation, I would have no hesitation. Here it is: a combination of DHEA, carnosine and SAMe, with added high-dose Q10, ginkgo biloba and isoflavones.

- At present, there is nothing stronger and better studied than the ingredients of this combination, and nothing that covers such a wide range of age-related damage. All the products are also relatively easily accessible.

- I can't foresee any other products which can surpass the combination of these six in the next 10 or 15 years. Only DNA manipulation, possibly with telomerase, may prove superior.

- It bears repeating once more that you should only take supplements under medical supervision.

Conclusion

As you have seen, there are many pros and cons regarding living longer. You'll need to make up your own mind and decide which path to follow.

Aging is both good and bad. The angel of aging brings us long-lasting health, productive life, an active brain, an envious social life, precious wisdom and excellent opportunities to help others. It brings us enjoyment of physical, mental and spiritual pleasures, over and over again.

The ferocious beast of aging has a insatiable appetite for lives. Sometimes we feed it, sometimes we fight it. Courageous people brandish their banners of defiance, surgeons waggle their scalpels, scientists rattle their test tubes, nutritionists fire their pills like magic bullets, gerontologists throw their theories like spears, all trying to defeat the dragon. In all the stories my grandmother told me, the dragon was always defeated in the end.

Glossary

acetylcholine
an essential chemical messenger molecule necessary for good brain function. Its concentration is low in the brains of patients suffering from Alzheimer's disease.

amino acid
a building block of a protein. If a protein is compared to a wall, an amino acid is a brick.

antioxidant
a chemical substance which inactivates or prevents the formation of free radicals.

average life span
the number of years most people live.

biological age
the apparent age of one's tissues, organs and biological processes.

chronological age
the number of calendar years (or months, etc) since birth.

cloning
a procedure in which a new organ, organism or group of organisms is formed from one original cell, seedling or stock.

collagen
a molecule which supports the skin and arteries, among others.

DNA
deoxyribonucleic acid – the molecule which carries the entire genetic code necessary for reproduction.

free radicals
active by-products of everyday metabolism which usually cause damage to tissues.

germ cells
cells in the sperm or ovaries.

gerontology
the scientific study of old age.

health span
the length of time during which one is reasonably healthy.

longevity
long life.

maximum life span
the maximum age ever reached by a human.

molecule
a structure representing a chemical identity. A molecule can be a protein, a drug, a compound, a vitamin, a hormone, etc.

nanotechnology
the science of miniaturization.

nootropic
a drug acting on the brain and purported to improve memory and cognition.

nutritional (or dietary) supplement
usually a pill, not requiring a doctor's prescription, and legally not a 'drug', which is taken in an effort to fortify chemicals missing from the normal diet.

receptor
a chemical lock on a cell or on a molecule. Only exact chemical keys can activate it.

regeneration
forming afresh, or coming into renewed existence.

rejuvenation
becoming young again.

soma
body.

youthing
growing young. The opposite of aging.

Further Reading

Blackman, Honor, *How to Look and Feel Half Your Age for the Rest of Your Life,* Virgin, London, 1997

Chee Soo, *The Chinese Art of T'ai Chi,* Thorsons, London

GHB: The Natural Mood Enhancer, Smart Publications, California (*see* 'Resources')

Hewitt, J, *Teach Yourself Yoga,* Teach Yourself Publications, London, 1992

Khalsa Dharma Sing, *Brain Longevity,* Century, London, 1997

Kirkwood, Tom, *Time of Our Lives,* Weidenfield & Nicholson, London, 1999

Restack, Richard and Mahoney, David, *The Longevity Strategy: How to live to 100 using the brain – body connection,* Wiley, London, 1998

Rose, Marc and Michael, *Save Your Sight: Natural ways to prevent and reverse macular degeneration,* available from the Life Extension Foundation (*see* 'Resources')

Spillane, Mary and McKee, Victoria, *Ultra Age,* Macmillan, London, 1999

Warrier, Gopi and Gunawant, Deepika, *The Complete Illustrated Guide to Ayurveda,* Element Books, Shaftesbury, 1997

Wong Kiew Kit, *Chi Kung for Health and Vitality,* Element Books, Shaftesbury, 1997

Yanick, Paul and Gianpapa, Vincent, *Quantum Longevity: Living to 100 and beyond,* Promotion Publishing, 1997

For a complete list of publications on all aspects of complementary medicine contact:

Element Books Ltd
Longmead
Shaftesbury
Dorset
SP7 8PL
UK
Tel: 01747 851 339

Resources

This list will help get you started in your exploration of the subject.

Australia

The Australia Wellness Centre for Optimal Health and Longevity

www.wellness.net.au/parijat/aprijat. htm

For information on complementary medicine:
Maharishi Ayurveda Health Centres
PO Box 81, Bundoora
Victoria 3083

The National Herbalist Association
PO Box 61, Broadway
NSW 2066
Ayurvedic Practioners

www.practitioner-
listing@ayurveda.com

Belgium

A conference on longevity medicine is organized by:
The European Academy of Quality of Life and Longevity Medicine (EAQUAL)
Avenue Albert Giraud 95
B–1030 Brussels

e-mail: medical.conference
@euronet.be

Switzerland

A private clinic well-known in the field of alternative anti-aging therapies·
Baxamed Medical Center
Hauptstrasse 4
CH–4102 Binningen

UK

For mainly written information on all areas of aging or to contact me:
The British Longevity Society (BLS)
PO Box 71
Northampton, NN1 5HJ,

www.antiageing.freeserve.co.uk
e-mail: kyriazis@antiaeging.
freeserve.co.uk

Journals, conferences and meetings on complementary medicine are published/organized by:
The Department of Complementary Medicine
The University of Exeter
25 Victoria Park Road
Exeter, EX2 4NT
e-mail: fact@exeter.ac.uk

A range of both established and innovative anti-aging therapies is available from:
Optimal Health Clinics Ltd
114 Harley Street
London W1N 1AG
e-mail: ohc@phealth.demon.co.uk

A clinic famous for its holistic approach to treating cancer, established 20 years ago, patron HRH The Prince of Wales, using complementary ways which may also be useful to those who want to explore mind–body medicine and holistic immunity enhancement:
The Bristol Cancer Help Centre
Grove House
Cornwallis Grove, Clifton
Bristol, BS8 4PG
Telephone: +44 117 980 9500
e-mail: info@bristolcancerhelp.org.uk

For a surprisingly extensive range of smells contact:
Dale Air Ltd
Unit 23, Arkwright Court
Blackpool & Fylde Industrial Estate
Blackpool, FY4 5DR

THERAPIES AND DISEASES
Ayurveda
For more details visit the Ayurvedic website:

www.ayurvediccompanyofgreatbrita
in.co.uk

Glaucoma
For more information on glaucoma visit the website of the International Glaucoma Association:

www.iga.org.uk/iga/

Osteoporosis
For more details, visit the UK Department of Health website on osteoporosis:

www.open.gov.uk/doh/osteop.htm

The United States of America

For information on aging:
The American Academy of Anti-aging Medicine (A4M)
1341 W. Fullerton Suite 111
Chicago IL 60614,
Tel: +1 773 528 4333

www.worldhealth.net

For details on holistic treatments and practitioners in the USA:
The American Holistic Medical Association
4101 Lake Boone Trail, Suite 210,
Raleigh
North Carolina 27607

For a full list of products and books on every aspect of aging and living longer (members only) contact:
The Life Extension Foundation
PO Box 229120, Hollywood
FL 33022–9120, USA

www.lef.org

Journal of Anti-Aging Medicine:
Mary Ann Liebert Inc.
2 Madison Avenue
Larchmont NY 10538

www.liebertpub.com

An innovative medical clinic affiliated to the Committee for Freedom of Choice in Medicine:
American Biologics
1180 Walnut Avenue
Chula Vista, CA 92011

The US branch of Baxamed Medical Center (see 'Switzerland'):
Jeunomed International Corporation
50 West Mashta Drive, Unit 3
Key Biscayne, FL 33149
Tel: +1 305 361 6755

Smart Publications
PO Box 4667, Petaluma
CA 94955
Tel: US toll free 1–800–976 2783

www.smart-publications.com

THERAPIES AND DISEASES
Chelation
www.chelationsouthflorida.com

Homoeopathy
National Center for Homeopathy

www.homeopathic.org

Osteoporosis
National Osteoporosis Foundation
12342 22nd Street NW
Washington DC 20037-1292
Tel: +1 202 223 2226

www.nof.org

Index